A PRICE TOO HIGH

A PRICE TOO HIGH
An Autobiography

Peter Rawlinson

Weidenfeld and Nicolson
London

For Elaine

George Weidenfeld and Nicolson Ltd
91 Clapham High Street, London SW4 7TA

ISBN 0 297 79431 0

Printed by Butler & Tanner Ltd
Frome and London

Contents

Illustrations

My grandfather, Sir Henry Mulleneux Grayson
My brother, my father, my mother and myself in 1940
Pilot Officer Michael Rawlinson
Lieutenant-Colonel A.R. Rawlinson
Rosa Lewis in her hotel (*Douglas Glass*)
A candidate in the 1951 general election (*The Photo Source*)
General Wladyslaw Anders (*Popperfoto*)
The new Solicitor General, 1962 (*Camera Press*)
With Harold Macmillan in 1964
Daily Express sketch of the ministers at the centre of the Profumo affair
    (*Daily Express*)
Elaine on her way to a ball (*Daily Express*)
Elaine after the ball
Attorney General, 1970
P.R. with John Mitchell, Warren Burger, Quintin Hailsham and Selwyn
    Lloyd
Leila Khaled (*Associated Press*)
Arthur Hosein (*The Photo Source*)
Dawson's Field, Jordan (*Associated Press*)
On my way to the Rudi Dutschke Tribunal in 1970 with Gordon Slynn
    and Tony Hetherington (*The Photo Source*)
IRA bomb attack on the Old Bailey, 1973 (*Associated Press*)
Ted Heath with Elaine and our children
With Quintin Hailsham and Peter Carrington, 1978
Chairman of the Bar, 1975 (*photo by Jeremy Grayson*)
Elaine and Geoffrey Howe
Anthony and Shirley Fanshawe, Elaine and P.R.

PART ONE

Prologue
An Invitation to Admiralty House

I picked up a taxi in Fleet Street by El Vino's, near to the lane which leads into the Temple. 'Admiralty House,' I said. 'But not the Whitehall entrance, the back entrance – in Horse Guards.' These had been the instructions from the Private Secretary. In the cab I rehearsed. I must not, out of confusion or nervousness, accept what I did not want.

In Horse Guards I found the door and went inside. I sat in a waiting room, still silently rehearsing. At last I was shown into the long thin room, down the length of which ran the mahogany Cabinet table. In its centre sat the Prime Minister. Downing Street was under repair and he was occupying the far more handsome Admiralty House. As I sat opposite him in the chair into which he waved me, my eyes settled on his moustache, now becomingly trimmed down from the bushy walrus which it had been five years previously. Credit for the trimming was claimed by Henry, the talkative barber of Bond Street who cut my own hair and my father's military moustache – and who, consequently, claimed sole credit for all 'Supermac's' subsequent success.

After graceful apologies for keeping me waiting (a tedious foreign luncheon guest) the Prime Minister, a hand now and then brushing an eye as if to forestall an uncontrollable tear, got down to business. Sad business, he called it, sad business: the pain of having to part with old comrades, lifelong friends. For the day was Monday 16 July 1962, and forty-eight hours earlier he had sacked a third of his Cabinet and ruthlessly slipped the political dagger between the ribs of many old friends. So far, in this general and melancholy preamble, there was not yet revealed the exact purpose of my personal summons. I waited, and then came the clue. For the Prime Ministerial musing had now centred upon the cruel parting with David, dear David, such a valued colleague but who had, after all, for some time wanted to go. And David, I knew, was David Kilmuir – formerly David Maxwell Fyfe and, until the previous Friday night, Lord Chancellor. David, as he himself later made crystal clear, had certainly not wanted to go. But gone he had, leaving a vacancy among the law officers in the post of Solicitor General. I prepared my acceptance of the offer which I now knew was poised to come.

'I hope', said Harold Macmillan, 'that you may consider joining my administration as Solicitor General.' I opened my mouth to reply. He raised his hand, a pale hand with long sensitive fingers, its palm toward me.

'But before you give me your answer I must remind you of the special position of the Law Officers, who are the last, the sole survivors in the long line of public servants of the Crown who sit in the House of Commons.' I swallowed back my words of acceptance and was honoured by a scholarly review of mediaeval office holders, a review which flowed into the sixteenth and seventeenth centuries, embraced approvingly the career of Samuel Pepys, and concluded with the admonition that the loyalties of a Law Officer must be first to the Crown, second to Parliament, and only thirdly, almost incidentally, to the administration. And now, concluded the Prime Minister, would I do him the honour of joining his administration as Solicitor General?

I certainly would. But then came a note of anti-climax to what had gone so elegantly before. For I had to ask him to allow me forty-eight hours' grace. He looked surprised, a little nettled.

I said that I was due to appear next day as counsel at the Old Bailey to speak on behalf of a former colleague, Sir Ian Horobin, who at the time of his arrest had been nominated by himself, the Prime Minister, as a life peer. The following day Sir Ian was to plead guilty to a number of serious offences with young boys at the club and hostel over which he, a bachelor, had presided for decades. To represent him was a long-standing professional engagement that I was bound to fulfil.

A look of pain passed like a shadow over the handsome features of the Prime Minister; a long finger floated down to the table and pressed a bell. 'Tim,' he said to the Principal Private Secretary who appeared, like a genie, through the door behind my chair. 'We must delay the announcement of the appointment of the new Solicitor General. He has to undertake tomorrow an unusually distasteful task which on no account can he avoid.' He explained fastidiously the general nature of the task to Tim Bligh. Then he paused, for quite a time. 'Why on earth did not the wretched fellow flee the country like poor old Willie Beauchamp did so many years ago?' I was unable to enlighten him, and shortly thereafter I floated out of the room.

The following day I performed my 'unusually distasteful', and extremely difficult, task. My client had at one time wanted me in my speech in mitigation of his offences to impress upon the judge that in the East, when a city had been stormed and sacked, it was not only the girls who were raped. But I had explained that on the whole I did not think that this would help him. Then he wanted me to say that often the boys he had seduced in their youth had later brought their own sons to join the club, so where was the harm? Again I suggested that this line might not altogether appeal to the sentencing judge. In the event the trial lasted only a few hours. Sir Ian pleaded guilty and was sentenced, as he had been warned, to a substantial term of imprisonment.

As I walked away from the Old Bailey on the day of that trial I was photographed; there was speculation about who was to be the new Solicitor General. I could make no announcement but I could not take any fresh private work. So, without explanation, I just stayed away from my Chambers, to the puzzlement of my clerk. The next day I spent with my wife Elaine, in Richmond Park, picnicking and from time to time listening to the news bulletins on the radio, waiting for the announcement of my appointment which would come that afternoon and explain my sudden idleness. It came about four o'clock. We packed up the picnic and rather solemnly wandered across the park, past the herds of deer, back to the car. We drove off to London to start an official life which came to a final conclusion twelve years later, with armed police guarding our home and our children.

Chapter 1
Monks and Actors

The hamlet where we lived as children consisted of our farmhouse and, across the lane, the twelfth-century church and the large house, the Abbey. It lay between Midhurst and Petersfield. The River Rother ran through the Abbey grounds and passed the end of our garden. Into it flowed the Hammer stream, where we bathed in the pools and built a raft, and the otter hounds would come splashing by, the huntsmen in their green coats and white breeches. In the eighteenth century a vicar on his way from our hamlet to Iping church across the fields had been murdered and robbed. It was said that there was a secret passage leading under the lane from the farmhouse to the church, constructed and used by smugglers in the days when the real sea came up to Chichester. Sixty years ago such parts of the Sussex countryside were truly isolated.

We had moved to this secret and buried part of the world because my father, who had served in the First World War and had at one time taken a regular commission, had left the army, gone unsuccessfully into business and then had conceived the idea that he was going to become a writer. My mother, who had come to him on their marriage in 1916 with a French maid and a pekinese, left all that behind as he settled down to write in the isolated house with no electricity where the water was pumped by hand from a well in the garden.

He began with short stories. Some were about the countryside and the church, and they began to find publishers. I cannot after all these years distinguish fact from his fiction. Was the story of the bones of an exciseman found in the well in our garden, or the rotting kegs found under the floor boards beneath the pews of the old church, local legend or part of one of his tales? I do not know. But the house was certainly haunted. I remember asking him one morning why he had come into my room to wake me carrying a light. (After dark, candles in old bottle-green candle-holders had to be carried by everyone, for there was no electric power.) He made some non-committal reply. I can see that white figure at the door of my room as if it were yesterday. Years later he told me that he had never come to me that night, and that mine was a happening experienced by several others, adults, including an aunt whose sobriety no one all her life had ever doubted.

I and my brother Mick, fifteen months my senior, loved the place, its secrecy, the absence of people, the silent mysterious woods, one of which was planted with exotic oriental trees and shrubs, a plantation which had long been neglected and grown wild. It was said that the owner had been a sea captain who had bought the land to build upon it. He had planted the shrubs which he had brought back in his tall ship from the Far East. Then he was lost at sea, and his bride drowned herself in the Hammer pond. Fact or fiction? The place draws me to this day and I often return.

In the meantime my father's short stories had led to a novel, then to plays produced in London, and later to early British films made at the studios at Elstree or Denham. This success led us, sadly for my brother and me, to leave our river and the secrecy of our haunted farmhouse and there began a new life, a more racy period, first in London and then at a house close to Sutton Place near Guildford. Sutton was at that time owned by Geordie, the then Duke of Sutherland, who allowed us to use his private golf course and swimming pool and covered tennis court. He rather fell for my young aunts, who lived with my grandmother in Sutton Park House.

Dutifully we attended all our father's first nights, the early ones in our blue suits straight from school. There were several disasters. One was at the Haymarket. The leading lady was the famous light-comedy actress Marie Tempest, by then well into, if not over, middle age. She forgot her lines; not just a few, but all of them. The first-night audience was at first embarrassed, then appalled, and then enthralled. Even we, fierce partisans, noticed that something seemed a bit odd about our father's splendid play.

On another occasion he had another play produced at the Adelphi Theatre in the Strand. It was an adaptation of a best-selling novel by Louis Golding. It was directed by the distinguished (but to us quite mad) Russian Komisarjevsky, and it was staged by the great impresario C. B. Cochran. We were disillusiond when we met the latter at the party after the first night. For 'Cochran's Young Ladies' were legendary, the chorus girls whom he selected and made into stars; but he came alone, youngladyless, bald and round like a bank manager. He was not nearly so interesting as Komisarjevsky, who at the first-night supper party kept drinking what I thought was water. The more he drank of it the sadder he became. But it did not require the lugubrious supper to tell me that the first night had been a flop. I knew, because in one scene set in a street, the lamp kept flickering off and on. I sat in the dress circle praying that it would stay lit. But it didn't, and I experienced my first doubts about the efficacy of prayer.

Among the friends of our family were Rudyard and Carrie Kipling. Their son John had been killed in the Irish Guards in France in 1915, while serving alongside my uncle, Rupert Grayson. When my father began to write and was achieving some success, he approached Kipling for advice. Kipling wrote to him in reply that the only way to learn to write professionally was to do your own work in your own way and then to keep on trying it on the market with the editors, 'who will give absolutely unbiased advice'. He added that to go to anyone 'in your own calling' (a flattering touch for the tyro) 'will only cramp your own style. I have seen that happen in too many cases ever to give advice to a beginner.' Seven years later he and my father were hired to work together professionally on a film script.

As children my brother and I used to be taken to visit Rudyard Kipling when he came to London at Brown's Hotel, where he usually stayed. We used to stare in fascination at his enormous, luxuriant eyebrows. Before each visit we would speculate whether the undergrowth (or rather over-growth) would have grown since last we saw him. He must have noticed our preoccupation, because his eyes used to twinkle behind his glasses – as though he were saying 'That's right. Take a good look. They *are* extraordinary, aren't they?' And we would come away full of tea cakes and clutching boxes of tin soldiers wrapped in serviceable brown paper tied by string.

After the death of her mother and father, his daughter Elsie Bainbridge in the early 1960s would come and visit my father at Chelsea Square where Elaine and I lived. She jealously and fiercely guarded the reputation of her father, which by then was in the shadows. She would permit only my father to adapt her father's work, and he wrote a series of the Indian stories for BBC television. Later he was approached by the publisher Hamish ('Jamie') Hamilton, who hoped he could persuade Elsie Bainbridge to lift her ban on Freddie Birkenhead's life of her father, of which she vehemently disapproved. He failed.

Among the closest friends my father made in the film world when we were boys was the actor and producer Tom Walls – the principal in the Aldwych Theatre team of Tom Walls, Ralph Lynn and Robertson Hare who starred in the series of great farces written by Ben Travers. My father and Tom had met when Tom had accepted one of my father's stories for a film script; later they adapted together *Rookery Nook*, one of the most successful of the Aldwych farces. We were taken on occasions to the film set. Once, extremely bored, we watched a 'shot' of Tom Walls repeatedly walking down a flight of stairs and into a yellow Rolls-Royce. In those days there were no union restrictions upon hours on the floor, each shot seemed to be repeated a hundred times, and shooting went on into the small hours of the morning.

But to us the great attraction of Tom was not his films but his horses. In 1931 he won the Derby with April the Fifth, trained by himself, and that September we all went up to the Downs near Slindon in the early mornings to watch the preparation of April the Fifth for the St Leger. I noticed that on these occasions my father always seemed remarkably stimulated. According to my mother he always was whenever he was with Tom in the morning; for Tom's breakfast was exclusively champagne. But April the Fifth could not repeat his Derby success. Tom's taste in horses, vintage champagne and attractive women, and his failure to repeat the success of the Ben Travers Aldwych farces, led him into deep debt. But the charm remained to the end. He was very bad for my father.

When we were older, on the first day home from school, we were often taken to luncheon at the then Kensington Palace Hotel, which was at this time the watering hole of many of the personalities in the British film industry, especially Gaumont British. My father had written the script for Alfred Hitchock's first, and better, version of *The Man Who Knew Too Much*. At one of these luncheons, Hitchcock was with us, and as with Rudyard Kipling we were struck dumb in wonder – not at something as exotic as eyebrows, but at his sheer bulk, shape, and appetite. He knew that we were home from school at Downside. The only conversation he addressed to us appeared to be quotations from the Latin Mass and a few statements, *ex cathedra*, of a religious character, all of which profoundly embarrassed us. Then a man who looked to me to be at least an ambassador, or a bishop in plain clothes, came over to our table. He was, in fact, the then doyen of English film actors, George, later of course Sir George, Arliss. His speciality was in historical roles and he portrayed both Benjamin Disraeli and the Duke of Wellington; the only difference in his performances, as far as I could judge, was that when he was the Duke he sat on a horse. It was said that by the vast fees paid him for each film he materially contributed to, if he did not actually cause, the pre-war collapse of the British film industry. Hitchcock did not seem to warm to him.

The most expensive British film prior to the Second World War was rumoured to be *Jew Süss*. We had gone down to Sidmouth to play cricket when my father was suddenly summoned home. He had been invited to write the script. This introduced us to two characters the like of which we had never previously encountered.

Hitherto the theatre people he had invited home were generally in the style of Tom Walls, rather rakish figures who shared his taste for the countryside; for my father was passionately devoted to field sports and had been brought up to love both gun and rod. His grandfather had taught him to fish as a boy and would sometimes take my father with him to Norway where he rented annually a stretch of a salmon river. In his turn my father always rented shoots and armed us with four-tens. My brother Mick was a good shot, but I was not, and I used to stand trembling with cold and apprehension as the bids rocketed off the Hog's Back and over the guns in the valley. Mick was also a musician, but his passion for jazz proved his undoing when at the age of nineteen he tried to become a Benedictine monk at Downside. He found a room with a piano and he would sit there, in his black monk's habit and shorn head, and play ragtime. The Novice Master came to hear of it and shook his head. My brother was told that he lacked sufficient vocation, so he left and joined the RAF and became a fighter pilot. He said it was the next best thing. He was killed in France in 1940.

But the two extraordinarily different personalities which the film *Jew Süss* brought into our lives were Lothar Mendez, an expatriate Hungarian from Hollywood who was to direct the picture, and his constant companion and amanuensis, Heinrich Fraenkel, expatriate Berliner. Both were short and squat, their English heavily accented, their humour incomparably Jewish. They and my father, with his military moustache and sporting tastes, made an incongruous trio. But they became firm friends and were often with us in the country.

At about this time I had been cast at Downside as Henry v. On the school stage I had waved my sword and bellowed out, 'Once more into the breach, dear friends, once more.' In semi-darkness, wrapped in a cloak above my armour, I had mused, 'Upon the King! Let us our lives, our souls, our debts, our careful wives, our children and our sins lay on the King.' By all this, and especially by my performance, I had been greatly moved. I was convinced that a star had been born. So I announced to the family that the career at the Bar (hitherto my fixed ambition) was to be abandoned. I would go on the stage. Would my father arrange interviews with Alfred Hitchcock and C. B. Cochran, preferably both? My mother paled, so my father sent for several friends, in particular for Lothar and Heinrich. They set to work – not on me directly; oh no, just when I was present. I discovered that no one thought much of actors. Actors were the interpreters of other men's words, chameleons, confused about their identity, vain and usually hungry. During all this talk Henry V sat silent, ignored, as the accented anecdotes swirled around the dining-room table. Soon the Great Actor stole away to his own room where he picked up the life of the great advocate, Edward Marshall-Hall, and nothing more was heard of a life on the boards.

The school years rolled on. At that time Downside was a sophisticated institution, too sophisticated for some. A new headmaster succeeded the remarkable Sigebert Trafford, who should have become the Cardinal Archbishop of Westminster. The new man acquired instant unpopularity by requiring the popular Head Boy to return to London his car, his dog and his mistress. This was considered highly unreasonable.

The community of Benedictine monks at Downside included a good share of eccentric English gentlemen, some former soldiers or parsons, a sculptor or two, and one who shared my surname, a connection who always referred to me as his nephew. He told me that when he joined the monastery in the 1890s he had rolled up in a hansom cab, and as he left the carriage he had thrown away what he then genuinely believed would be his very last Havana cigar. In the 1914 war he became the Senior Catholic Chaplain to the forces, founded the boys club which still flourishes in Bermondsey, and was rarely without a cigar – except in church.

In the 1930s the high roof of the Abbey church rang to the age-old sounds of the great Masses of the European tradition, and to the notes of the plain chant as the Community sang the office. Of an evening, once a week, the school attended Compline, which was followed by Benediction. At its end the candles were doused one by one until only a last, solitary light lit the high altar, and the cowled figures of the monks would slip away into the darkness and the silence. An eternity of centuries-old tradition was represented in those rituals. Little could anyone then conceive that only thirty years later they would be abandoned. It was an Anglican, Quintin Hailsham, who many years later sadly commented to me on the change which he himself had witnessed, as an occasional visitor, from the great rituals of tradition to the functionalism after the reformation of the Second Vatican Council, that Council in which the Abbot of Downside, Christopher Butler, had played so significant a part.

At the school there had always been a strong military tradition, perhaps coming from the days when only a military career was open to the English

Catholic. At any rate this resulted in much importance being attached to the school Officers' Training Corps, in which service was compulsory. During the 1930s, as the war clouds gathered, this importance increased. The Downside corps uniform, while not quite so distinctive as the pink tones of Eton, sported smart red piping. The corps was commanded by a retired lieutenant-colonel, who at the annual camps perennially outranked the commanders of other school corps. It was rumoured that Downside brought servants to the camps to clean our uniform buttons, and that we received special rations ordered from Fortnum & Mason. True or not, in the last years of that period the focus on the OTC, and the need to pass the proficiency exam, Certificate A, intensified. Fifteen months after my last camp as a schoolboy soldier, I was receiving the King's shilling (two shillings, in fact), a soldier in earnest.

But before this, I had one enchanted year at Cambridge. The uneasy peace that had followed the Treaty of Versailles of the year of my birth was coming inexorably to an end, and I experienced the same fate as had my father a generation earlier. He had had two years at Pembroke, Cambridge, before he went to his war mounted on a charger and carrying a sword, with which he later cut his wedding cake. That was the only practical use to which it was ever put. In my turn I had only one year at Christ's, going up after the Munich crisis of 1938 and coming down at the outbreak of our war in 1939. By virtue of my OTC Certificate A, I was on the Officer Cadet Reserve and I was accepted by the Irish Guards, the regiment in which one uncle was then serving and two others had served in the First World War. By the autumn of 1939 I was at the Royal Military College at Sandhurst.

It had been an unsettled year at the University. War had seemed so certain, study so irrelevant. There was a climate of fierce political argument, with the left overwhelmingly dominant in the Union. We on the right were few, making up in quality, we smugly declared, what we lacked in quantity. I joined the group which invited Winston Churchill ('Can't trust him', said my father at that time) to speak at the Corn Exchange in favour of national conscription.

I and my particular friends Christopher Dodd and John Hunt (later Secretary of the Cabinet) knew that the sands were running out. It was a time of waiting for the battle which we knew was coming; time was precious and we made the most of it.

That fallen star, Henry v took himself off into the Footlights. My father had been a member in the summer of 1914 when Jack Hulbert had been the star. Jack Hulbert never went to war, but danced his way on to the London stage. Some of his friends never spoke to him again. Anyhow I found my way into that upstairs club room, with the old photographs on the stairs and walls, and wrote and performed in a smoking concert. 'Three little tarts from the Maid's Causeway who never did things in a coarse whore's way', we warbled. One of the singers was Bill Mars-Jones, now a judge of the High Court. Disguised behind a handlebar moustache, I sang interminable verses of a folk song 'As I was Going to Strawberry Fair', while Jimmy Edwards came on stage with a ladder, a mop and a bucket of water, most of which eventually was emptied over me and my moustache. In the May Week Review, in top hat and habit, I performed my own lyric as a Horsey-Horsey Woman. Then, when the curtain fell, it was away to the May Week Balls. I had invited up a girl whom John Hunt immediately fell in love with – and later married. Meanwhile I pursued another, a student at the Webber-Douglas School of Acting in London. I had to climb a wall and gatecrash another dance in order to retrieve her and bring her, triumphantly, to join our party on the river in punts, and then on to Grantchester. We walked through the tall grass in the early-morning sunlight, the girls in their long dresses trailing in the dew and we in our tailcoats. So to breakfast – the final act of a magical year.

The next time I saw Cambridge I was attending an Army Medical Board, my tailcoat replaced by an ill-fitting battledress with canvas, anklets and hobnailed boots. In the west along the Maginot Line there was silence; the only war was at sea and in the air. My brother was with his fighter squadron in France. In the east my Polish schoolfriends and their families were being slaughtered by Nazi and Communist alike. Boyhood was over.

Chapter 2
The King's Shilling

It was nine months after my arrival at Sandhurst before I had my personal inoculation in real war – and then it was on English soil. Battalions of the Irish Guards had been to Norway and back, to Boulogne and back. But it was with the Training Battalion that I went to guard the heights of Dover in 1940 and to lie in the ancient redoubts to be shelled by the German long-range guns and to be machine-gunned by their aircraft. We watched the destroyers being driven out of their Dover station and we sat waiting for the invasion fleet to swim out of the summer haze which that July floated over the English Channel. Dunkirk had come and gone, and my brother had been shot from the skies above Flanders, not before he had accounted for three German fighters. It was only when Belgium was liberated four years later that his grave was found. The love between brothers, especially those separated in age only by months, can go very deep. He was the only man with whom I was ever utterly open, and although it is nearly fifty years since he crashed to his death I still feel as though a part of me had been amputated.

I spent seven years as a soldier, a not inconsiderable portion of any man's life. Parts of that time remain clear in the memory; parts have gone. Suddenly, for little or no reason, the curtain rises and a scene is revealed, vividly lit. The curtain then falls, and then rises again. The scenes have little continuity. If I attend the annual dinners of the regiment in which I served, then on the following days the curtain rises more often.

The Irish Guards is a regiment which is part of and is yet different from the sister regiments in the Brigade of Guards. 'There is something about the Micks', the Queen Mother, who has almost adopted the regiment as her own, is reported to have said. Indeed there is. There is an air to them, a style that is quite unique. It is a regiment which has all the pomp and starch which befits all Household troops; but superimposed is élan, a dash, a swashbuckle that sets them apart from all the other regiments. 'I may not come from Ireland,' said a sergeant serving in 1944 in the bloody Anzio battle, 'but I am as fine a —— Mick as you are.'

At these dinners there are, annually, more inches around the waists and less strands of hair upon the heads of the diners, yet each sees in the others only the dashing young ensigns of forty years ago. They are evenings of transformation. The link between men who have shared personal danger is stronger than almost any other: it is a bond which neither time nor change in fortune sever. The heroes of that time (and there were many of them) remain to me heroes still. Courage, after all, is the first of qualities and those of us with less of it naturally worship those with more.

But living under fire in Dover in 1940 did not last beyond the autumn. Soon there was fire from the skies over all the cities. In December of that year I stood on the top of the old Junior Carlton Club in Pall Mall and watched the second great fire of the City of London, wondering how it all could ever end. It is said that human memory often rejects what is painful. That is not true of all experience, although it is mainly the happy times which, I suppose, are remembered. So the memory of those days of Blitz retains vividly the pleasures of leave on a Saturday evening in London, which had a routine fixed whether or not bombs were falling or the blacked-out night remained silent. One had to be lucky enough to be in London from camp or hospital, or home from overseas; then there was a circuit which girlfriends demanded, and they became exasperated if idleness or inefficiency had failed to arrange it.

It began with drinks in the old Berkeley Hotel with its entrance in Piccadilly over which Ferraro had presided until he evacuated himself to the Hind's Head in Bray. Then it was across the road, sometimes dodging the shrapnel which fell from the anti-aircraft shells, to Jermyn Street. Then to turn down Duke Street to Quaglino's for dinner – at a legal maximum cost of five shillings a head with extra shillings for music and dancing. From there it was on to the Four Hundred nightclub in Leicester Square, to dance in the stygian darkness to a real live band, entwined on the small dance-floor or seated with heads close together at the wall tables with their dim pink-shaded table-lamps. Once I had to return there late on a Sunday morning to collect something which I had left behind in the small hours of the morning, a cigarette case I believe. Now the overhead lights were full on; large women were at work with mops and dusters; Rossi, the proprietor, stripped to his shirtsleeves, was at work in his office. I grabbed what I had come for and fled, unwilling to see that romantic place as it really was.

The Training Battalion was then at Hobbs' Barracks, a few miles from the hospital near to East Grinstead where Archie McIndoe treated and operated on his 'Guinea Pigs', the men whose skin had been horribly burned and scarred by war. Some used to come and dine with us in our Mess or join us at the local hotels where wives or friends were visiting. One of those whom I got to know was Richard Hillary. Because my pilot-officer brother had been lost a few months earlier and none then knew what had happened to him, I used to talk with him about the fighting in the air and through him try to discover more about the air war in France before the retreat.

Richard Hillary was then writing his book, *The Last Enemy*. He was scarred not only by the terrible burns to his face and by the claws which his hands had become. He also suffered bitterly from his disfigurement. He must have been very conscious of his former physical beauty and its loss tormented him. Understandably he was ambivalent towards us, towards us in our wholeness, towards us who had then experienced so little of the war which he had been fighting and which had so cruelly transformed him into what he felt was a monster. He wanted our company, he liked being with our girls, but he resented us. He wanted to join in a part of the gaiety of our youth, but as his had been burned away he would also sneer and scratch at us. We probably deserved it, but we had the grace to understand and to tolerate the savagery of the wounded man.

Sometimes he would come with us on short trips to London and when he came he would wear large dark sun-glasses. If a girl attracted him, after he had been talking to her he would suddenly sweep off the glasses and she would then be confronted not only by the scarred skin and features but by hollowed-out caverns from which protruded the naked bulbs of his eye-balls, the eyelids burned away and not yet rebuilt by the surgeon. He would watch the girl for her reaction, taking a perverse satisfaction should she react with undisguised horror. He seemed to want to play in reverse the role of John Wilkes, who needed time to talk away his squint and his ugliness, for it was only after Richard had begun to captivate by the interest and intensity of his talk that he would then make his demonstration. But we would usually have warned her, and she would be prepared.

I did not see him again after I left to join the 1st Battalion, and soon all the scenes of leave were replaced by sterner ones; the Four Hundred by the Combined Operations Training School at Inveraray and the uniform for London – of blue patrol with high collar, double set of four brass buttons and blood-red stripe down trouser leg – by combat dress. It was at Inveraray that the battalion trained for its intended role in Assault Force 125. There we practised landing from assault craft, wading up to the armpits in the icy sea on to the beaches below Inveraray Castle.

The then Duke, a kindly, rather fussy man with a high-pitched voice, enjoyed showing the treasures of his castle to the troops training beneath its walls. He declared that he found the Irish Guardsmen whom he showed round by far the most courteous and interested of all of those whom he had ever welcomed to his home – until he discovered several dirks and snuffboxes missing. They were retrieved, and the Duke puffed off – disillusioned.

The assault for which we were training never materialized. The orders were changed. At 10.30 p.m. on 1 March 1943 the P&O liner *Strathmore* sailed in convoy from the Clyde, taking the Irish Guards back to war. Eight days later we docked at Algiers, just before nightfall. The rain began to fall, and with the rain came an air raid. We then marched more than a dozen miles, fully laden, to an open field and lay on groundsheets in a sea of mud – hungry, weary and, above all, very wet. Now the curtain falls and rises on kaleidoscopic scenes in my memory, without accurate continuity, until I arrived back in that city weeks later, in the summer heat.

Thereafter comes the memory of a nightmare drive in the dark through a storm across the mountains towards the flashes and the sounds of guns. I commanded the battalion carrier platoon. A Bren-gun carrier was a tracked, open-topped vehicle which at the best of times was hard and heavy to steer. At speed, around mountainous hairpin bends, with precipices to one side and in bitter driving rain, the task was devilish. Vehicles in the convoy careered over the cliffs; we stopped each half-hour for the drivers to get out and run round the vehicles to keep themselves awake. When at last we rejoined the battalion, which had come up by sea, it was like coming home – save that home was to be in the line at Medjez-el-Bab – 'The Gate of the Path', the path which led to the plains and to Tunis. 'Who holds the pass, holds Carthage', said Hannibal. And in March 1943 the British First Army tenuously held the pass to Tunis, the city near to Carthage which was the last foothold of the Axis powers in Africa.

A few years ago I felt discomfort and irritation in my thigh. On examination, beneath the skin and near to the surface, there appeared dark pieces of metal. They were small pieces of shrapnel which had lodged in my leg forty years earlier, the survivors of what had then mostly been removed. They were at long last working their way to freedom. I was rather sad to see them go. But they evoked memories; of a tracked vehicle, a carrier, in a wadi, and on the ground beside it a pair of boots. Above the boots, neat canvas anklets; above the anklets, two legs in khaki trousers – and above the waistband a bloody stump, sans arms, sans head, sans everything. It was the remains of my personal driver, beside whom I had been sitting but seconds earlier. I remember looking down matter-of-factly, unmoved by a sight which seemed quite in context with all that was happening. As indeed it was. The intense preoccupation with the extraordinary circumstances of battle makes all such spectacles usual and everyday. Later, another scene: this time an overturned carrier, with its tracks trapping the legs of Guardsman Price (suddenly that name comes back), pinning him to the ground. I and a companion tried to free him, tugging at him until he screamed, the sound rising above the noise of the mortar shells which were bursting around us. We had to leave him, with water bottle and cigarettes; and we ran back under covering fire.

During this battle it was very hot by day. The North African summer had begun at last, congealing the mud. We had started off in shirtsleeve order, but by night it was bitterly cold on the hills, and jackets or blankets could never reach us. I had gut-wracking dysentery which had commenced its attack after I had lain in the mud in that field outside Algiers some weeks earlier. (Back in England I had had serious stomach trouble requiring a nauseating diet, mainly of milk, which I have loathed to this day. I had been downgraded medically and had eventually got myself upgraded. It is trouble which has recurred off and on ever since childhood. Now the African dysentery was ripping at my gut.) Its inevitable consequence created an extra sense of vulnerability on a battlefield. I did carry, like all officers, some grains of morphine. But I had treated one badly wounded Guardsman. He was lying out on the hillside; I could reach him only at night. I fed him some of the morphine but I could not move him and there was no one to help. He had taken the grains and then he had begun to laugh and the laughter rang out all the night until, just before first light, it ceased. So I did not try the morphine on my gut.

The Commanding Officer was a much loved figure, Andrew Scott. He was imperturbable. He began the war as a subaltern and towards its end was acting commander of a division. Once I had to report to his headquarters, which were in a cave whose entrance faced the enemy positions and so was sporadically under fire. Prudently I crawled towards it, hugging the rocky ground. Andrew was seated cross-legged at the entrance. 'Hello, you old bugger', he said. 'Have a gin and tonic.' I stood up. I felt that I was in White's, 'The Parson's Rest' as Andrew called it. At the HQ was

Father J. R. (Dolly) Brookes, monk of Downside, a former regular officer and now the Chaplain. He was everywhere in that battle, carrying his blackthorn stick. But he was never far from his Mass-box, which Andrew called his 'box of tricks'. He captured three Germans and turned them into stretcher-bearers.

The remnants of the battalion were by then high up on Point 212, famed as 'the Bou'. The possession of this hill was the key to the battle and would allow the armour to break through and into the plain and victory at Tunis. They were holding the hill against desperate German counter-attacks with small arms, since nothing heavier could reach them. They were under constant attack. My command, the carriers, had the task of ferrying ammunition and water to the foot of the hill, up which the carriers could not possibly mount, and bringing back the walking wounded. I remember thinking to myself, 'If you are ever tempted to think battle glorious, remember these moments!'

Then there is lit, again vividly in memory, a scene in an olive grove behind the line. Our fifteen-hundredweight trucks were parked under the trees. The bedding was laid out on the back of each truck, covered from the night by the vehicles' tarpaulin hoods. But the stars were visible. Under the ring of olive trees stood the table and the camp chairs. On the table were the tin mugs and the whisky. Sitting there was Gilbert Kilmarnock from Divisional Headquarters. He became a life-long friend. As we talked there was the friendly scent of tobacco and the sound of the hissing gas hurricane lamps casting shadows, while in the distance was the rumble of the guns. Then snug into a sleeping bag on the back of a truck, watching the shooting stars, feeling safe, safe, safe.

Another olive-grove scene. It was of the grove which was used as the park for the battalion's carriers and transport as the assembly point just before battle. We were waiting for the barrage to begin. The wireless picked up a broadcast of news on the African Theatre Forces Network. One item was the report of a strike back in England. Somebody turned it off with an oath.

The last scene is of a snow-white hospital ship, with large red crosses painted on her side and, unlike the *Strathmore*, with all her lights blazing. It brought me home – dreaming at night of battle and by day composing melancholy poetry, pale imitation of Owen and Sassoon. A German aircraft, a Focke-Wulf, circled the ship and swooped in low as though to attack. But it flew away and let the white ship steam on undisturbed until she docked, silently with no flourish of trumpets, and disgorged her cargo into hospitals and homes.

So followed leave, and medical boards; command of our Regiment Recruit Company; adjutancy of our Training Battalion; and finally a staff job with Colonel Andrew, now home and commanding a district of London. This staff job gave the opportunity for long nights of study, burning the midnight oil, so that I could read and get called to the Bar. As a result, when I emerged from the army in 1946 and was discharged, there was a gap of only two months between exchanging the forage cap and long grey greatcoat of a Guardsman for the pristine white wig and stuff gown of a newly fledged barrister.

Chapter 3
Rosa Lewis's Impecunious Tenant

Save for my brief flirtation with acting, the consequence of waving my sword on the school stage as Harry of England, I had always wanted to be a barrister, as many of my father's family had been, as far back as the eighteenth century. They are buried in Combe, Berkshire, and their graves, let into the stone floor of the parish church, were shown to me as a child by my mother, who wanted to encourage me to follow in their tradition. My father himself had been destined for the law, until the First World War interrupted his time at Cambridge.

On one early morning in October 1946, seven years after reporting to Sandhurst, and now clad in a dark suit, white stiff collar, topped by a curly Lock bowler hat, and a Brigg's umbrella clasped in my yellow suede gloves, I found myself boarding a No. 9 bus in Kensington, paying the lawful fare of tuppence ha'penny and dismounting in Fleet Street. From there I walked into the Temple, then still badly scarred with bombed-out buildings and a concrete barrage-balloon emplacement in the garden. In Paper Buildings I climbed the stairs to the chambers of Walter Monckton.

Walter's son, Gilbert, had been a friend of mine at Cambridge. A chance meeting with Donald Somervell, Attorney General in Churchill's wartime coalition government, led to my finding a place as a pupil in Walter's chambers. It was a fortunate start. Walter had been a close friend and counsel to King Edward VIII during the Abdication crisis, and he was the most distinguished barrister then at the Bar. He was a man of great personal charm, and when he spoke to anyone he conveyed the impression that he or she (and especially she) was the most important person he had ever met. Years later, chatting together in the Smoking Room of the House of Commons, he confessed to me that it was very exhausting always being pleasant and he mused about passing a lifetime doing what he greatly disliked, making speeches. But he was very good at both.

He had a most attractive speaking voice, and I learned that as a young man he had had elocution lessons. So, of course, off I went and located a teacher, a very old man with rooms near to Marylebone Station who made me read poetry to him. I enjoyed this, but apparently he did not, because after a time he told me that I must learn to throw my voice and that in order to test me he would leave the room and go down the corridor to listen. Meanwhile I was to continue to read. I did so, but then I happened to glance out of the window. I saw the old gentleman scurrying across the road and into a public house. I suppose that it had been due to that thirsty old Professor that shortly afterwards, during a case at the old Bailey, the then Recorder of London, Gerald Dodson, sent me a note in which he said that my voice pleasantly reminded him of the then Archbishop of Canterbury. I was not quite sure what to make of that, but I endeavoured to look pleased.

Walter had an immense practice. He had been for a few months Solicitor General in Winston Churchill's Conservative government after the end of the coalition and before the electoral defeat of the Tories in 1945. But Walter had had no seat in Parliament. Winston was anxious that he should find one, and he was applying to local constituency parties. It is a measure of their independence and power (which they retain to this day) that despite the Leader's expressed recommendation and wish, the local Conservative Associations regularly rejected this distinguished figure and confidently selected others who thereafter mouldered in dim parliamentary obscurity. It was believed that Walter's frequent rejection was because he had been cited as co-respondent in a divorce. Other days other ways. Eventually Walter found a seat in Bristol.

At the hearing of the divorce suit (which would lead to his happy marriage to Biddy Carlisle) he asked me to attend and to report. I did so, and received a useful lesson – namely, to extend the great Jowett's advice over checking references to checking the facts in a brief. In an undefended divorce all the facts are meant to be agreed and nothing is in dispute. All that had to be done was to establish the marriage and prove the matrimonial 'offence'. So the petitioner husband was called to give evidence and duly sworn.

'Are you', he was asked by counsel, 'George Josslyn L'Estrange, eleventh Earl of Carlisle?' 'I am', the witness replied. After establishing the date of the marriage, counsel came to the time when Walter and Biddy, Lady Carlisle, fell in love during the war in Cairo. 'In 1943,' said counsel grandly, 'were you Commander-in-Chief Mediterranean, Royal Navy?' 'Don't be a bloody fool,' came the choleric reply, 'of course I wasn't.' Despite this bumpy start, the divorce was granted.

Walter permitted me often to sit in on consultations which he had in his chambers. So I would sit well to the back of the room, and not infrequently the complex nature of the matter under discussion led me into agreeable reveries upon with whom or where I was to pass the evening or the coming weekend. But I soon learned that this was dangerous. For Walter, with the kindly purpose of bringing a humble presence and unknown name to the attention of the grand solicitors then in the room, would sometimes disconcertingly call for the comment of the youngest person present. The grave, grey heads would turn and cock, and await a hesitant contribution from the back of the room. It was not good for the nerves.

At that time almost every man wore a hat. Walter was often briefed to argue cases in the Privy Council, which sat in a building in Downing Street. After luncheon, which counsel ate in a room in the House of Lords, he liked to take a brisk walk down Whitehall before returning to court. It was then still the custom for a man, as he passed the War Memorial to the Fallen in Whitehall, to raise his hat in acknowledgment of the sacrifice of 'The Glorious Dead'. As Walter and I were walking and talking, a man scurried by and raised his hat to the War Memorial. 'Hello,' said Walter, raising his, 'hello, how are you? How are you?' He could not bear to slight anyone by letting them think that he had not recognized them. So he took no chances.

In the court he would stand, graceful and outwardly at ease, the tones of his attractive voice lapping around the ears of the judges, one of whom was an Indian whom I noticed was daily shrinking physically. It was the bitter cold winter of 1946–7. There was a fuel crisis, for which Emanuel Shinwell the Minister was, of course, blamed. Artificial heating during the day was forbidden by law, so the judges brought in rugs to wrap around their old bones. The Indian, sensibly, used his rug as a headdress and a shawl. He did, however, leave one ear free.

When Walter came to the end of a particular part of his argument, he would pause and then turn away from the judges and bend. At this his opponent, who was usually Cyril Radcliffe, would purse his prim lips and make a faint, very faint, cluck of his tongue. Meanwhile Walter's junior, my pupil master, undeterred by the cluck, would advance, crouch beside Walter and pour into his receptive ear the requisite law and propositions for the next stage of the argument. Walter would absorb, then turn back to the judges and out would flow the propositions of law provided by his junior but now dressed in Walter's unique and graceful style.

The supplier of the law was Brian McKenna, later a High Court judge, who was one of the best lawyers of his day, and a man of endearing eccentricity. He was a person of great kindness, shy and generous, who even when a judge and in his late seventies would tramp through the countryside and London, rucksack upon back, dressed and looking like a down-and-out tramp. He tried to teach me some law, but he also knew that it was the advocacy to which I was so attracted. Brian would send me over to the Law Courts to sit through prominent cases, one of which was a political libel suit in which Sir Patrick Hastings, a one-time Labour Attorney General, cross-examined Harold Laski who had been chairman of the Labour Party during the 1945 general election. In reply to an offensive and pugnacious question by Hastings as to whether there were any privileged members of Society in the Labour Party, the grossly provoked Laski began to reply 'Why indeed, Sir Patrick, when you were a Member....' 'Don't be rude', snapped Sir Patrick. Hastings was so effective at the Bar because his manner was tough and unpleasant, Walter because his was so smooth and agreeable. I could see that you had to choose.

Brian secured for me the role of taking a note for Walter when he defended in what became known as the Chalk-Pit Murder. This meant that I sat behind him in court throughout the trial and attended all consultations. Thus, at this early stage of my life at the Bar, I was able to witness at first hand the onerous task of defending counsel in a capital murder case. It was an invaluable experience.

The accused had been a Minister of Justice in New South Wales and he had conceived a mad, obsessional jealousy of a young barman whom he absurdly believed was the lover of his elderly and infirm mistress. So he arranged that the young man should be lured to a house in Knightsbridge. There the victim was bound and, deliberately or not, throttled to death. It was a hopeless task for defending counsel, and all knew it. When the time came for Walter to make his final speech to the jury and while we were waiting for the entry of the judge, Rayner Goddard, the Lord Chief Justice, and for Walter to start his speech, he turned to me and asked if I had ever ridden in a point-to-point. I noticed that the knuckles of his hands were white. I replied that I had not. He said, 'I feel as though it were just before the off.' Walter inevitably did not prevail, and the accused was convicted of the murder. But the death sentence was commuted, and the ex-Minister was sent to Broadmoor, the criminal asylum for the insane, where later he died. For long years thereafter, indeed for all of my almost forty years of practice, I remembered Walter's words and that occasion. I took comfort that a man so experienced, so distinguished, at the height of his powers, could feel so nervous and apprehensive.

Each and every appearance in court is a personal performance for the barrister, demanding great co-ordination of brain and tongue in the effort to persuade, especially when the advocate's heart and the back of his brain know that his effort must surely fail. Right up to the end of my time at the Bar, I used to stand, looking, I hope, cool and at ease and in command as years of experience had taught, while my stomach leaped with apprehension and my body literally ran with sweat. At the end of each day, exhausted and drained like an empty vessel, the advocate crosses the Strand back to the Temple, back to many hours of reading and research and note-making to prepare for the effort of the next day. No wonder it has been said that the first asset for the barrister, the one most to be desired, is an iron constitution and a well-ordered digestion. This last I sadly could never command.

The first time that I actually wore my new white wig in court was when I was rushed over to sit behind a silk (a KC or King's Counsel, as they then were) whose junior counsel had been suddenly called away. I slipped unobtrusively into my place in the row behind the silk who was called Gilbert Beyfus, known at the bar as the Old Fox. He was making his final submissions in a civil action tried by a judge alone. Beyfus was obviously under pressure. As he addressed the judge, he was patrolling his row, a step or two one way, turn, and then a step or two back. He was rolling and unrolling the long black ribbons of his silk gown. As he passed me on his patrol in profile in front of me, I thought that he winked. I bowed politely. When he came back he turned his head towards me and he definitely winked. So I winked back. When he came back the third time he leaned over me and said savagely, 'What the devil do you want?' It was only then that I realised that the wink was, in fact, a facial twitch which became the worse the worse a case was going. I shrank back into my seat. He got his revenge, for he left me alone to face an anguished client against whom judgment had been given of twenty thousand pounds, then a very tidy sum indeed.

My first solo appearance was, naturally, in a magistrates' court and it was at Bow Street, where I appeared for a company to apologize for defective brakes on a lorry. I earned a guinea (paid six months later, which was considered prompt), and I celebrated at Claridge's where after luncheon for two I had still change in my pocket from my, as yet unpaid, guinea. So commenced a series of similar appearances, usually on behalf of a client without merit in causes without hope before a stipendiary magistrate with a defective digestion and an overcrowded list. One certainly learned to keep it short.

Then fortune took an unexpected turn. Patrick Hastings had written a play, *The Blind Goddess*, which centred upon a scene in the court of the Lord Chief Justice. It was about to be made into a film. Hastings demanded that a practising barrister should be employed as an expert adviser. One of those grave-faced gentlemen whose conferences I had attended, and into which Walter had so thoughtfully drawn me, now instructed the clerk that he wished me to act as this expert adviser. He, or rather the film company, would pay twenty-five guineas a day. In 1947 this was riches beyond the dreams of any pupil barrister. I at once rushed off to the Lord Chief Justice's court to take a quick look at it, for I was so green that I had never even seen it. Then off to the studio. There I met Michael Denison. He played the part of the young and wronged hero, who was about to be cross-examined by the fierce KC played by Eric Portman. Michael had served in my father's Intelligence section in the war, and from this meeting we became good friends. He says that later I became the model for his television character, Boyd QC. I do know that both Boyd and I fiddled with our watch-chains when engaged in cross-examination.

The director of the film was Harold French. Day after day the scenes were shot and reshot; each evening I happily ticked off my 'take'. But more than that, for when as happened now and then I had a genuine brief (if only marked 'one guinea'), Harold French would obligingly rearrange the shooting schedule to allow me, as he said, 'to do the real thing'. On my return he would enquire closely about the result. This was awkward since the cases seemed always to concern lorries which were overloaded. As George Arliss had before the war, I realised that I after the war was contributing, if more modestly, to the perennial cash crisis of the British film industry. We were, however, getting along comfortably enough until one day the author, Patrick Hastings, visited the set. Eric Portman in his KC's wig and silk gown was introduced. 'You are the last person whom I could ever imagine as a silk', said the author abruptly. Then, turning to me, 'For God's sake see that they don't shout.' Then he left. Suitably chastened we went back to filming.

But all good things come to an end. The court of the Lord Chief Justice was dismantled; another set replaced it. I said goodbye and returned to the Temple. My year of pupilage was also drawing towards its close. To celebrate, Brian my pupil master came to dine. Later that evening I took him to a nightclub, where the scene, to which he was unused, appeared to interest him. I introduced him to a friend seated at a table. The scholarly and courteous Brian bowed gravely – and very low. His behind struck a passing waiter who tipped a tray of drinks on to the lap of the Spanish Ambassadress. Next morning, feeling unready to face his usual daily stint dealing with the mountain of briefs stacked on his desk, he announced that we could pass that morning more profitably by listening to the often extremely uninteresting cases in the Divisional Court. I was uneasy. When at last we were seated in the back of that court, a rather noisy process, I noticed the surprised glances of various counsel and solicitors and even of the judges at the unusual spectacle of the noisy arrival in their court of this busy and well-known counsel, who then appeared to fall asleep. Tactfully I persuaded Brian to leave and led him away. Shortly afterwards I bade him goodbye as his pupil. We had got on very well, and I loved him. But I felt that, on the whole, he was relieved that my successor as his pupil was a sight more sober-sided.

Life in England in 1946 was still austere, and Sir Stafford Cripps, fruit juice and nut cutlet beside him, ensured that it remained so. Food was still rationed, wine hard to secure. But nothing could dampen the relief at having survived, nor the sense of life renewed and a future ahead. Despite the austerities and the drabness of the as yet unrebuilt cities, there was in the air an atmosphere of excitement, certainly for those recently released from soldiering. Ascot began again, after which I abandoned all betting on horses. Henry and Daphne Bath gave a ball at Claridge's, where Evelyn Waugh complained indignantly about the manners of the modern young man. They would, he said to me with grim menace, keep blowing air on the top of his head. I apologized hastily. Later I would encounter him in White's, where he would sit morosely smoking a cigar, while Randolph Churchill argued loudly at the bar.

In the summer of 1946, for my first peacetime holiday for eight years and before I started life at the Bar in earnest, I had driven in a small car to the south of France, down the old road south which in places was still pitted with shell holes. Burned-out tanks still lay beside the road. I went back two years later. In the little fishing village of St Tropez, we were dining on the quay at L'Escale, then the only real restaurant, when out of the darkness there slid the hull of a great black schooner which moored beside the quay. The little harbour was in those days full only of fishing boats and quite empty of yachts. From the schooner black crewmen lowered a gang-plank, down which staggered Errol Flynn and a drunken party. Long before Brigitte Bardot, St Tropez had begun to lose its innocence. There was then only one nightclub where taut, sad-faced lesbians danced together and a girl, Barbara, did a striptease with a look of utter contempt upon her face. The local inhabitants often emptied pots over the heads of visitors when they left the club. I was offered the local doctor's house for three thousand pounds. I did not have it, and so lost a fortune.

At Easter 1948 I visited Lydia Deterding in Paris and I stayed with her in her apartment in the Boulevard Suchet – for the first and last time. Lydia was the White Russian relict of Sir Henry Deterding, the oil magnate. During the war she had lived in rare opulence at Buckhurst Park; now she was at her apartment in Paris. Beneath the block was a garage equipped with great gates and with locks fit for the strongroom of a bank. For cars and petrol were then precious and needed to be protected. We all went to the Russian Orthodox Easter Eucharist. Up the aisle processed the Grand Duke and his Grand Duchess. As they passed, the women curtseyed and the men bowed. The Grand Duchess in real life presided over a ladies' cloakroom. After the Eucharist, Lydia, the only affluent member of the White Russian community, had invited many of them back to the Boulevard Suchet. Along the length of her great room ran a table groaning with food and wine. I had returned with my hostess before the guests had arrived. But I made the error of slipping into my room, literally for a minute or two, to check my luggage as I was leaving very early the next morning. Having seen all that food and drink I thought that the night might last long. When I got back to the drawing-room and sought some wine and some supper, the cupboard was bare. It was as though a swarm of locusts had descended; in a few seconds, there had gone every last crumb.

Next morning I got up early and crept carefully down to the fortress garage, opening the gates with the many keys with which I had been entrusted. They were, I knew, the only set. Beside my Ford was parked Lydia's shiny, black Hispano-Suiza which I knew was to take her next day to Chantilly to a picnic which she had organized for her community. I drove out of the garage, locking the security doors carefully behind me. I congratulated myself that I had woken no one in the household and I swept off on the road to Calais. It was only on the ferry some hours later that I found that the precious keys were still in my pocket.

I knew then that this would be the end of a very beautiful friendship. I gave the keys to the purser with instructions to post them when the boat returned next day to Calais. I neither saw nor heard ever again from Lydia, as I knew I never would. But I did hear later from Dimitri Romanoff who was with her later on the morning of my departure. He said that he sat impassively, smoking his yellow cigarettes with their cardboard holders, while priceless china smashed, rich fabric was ripped, and the Boulvard Suchet rang to Russian expressions of resentment.

On New Year's Eve the fancy-dress Chelsea Arts Ball had been revived at the Albert Hall. It was best to take a box – but on the upper tier some feet above the raised dance floor as this gave some protection from invading marauders. Our party in 1948 included the bald-headed Sir Philip Egerton, who had for many years served worthily in the Sudan Civil Service. For some reason we had christened him Sid. We had to hold on to the tails of his eighteenth-century costume to prevent him from descending on to the dance floor and clobbering the painted, pretty youths who seemed gravely to offend the baronet only recently home from bearing the soon-to-disappear burdens of the Empire. We could not stop him from shouting abuse, but fortunately it was in Swahili.

Also in our party was Duff Cooper, who had brought a very pretty girl. At one stage a real policeman, in real uniform, came into our box. He had come to make some routine enquiry concerning Ambassador Cooper's car. However, Ambassador Cooper's companion thought that he was a fetching fancy-dress policeman, and she started affectionately to unbutton his tunic. In this unbuttoning she had reached his regulation braces when she too had to be restrained. It was a difficult group. The policeman, however, had been understandably flattered by these attentions and when, after dawn, our party was gathered outside the Hall waiting for the Cooper car and taxis, the same policeman innocently approached the pretty girl, who, after all, must have seen something in him earlier in the evening for she had had her fingers on his buttons. So he gave her a wink and a nudge. But by this time she had reached the tearful stage in her New Year's celebrations, and she fled piteously from the friendly approach of the law and came to anchor weeping upon Duff's arm. 'How dare you', he thundered, 'insult this lady who is under my personal protection!' She certainly was. 'Send', the Ambassador bawled, 'for your superior officer. Send for the Commissioner of Police'. Fortunately at this moment the car drove up and Andrew Scott bundled in the Ambassador and the tearful girl, followed in a heap by Sid, who eyed the chauffeur pugnaciously as if to check that he was not wearing lipstick. The driver passed the test and the car bowled off. Like the officer of the law in *Albert and the Lion*, our policeman was quite nice about it. I was glad to get home.

During the war I had drifted into an engagement. In the summer of 1940 after the fall of France and the rout of Dunkirk, invasion and the German paratroops were expected daily. England was alone and under siege. Few believed then that we could survive the onslaught from the air and from the massive forces which were then being assembled across the Channel. Even if the invaders were beaten back, the devastation would be immense.

Haidee and I decided to break off our engagement. We were very young and we both knew that it had arisen out of the unreal atmosphere of the Phoney War in a London which had not yet had to come to terms with what war meant. Soon it would. We realised that we had been caught up in the frenetic yet romantic mood which existed in the days before any real battle had been joined. So we decided to end our engagement, and we announced it to our parents. But my parents were then grieving the loss of my brother, shot down over France a month earlier. For some reason they took this decision as an extra blow and they urged marriage upon us. Haidee's mother supported them. She thought that we were overreacting to the times and she told Haidee not to be so foolish.

Because of the invasion threat, all troops were confined to barracks and were put on regular stand-to. Haidee telephoned and asked me to try to get permission to come and see her for an hour. I succeeded and I went to the hotel in the village to which she and her mother had come. We talked. What were we to do? We flinched from adding to the pain which apparently our decision had caused. We thought, as did everyone, that the battle on the beaches and in the English fields could not be long delayed. Life did not seem to have much expectancy, certainly not for a life of home and marriage. Finally we made the decision to go through the form of the marriage and then she should go home to Ireland. So it was done. After the ceremony, the bride took aside the startled priest and told him that it was no marriage, that it was all a sham, and that she had never truly given her consent. She was in tears, and he was understandably distressed. But of course he remembered. Haidee went back to Ireland and I to my battalion.

But the Germans never came. The Battle of Britain was fought in the sky. Later I went at intervals to Ireland on leave. Haidee came for periods to England. We started a family, but it was never an easy or happy relationship. That original decision was rarely out of mind. Our three daughters were a great joy but in the event I did not see much of their childhood. We had a house for two years in London after the war and then rented one in the country. But by then she had fallen in love with the man whom she eventually married. She took the children away, first to France then to Swizerland, where the children later went to school. Finally they settled in Rome.

A civil divorce followed. The priest had remembered what Haidee had said to him after the ceremony in 1940, that it was all a sham, that she had never really consented. So after many years the marriage was annulled by the Sacred Rota in Rome.

I had gone to live in a flat in Jermyn Street; it was next to the old Cavendish Hotel. The flat was reached by a flight of uncarpeted stairs. My landlady was Rosa Lewis. I had known her for several years and I was often summoned to sit with her in her drawing-room on the right of the hall as you entered, and opposite the portrait of Rosa's patron, Lord Ribblesdale, in his hunting clothes. Once during the war some of us on leave had taken Rosa with us, dining and dancing. Towards the end of the evening it was clear that the bill would be enormous. Rosa had noticed our consternation. ''Ere,' she had said. 'Isn't that young Arkwright [or some such name] sitting over there with a tart?' We peered through the gloom and saw a bald-headed colonel in the Brigade of Guards sitting at a table with a highly respectable-looking woman in her forties. 'Ask young Arkwright to come over 'ere and 'ave a word with me.' We did. The colonel came, promptly. He and Rosa put their heads together, talking animatedly. After a time all fight seemed to go out of young Arkwright. He paid our bill. He didn't react very effusively when I bade him goodnight.

During the war Rosa used to sit in her chair through the fiercest of the bombing, steadily drinking the excellent champagne from her cellar and muttering obscenities about Hitler. On VE day her long, heavy Edwardian skirt went cartwheeling into Jermyn Street.

After the war I was often in the Cavendish and talked with her and her companion Edith Jefferies, who was never parted from Skippy her testy small dog, and with Charles the butler-headwaiter. I used to dine there with a friend, George Sullavan, a former Mick who lived in the hotel. When Rosa rented me her flat, I used to pay the rent weekly by taking my cheque personally to her accountant who sat in an upstairs office in the hotel. We had become friendly, and he knew that I was just starting at the Bar. One day he said to me: 'You know, you are really paying too much rent. The old lady does not need it. Let's reduce it.' And he did, substantially. I was suitably grateful. After I had left him I went downstairs. Rosa beckoned me into her drawing-room, where she was sitting in her chair, behind her the screen decorated by Edwardian 'cut-outs'. She was still handsome, her silver hair piled on top of her head. ''Ave a drink', she said. Drink was, of course, champagne. While we were chatting and drinking, the middle-aged accountant on his way home put his head through the door. 'Goodnight, Rosa', he said cheerily, 'goodnight.' Rosa ignored him. He disappeared. Then she leaned towards me and said, conspiratorially, ''Ere', she said, 'that young man, 'e's ruining me.' I had sufficient conscience to choke a little on my champagne.

At her funeral hundreds flocked to the service at St James's, the church opposite her hotel. She was one of the last Edwardian institutions in a London changing out of all recognition. Edith carried on the hotel for a while, but when she too went the building was pulled down to make way for a hideous replacement. And with it went my flat. But I had already moved west, to Chelsea. The salad days were over.

Chapter 4
Fleet Street

The accountant was, of course, correct about the shortage of resources of a newly called barrister. There were many briefs, but they were not highly paid and they were paid late. The rules of the profession did not permit combining practice with employment. A non-executive directorship, writing or teaching were permitted. But the most sought-after permissible means of supplementing a barrister's income was to be taken on as a libel reader on a newspaper. This was the practice which the more lively press followed, of having a barrister come each evening to the newsroom to read all the copy, with the duty to advise the editor or managing editor if any piece might involve the newspaper in libel suits or, more importantly, involve the newspaper and the editor personally in proceedings for contempt of court.

Because my brother had been a fighter pilot, I had met Max Aitken, 'young Max', Lord Beaverbrook's son. I approachd him, and I was taken on for a trial as the 'night lawyer' on the *Daily Express*. Later I also read for the *Sunday Express*. The work required leaving the Temple in the evening at about six, crossing Fleet Street to the black glass building, and remaining there until about two in the morning. It made for a very long day, but it was a stimulating experience. I was effectively a bachelor. I was lonely and the work paid well.

The legal manager of the Express Group at this time was James Critchley. He had a halo of white hair, a florid complexion and a deceptively mild manner. He had unrivalled experience in newspaper law. He was close to 'the Lord', Old Max, Beaverbrook. He had advised Winston Churchill to issue a writ against the *Daily Mirror* when it printed its 'Whose finger on the trigger?' edition on polling day in October 1951. It was reckoned that that headline had cost the Tory Party several seats.

Critchley's room at the *Express* was filled with Victorian paintings in heavy gilt frames. Those which could not be hung on his walls were stacked against desk and chairs. At night he invariably played chess at the Reform Club. The editor of the *Daily Express* was the legendary Chris, Arthur Christiansen; the managing editor was Ted Pickering.

The night lawyer sat at a back table behind the night news editor and beside another *Express* character, Willie Crumley, a blunt Scotsman who read the copy to ensure that all complied with *Express* 'style' – e.g. 'Socialist' for Labour, 'Tory' for Conservative, and so on. The night lawyer's duty apart from watching for libel was especially to prevent anything which might lead to proceedings for contempt of court. In 1949 Sylvester Bolam, the editor of the *Daily Mirror*, had been jailed by Lord Chief Justice Goddard for publishing a story compromising the accused Haigh, who was awaiting trial for 'the acid-bath murders'. As a consequence of Mr Bolam's unpleasant experience, editors were very wary and careful about the dangers of publishing material which might prejudice a forthcoming trial and land them in court for contempt.

This was the heyday of the Beaverbrook *Express*. I would watch Osbert Lancaster come into the office, lay down his hat, stick and gloves, draw his cartoon and leave, on occasions all within one half-hour. In 1951, when I first stood for Parliament at Hackney, he drew a cartoon for me for my election address. It was meant to illustrate the contemporary split in the Labour Party (times don't change!). He drew a picture of Clement Attlee and Herbert Morrison, behind them an enormous Nye Bevan; the caption was 'Look out, Clem, I think we are being swallowed.' Good, simple election stuff.

Mid-evening I would go to the pub with Willie Crumley; later to the Press Club with Ted Pickering. Then in the early hours I would walk home to save the cab fare, through streets deserted save for the tarts. At weekends the routine on the *Sunday Express* was different: a short Friday evening, and then Saturday midday to midnight. I kept this up until I was married and selected as parliamentary candidate for Epsom, long after my Bar practice had grown so that I did not need the extra income. I enjoyed the work and the company, and in the long run the knowledge gained of newspapers and of journalists was a great advantage when later I was briefed in many libel actions and represented, at one time or another, most of the national newspapers.

The most taxing session on the *Sunday Express* was, naturally, with the editor-in-chief, 'Man of the People' John Gordon. He was a Scotsman like his successor John Junor, and he usually selected as his column's target,

or victim, the magistracy. Week by week he would compare the sentences
and penalties imposed by the magistrates' courts mostly in motoring cases,
and he vigorously denounced the irresponsible leniency which magistrates
regularly displayed. Motorist ofenders, he thundered, must be severely
punished.

Then came a day when this scourge of the magistracy was driving his
Rolls-Royce along Queen Victoria Street on his way to his office. John
Gordon's mind and attention were, I assume, so concentrated upon the
irresponsible weakness of some local bench of magistrates which he
intended to expose in his column that he wholly failed to see an approaching
motor cyclist, turned straight across his path, and knocked him over. John
Gordon was accordingly summonsed to appear before the court at the
Mansion House, charged with dangerous driving (more serious) and alternatively careless driving (less serious). He asked if I would represent him.
I was duly instructed by his solicitors, who, on the instructions of their
client, bargained fiercely with my clerk so that I was booked to appear to
defend the editor-in-chief for a very modest fee. As the hearing date
approached, the 'Man of the People' column, which every Sunday usually
served up a dish of devilled magistrates, dropped this and concentrated
rather upon the sins of those members of the House of Bishops who
failed to preach sufficiently vigorously the more awful tenets of the Old
Testament.

The day of the trial arrived. The tribunal consisted of a single magistrate,
a City father, an alderman, sitting alone. The prosecution produced a
blackboard and chalk and demonstrated the paths of the Rolls-Royce and
the motorcycle. The motorcyclist swore that the driver of the fancy car
had cut across his path and obviously had not been looking where he was
going. The case for the prosecution rested. As I was preparing to call my
client to give evidence in his defence, the magistrate suddenly announced
that he found that the charge of dangerous driving was unproven; he
dismissed that charge, but he found the defendant guilty of the lesser
offence of careless driving. This was too good to be true. Up I jumped.
The Court, I emphasized, had not even heard the evidence of the accused
and while the Court could, as now it had (this I emphasized), dismiss
(more emphasis) the serious charge of dangerous driving, it could not
convict of any charge before hearing the defence. A cloud much larger than
a hand passed over the Alderman's brow. He realized that he had erred.
He could already hear the comments of the Divisional Court when the case
went to appeal on the inept and incompetent behaviour of the magistrate.

'Ah yes,' he said, 'slip, an unfortunate slip. Please proceed with the defence.' I hustled John Gordon through his evidence. He was piqued, since he had been rehearsing it for days. Even his shorter version of the accident, however, sounded singularly unconvincing. For how had the unfortunate motorcyclist come to be bowled over by the huge car? In my concluding submissions, I reminded the magistrate, with much regret, of his slip. I insisted that I and my client were confident that he would eliminate entirely from his mind what he had earlier said. The magistrate nodded unhappily. He was now only too anxious to be done with the case. He acquitted Mr Gordon on all charges. I asked for costs. The magistrate winced, agreed and rapidly retired.

Over lunch John Gordon attributed this satisfactory result entirely to his performance in the witness box, which, he declared, had done the trick. It was lucky, he felt, that we had encountered a magistrate of above-average intelligence. There were, he opined, very few. Then he told me stories of the last mad days of Lord Northcliffe, and of his early association with Lord Beaverbrook. The following Sunday, and thereafter, the readers of the *Sunday Express* were returned to their usual diet of boiled justices of which, for a few weeks, they had been deprived. The very modest fee was the only dividend which I received from the successful defence, for thereafter my advice on any controversial pieces in his column was rejected even more confidently than before.

During these agreeable and instructive years as 'the bloody lawyer' reading for libel on the *Express* I made one particular friend, Derek Marks. He was then political correspondent and he later became the editor. Physically he was enormous, with a gargantuan capacity for food and drink, his appetite for which was matched by his knowledge of and fascination with the world of politics. He was astute and especially irreverent about the people who practised that black art which he himself so dearly loved. When he was the paper's Lobby correspondent at the time of the Suez crisis his reports of what passed at the dramatic private meetings of the Tory Party were particularly accurate and caused the Whips great embarrassment. But Derek was scrupulous to avoid compromising his friends. A mole was sought and thought to be found in the person of the admittedly sinister Conservative MP, Henry Kerby, a hugely unlikeable man, trusted by few. Whether or not he was Derek's informant, no one ever knew – for certain.

Beaverbrook, always known on the *Express* as 'The Lord', invited me to luncheon. I was, like many others, immediately bewitched. He spoke of trials and barristers and especially of F. E. Smith, whose father had once lived in a house in Birkenhead on the property of my great-grandfather.

At the end of luncheon we moved into his study and as we talked he picked up a sheaf of memoranda and glanced through them. When he read the first he let it float to the floor. As the first fluttered to his feet I thought that he had dropped it accidentally, and I was about to get on my knees to retrieve it when another floated down, followed by others. Soon the carpet was a snowfield. I was glad that I had not stooped to collect that first sheet.

Later I saw much more of him, for his home Cherkeley was in the Epsom constituency which I represented. At my first election he sent me £100 for my 'personal expenses' – not, he instructed, to be included in the campaign funds or attributed to him. After the poll he telegraphed, 'Splendidly done and I am certain entirely due to your wife.' I had married at the end of 1954 and he, like all the world, greatly admired Elaine. We used to sit on the patio at Cherkeley drinking his rum cocktails. Elaine came from Rhode Island in the United States, whose capital Providence was where Max Beaverbrook had made his controversial fortune. He called it 'Rogues Island'. He would ask me about Winston Churchill, with whom I would sit from time to time in the House of Commons smoking-room. Max would enquire about Winston's health and state of mind and lucidity, and he asked whether Winston pined for the despatch-riders bringing the red boxes and the loss of power which had been so reluctantly surrendered only a year or so previously. It was like one faded beauty enquiring about the looks of another and taking pleasure if the report were sad.

At the time of Suez in 1956, old Max gave a dinner party at Cherkeley. Among the guests were George Drew, then leader of the Conservative Party in Canada; Beverly Baxter, a Canadian and a former Beaverbrook editor and at the time a colleague of mine at the House; Anne Sharpley, an attractive columnist on the *Evening Standard*; and Lionel Cohen, the judge. The attitude of the Canadian government to the Suez adventure was then arousing controversy, like everything about that adventure. When dinner began, Max began to stir things up. He asked George Drew whether 'we Canadians' were going 'to rat'. The dinner party erupted. Whenever Lionel Cohen judiciously sought to calm the uproar, Max would stir it up further. I watched the feline grin on the broad face and his obvious pleasure at the row he had inspired. Once he slipped away and when he returned and found that the dispute was flagging, he revived it so that it raged on until the cars came at the end of the evening. As he waved us goodbye from his doorstep, he was shuffling his little feet as if in some celebratory dance of satisfaction.

Many years later, in the summer of 1970 and after his death, Elaine and

I spent a day at his villa La Capponcina in the south of France. Young Max used to loan it to his editors for holidays, and we were the guests of Derek and Jeannie Marks. Elaine and I went for a walk through the grounds which led down to the sea wall. In various positions in the terraced garden, rails had been constructed which had permitted old Max at the end of his life to move around the garden in his wheelchair. The whole place was permeated by his spirit. As we walked, a large black rabbit hopped out of the bushes and on to the path ahead of us. It looked at us. It had one ear cocked; the other flopped. It had a grin on its face – or so it seemed. As we got nearer it hopped out of sight. A few minutes later it repeated the performance. Then again, and again. At each corner it was there to greet us. Then it finally disappeared. We were quite certain that it was Max.

Chapter 5
First Lessons in Electioneering

From my schooldays I had been fascinated by politics. But when I asked my father if he would not like to be a Member of Parliament, he said angrily that he could think of nothing on earth which he would like less. I was rather shocked. I was driven to consult my fierce but beloved grandfather, my mother's father, Sir Henry Mulleneux Grayson. She was his eldest daughter, his second child, and had inherited his indomitable character and will. But even she when a girl took no chances with him. At dinner she was always seated on his left, with her current boyfriend on her left. On the ear next to the boyfriend glistened an earring, but grandfather's ear had to be left unadorned. For a short time he had sat in the House. He had loathed it and soon, snorting contempt, had left. He advised me strongly to have nothing to do with it.

One of his colleagues had been J. F. P. Rawlinson kc from my father's side of the family. He had sat for Cambridge University for twenty years from 1906. He eventually became a Privy Councillor, but he held only junior office. He had appeared for the Treasury in 1896 in the enquiry in South Africa into the circumstances of the Jameson Raid, and was described by Edward Marjoribanks as a very muddled advocate but a great gentleman. He would have liked it that way round. There is a 'Spy' cartoon of J. F. P., entitled 'Eton and Cambridge'. He lived in Crown Office Row in the Temple, but at the end of his days he left his fortune to the hosptial nurse who had tended him. She was rather nice to my brother and me when we were children. She used to have us to tea, and would make a point of showing us the family crest on the silver spoons.

At the time of the 1945 election I was still serving in the army. But in 1950 I was at the Bar and living in Sussex, and when Clement Attlee announced the election that year I went to the local Tory headquarters and volunteered to help.

I duly helped, if that is the correct word, Tufton Beamish, whose constituency was Lewes, which consisted of many villages and a few small towns. I was cast in the role of preliminary speaker, the outrider whose task was to precede the candidate on his nightly stint of a dozen or so village meetings. I had to hold the fort by trying to keep the village audiences occupied, if not entertained, during his nightly circuit. That election preceded the television era and the meetings were well attended. My task was to start off the meetings with a harangue, and to stop as soon as the candidate had arrived. I would then leave to go on to the next village while Tufton made his speech and answered questions. At the next village we would repeat the procedure, and so on throughout the successive evenings of the campaign.

It was impossible to gauge how long the candidate might be kept in each village. It depended on the reaction of the audience to his speech and on the number of questions. As the night wore on the candidate's timetable often fell behind. There was no warning of delay, and my harangues had to be shortened or prolonged without notice. It was good training. The audience did not want to hear me; they wanted to hear Tufton. But a political meeting had been arranged; something had to be done to keep the electors occupied until the great man arrived.

The person assigned as the driver to take me on from village to village was Lord Hindlip, Sam, whose enthusiasm for the Party and the cause was not generally thought to be matched by any aptitude for platform performances, even those demanded by fifty or so villagers. Indeed Tufton's agent instructed all of us on no account and on pain of death to permit Sam to open his mouth on the platform. In the agent's opinion, and that of other organization men, a public performance by Sam could seriously jeopardize even the vast Tory majority in this safest of Tory seats.

One evening, Tufton was falling farther and farther behind his schedule and my voice was growing more and more hoarse, and the audience in successive villages more and more bored and impatient. At the final meeting my set speech was exhausted, and I had clearly reached the end of any conceivably acceptable contribution. During a pause in which I sipped some water and longed for something stronger, I read a note which had been laid before me. It read. 'We have some Reds here. If you like I can give them a few minutes on the State of the Poll.' It was signed 'Sam'. The orders of the agent, the fears of the organization men, deserted me. Suddenly all that I now wanted was to hear Sam, who had spotted some

Reds and who wanted to talk to the village on 'the State of the Poll'. 'What state?', I wondered. Which poll? What had the Reds to do with it? I felt that I must know the answers. The crisis of Tufton's delayed arrival called for crisis measures. So I took the plunge.

'And now,' I said, 'before you have the privilege of hearing your Conservative candidate, who will shortly be joining us' (some shouts of 'Where is he?'), 'I am pleased to announce that Lord Hindlip is going to speak on the State of the Poll.' There was an immediate stir of interest. Sam was known and well liked locally, particularly in the village pubs. A buzz of anticipation arose. Sam, red-faced, trembling with excitement at the chance offered to him, stumbled noisily centre-stage from the wings, tilting as he went the hat across the face of the lady chairman on the platform. The interest in the hall visibly increased. I handed over the centre spot. Sam took up position, his face now almost purple, his body bent fiercely forward, his fists clenched, his eye fixed presumably on the Reds, both arms engaged in a curious sawing motion. There was a momentary silence, which seemed to last quite a time. Then 'Ladies and Gentlemen,' he thundered, causing an elderly woman in the front row literally to jump at this sudden change in pitch and volume.

At that precise moment Tufton bustled into the hall. There was an audible sigh of disappointment from the audience as though a balloon had been deflated. Sam said not another word. Organization men took over smoothly. Sam and I were politely moved back into the wings. The Clowns were removed, and the Hero began the speech he had already delivered a dozen times earlier that evening in a dozen similar halls. I would never hear Sam on the State of the Poll. All Sam said to me after the meeting as he drove me to the pub was 'I spotted those damn Reds all right. I'd have dealt with them.'

We got a chance at 'the Reds' an evening later. In a sense he and I had our revenge on the organization men, although the victim was poor Tufton. It was at Newhaven, a small port and perhaps the only place in that constituency where the Tory candidate might expect some excitement. It was the last of our nightly meetings. When we arrived and I was going to mount the platform and start the meeting, Sam whispered loudly, 'The place is stiff with Reds.' I then proceeded to commit the cardinal sin of the warm-up speaker for a candidate engaged in a wearisome circuit of meetings. I stirred up the audience. After a time the front rows were cheering and the back rows were booing. And in the back rows were men in long sea-boots which they began to stamp and clump. They out-noised the genteel front rows. Tufton later told me that he could hear the noise from the hall as he rounded the street corner. He was exhausted from three weeks of electioneering; the last thing he wanted was a stormy final meeting. But he got one all right. The thud of sea-boots reached a crescendo as Tufton arrived. I shamefacedly handed over the meeting to the candidate and I crept out with Sam for our usual drink. He was triumphant. 'Splendid,' he said, 'splendid.' And then wistfully, 'If Tufton had been held up a litle longer I could have had my go on the State of the Poll. Bloody Reds.'

Tufton Beamish was, of course, returned with a thumping majority, and he kept the seat until 1974 when he retired to the Lords as Baron Chelwood. He did all this despite his helpers – Sam and me.

After the narrow survival of the Attlee government in the February 1950 election, I managed to get on to the Conservative Party's candidates list. In the summer of that year I attended, at their request, on the Hackney South Conservative Association, who were seeking a candidate. Among my rivals invited to the selection meeting was David Napley. In his memoirs he has for some strange reason dressed me up, at this interview, in the prestigious uniform of the Brigade of Guards. He seemed to think that this gave me some advantage and swung the decision in my favour. In fact I had exchanged that uniform for that of the lawyer four years previously, and both David and I attended on equal terms, both soberly attired in sub-fusc. Old men forget; but old Presidents of the Law Society shouldn't.

The minuscule majority which Labour then held in the Commons meant that another election could not long be delayed. But before the election battle of Hackney began I had an encounter of another kind.

'Pray', said our host, 'have some tea.' He moved his delicate, almost feminine, white hand towards a small table, on which stood a silver tray with a decanter of whisky, a siphon and a box of cigars. We sat three abreast, our host in the middle, three of us in a row as though we were the sole occupants of the stalls in a theatre. We faced, however, not a stage but a long wall. On the wall were hung, and against it were stacked, literally scores of our host's paintings. He regarded them through the blue cigar smoke with unfeigned satisfaction. He invited us to select the one which we most admired. I chose a snow scene. I struck lucky, for he approved. It had been, he said, very difficult to paint.

It was August 1950, some fourteen months before Winston Churchill began his second and peacetime term as Prime Minister. I had driven over to Chartwell with my friend and contemporary Roger Frewen, the son of Winston's cousin Moreton Frewen, known as 'Mortal Ruin', of whom that afternoon Winston spoke with much affection. We had spent the afternoon alone with our host, walking in the garden, feeding the waterfowl, being shown the home-built walls. Now we were back in the house.

After the satisfactory review of the art displayed before us, he turned to politics. Roger had told him that I was at the Bar and had been adopted as the candidate for the Hackney South constituency. So he spoke about the notorious Horatio Bottomley, who had been a member for that constituency both before and after the First World War. He enquired whether I conducted a personal canvass. I replied that I did. 'I trust', he said, 'that you do not emulate the highly effective but not over-scrupulous style of him who I hope will be your predecessor.' There was precious little chance of my succeeding at Hackney, I thought to myself; even you, I thought, could not achieve that miracle. But he was launched into his anecdote.

Mr Bottomley, he explained, dressed in full fig of top hat and frock coat and carrying a cane, would make personal calls upon constituents in carefully selected areas. When he had gained admittance to a house and was seated and engaged in winsome conversation with the householder, he would lay his hat and stick on the floor beside him. After he had left and the front door had been closed behind him, there would then come another knock. It was, surprisingly, Mr Bottomley once again. If, as happened more often than not, the door was opened by a child of the family, Mr Bottomley, with an apology for his further intrusion, would explain that, alas, he had left his stick behind him on the floor beside the chair on which he had been sitting, where, of course, he had discreetly pushed it out of sight. Mr Bottomley begged the child to fetch the stick for him. If the parent had opened the door, Mr Bottomley asked that the child be sent on this errand. In any event, on retrieving his stick Mr Bottomley would thank the child, press a shilling into a willing palm, and the Member of Parliament raising his tall hat would saunter off to continue his personal canvass. These calls of the Member of Parliament were, accordingly, eagerly anticipated, the errant stick regularly retrieved, the shillings widely distributed, and Mr Bottomley's hold on the affections of the electorate firmly consolidated.

This mode of influencing the electors gave our host much satisfaction. The story led on to others about Bottomley and F. E. Smith, who together had formed an extremely effective litigation team, with F. E. representing Bottomley's dubious companies, and Bottomley representing himself. The memories of F. E. brought with them tears, which rolled untended down the cheeks of the past and future Prime Minister as he recollected what he had written about the death of his friend: 'Beneath the setting of the sun and the night there was only the briefest twilight. It was better so.'

But Winston's tears were soon brushed aside as I was cross-examined about how long I took in preparing my speeches. Not satisfied with my hesitant estimates, he told me sternly that if the citizens honoured me by listening, I must honour them by preparing. I thought of the half-dozen of the Hackney Association Executive Committee sitting in the bare constituency office and of the resigned look upon their faces whenever anyone addressed their weekly meetings for longer than five minutes. Then he turned to international affairs, which were troubling him and the world. He remarked that he did not care to sit in a room where a man was poking a rifle through the window, however earnestly the rifleman swore that he had no present intention of pressing the trigger.

The level of whisky in the decanter had now fallen, the cigars were extinguished, and the time to leave had arrived. Churchill stood in his siren-suit at the top of the steps outside his front door waiting as we two young men got into my awful open-topped yellow car. He remained there bowing, until his supremely insignificant visitors had disappeared down the drive. I manoeuvred the car rather awkwardly as I drove out into the country road, for I was still clutching the butt of the cigar which he had given to me. At home I kept it in my stud box, until my cleaner came upon it and threw it away. So, years later, when sitting with him and talking in the Smoking Room of the House of Commons, I purloined another and kept that as a substitute for the one which he had indisputably presented to me.

Hackney South, in north-east London, had a socialist majority of over 20,000. Within its boundaries lay Ridley Road, at that time the battleground for fierce street clashes between Communists and the recently revived Fascists, who would march and countermarch and attack each other with stones and bottles and stink-bombs. The Conservatives were few in number but, like any group surrounded by a sea of opponents, dedicated and courageous. It took courage to be a Tory in Hackney. A Tory hand-bill invariably meant a stone through the window-pane.

The Conservative Association had a president, a prosperous builder by trade and a Territorial colonel, who cheerfully led his candidate around the pubs on an electioneering pub crawl. After that, he felt that he had done his bit. The chairman was a Mrs Mary Wilson MBE, justice of the peace and a staunch Conservative who served her community selflessly in numerous non-political fields until she was dismissed from all her official local appointments by her shabby political opponents. There were also one or two local Conservative councillors. So the officers were fine; but the troops, save for a few Young Conservatives, were almost non-existent.

Accordingly the only possible strategic role for the Hackney Tories in the general election campaign in October 1951 was to make as great a noise and as much electioneering fuss as possible, in the hope of making the enemy run scared. We could not possibly come anywhere near to winning the seat, so our objective was to become so visible and so public on the streets that the enemy might be deterred from doing what they ought, namely send their own local troops across the borders into neighbouring marginals in which the general election would nationally be won or lost. If we could scare the local party into holding back their own workers because of the fear that we might be making some kind of unexpected impact, then it mattered not what was the ultimate result in Hackney. We would have made an effective contribution to the national campaign. Also, we might have a lot of fun.

And this is what we set out to do. We had, of course, no money, and so I took up a collection from the bar at White's organized by Ian Menzies. I then asked Central Office for any unemployed, even unemployable speakers and I recruited a team of enormous ex-Warrant Officers from the Irish Guards. Both of these groups were to play important roles in our local strategy. Then, with as much publicity as possible, we announced to a sceptical Hackney electorate through an even more sceptical local press that the Tories were coming to Ridley Road and would be setting up their platform to hold open-air meetings. A local editor enquired if we had taken out personal insurance. I replied that we had, but it was of a different kind from that which he had in mind.

The drill was now carefully prepared. At Ridley Road, local Young Conservatives set up our stand and guarded it. At our headquarters the team of Central Office speakers was briefed but, I must confess, not wholly taken into our confidence. They were unlikely performers for the dangerous task of trying to win the support of the street-wise inhabitants of Ridley Road. One of the team of speakers, smartly dressed in hacking jacket and cavalry twill trousers, said that as he thought the evening might prove exciting he had come in his gardening clothes. One or two had come straight from their stools in the smarter counting houses in the City; and there were several earnest academics. They were all led off to Ridley Road.

By now there had gathered round our stand a bunch of villainous-looking men of enormous size. At the sight of them, the visiting speakers grew thoughtful. Trouble started at once. Unfortunate speaker followed unfortunate speaker, all bravely explaining important aspects of Conservative policy as set out in the manifesto. The giants hooted and heckled and insulted. Soon, attracted by the row, a large crowd of regular Ridley

Roaders started to assemble. They soon grasped that the heckling was being led by a group of outstandingly large men. If, they reckoned, there was going to be trouble (as there usually was in Ridley Road), they would be on the side of the big battalions. At the height of the uproar the Tory candidate arrived. A signal was passed to the current speaker who, with the sweat pouring from his brow and tears in his eyes, gladly descended from the platform to a storm of boos and insults. With a bound the gallant candidate took his place. The heckling reached a crescendo. Here was excellent sport.

Then, something very odd happened. The noise began to abate. A close observer might have noticed that the large men, who had started all the trouble, suddenly began to fall silent. Indeed, after a few more minutes, they could be heard to say to all and sundry, 'Ah, but this fellow's talking sense.' As the candidate continued, the large men even began to nod agreement with the rhetoric flowing from his lips. Their conversion must have seemed to some as unexpected and sudden as that of St Paul.

Some of the hecklers at first did not notice that the big men had changed sides. They kept up the sport for a time. Then they began to look around them and suddenly they began to grow uneasy. For the big men who had so recently been their friends were now looking decidedly menacing, and the menace, for some reason which was beyond them, seemed now to be directed very unfairly towards them. The candidate at last leaped from the platform with a final cheery wave, the big men told all and sundry that this was the man for us and hoped it was the man for them, at which the Hackney hecklers swiftly agreed and the strange meeting drew to is close.

An hour later, just over the constituency boundary and away from any anti-treating restrictions, the large men might have been observed being served prodigious quantities of pints of stout by the candidate and his entourage. Unfortunately on one occasion I was at the bar ordering drinks when one of the speaking team who had earlier undergone a particularly rough time saw me and came over. 'That', he said, 'was the most unpleasant and terrifying experience of my life.... However did you manage to quieten those great louts?' Then he saw to whom I was handing out the pints. He never forgave me.

In the event the Labour majority hardly shifted (bad); but the Conservative vote swelled (good). It had certainly been fun. I had learned much about fighting an election. I could, of course, enjoy it all because there was no conceivable chance of getting elected. Next time round, it would all be very grave – and very respectable.

I went back to the Bar, to the great relief of my clerk who, like all barristers' clerks, thoroughly disapproved of this political skylarking when there was serious work to be done at the Bar and sensible guineas to be earned, guineas the shillings of which went smartly into his own pocket.

Chapter 6
The Towpath Murder Case – A Sequel Twenty Years Later

On 1 June 1953 the body of a young girl was found floating in the Thames near Teddington Lock. Where she had been dragged into the river were found not one but two pairs of women's shoes. Six days later the body of a second girl was found in the Thames. Both had been stabbed and raped. A month later Alfred Charles Whiteway was arrested for assaulting a fourteen-year-old schoolgirl at Oxshott and a middle-aged woman in Windsor Great Park. A further month later he was charged with the vastly more serious charges of the murder of the two girls whose bodies had been found in the Thames.

So began what came to be known as the 'Towpath Murder Case'. It is a reflection upon the changes in life and society that have come about during the past thirty years that the facts of these murders and rapes were greeted with great public horror, almost disbelief, that such an enormity could have been committed. The trial which followed was reported daily under banner headlines on the front pages of every popular newspaper. Television was then in its infancy, and what there was was polite and respectable. Everyone and everything on the box was rather decent. The nightly ration of blood and sex and cruelty and what was then barrack-room but is now drawing-room language was not yet dished out to every household. On the stage the Lord Chamberlain exercised firm control from St James's Palace; nudes had to be statuesque – and stationary. On the cinema screen couples, even married couples, were never shown to share a bed; violence was, generally, in the style of 'bang-bang-you're dead'. Homosexual acts between men, even in private, if discovered, led to prosecutions, and conviction to sentences of imprisonment. Authority, even age, was generally deferred to; youth was regarded benignly as rather engaging. Men gave up their seats to women on buses and trains; demon-drink was the only common drug; pregnancy usually led to matrimony. The penalty for murder was death.

So trials for murder were then occasions of real drama, for in the final scene a human being might be formally sentenced to die. These trials were accordingly much publicized in the press, and 1953 was a year of sensational murder trials. That summer had seen the trial of John Christie for the murder of women whose bodies were found at No. 10 Rillington Place, where four years previously had been located the bodies of Mrs Evans and the child Geraldine – for whose murders another man, Timothy Evans, had been convicted and executed. Now in September there was to begin the Towpath Murder Case.

Alfred Charles Whiteway's solicitor, Arthur Prothero, was a remarkable personality among those lawyers who were then practising in the criminal courts. He was a tall, well-built man with a short black beard. He usually sported a flower in his buttonhole; on St David's Day it was a daffodil, and at Twickenham, when Wales were playing, a leek. He was a former officer in the RNVR who enjoyed sailing Thames barges. He was the son of a distinguished police officer, and as a solicitor he was a fighter, but one wholly trusted by the police and scrupulously honest. In the early 1950s he began to brief me. I was not in chambers which specialised only in criminal work, and the briefs he brought were interesting and often exciting. Unlike many of his confrères, he paid counsel's fees promptly. We got on well and I liked and admired him.

When he was retained by Whiteway, he instructed me to defend. Whiteway's counsel, announced the press, was to be a 'thirty-four-year-old ex-Irish Guardsman and former Tory candidate for Hackney'. I was not at the time a silk (that is, a QC). Indeed it was less than seven years since my call to the Bar and in those days it was unusual for a junior counsel to be instructed for such a defence in such a sensational criminal case. That he was not – as I was not – a regular practitioner at the Old Bailey earned some sour looks. For, sordid as was the crime, the case involved technical points of criminal law concerning the admissibility of the evidence in the murder trial of a fourteen-year-old schoolgirl alleged to have been attacked on another occasion by the same accused; scientific evidence about the nature of stains on clothing which were said to be blood; and reflections upon the conduct of the enquiry by the investigating police. From the professional point of view there were hidden shoals and dangerous rocks which would have to be navigated and it was a case which any leading practitioner would have been very willing to handle.

In those days all criminal trials were shorter and juries far less tortured by doubt than today. Quite often, if invited by the judge, they would not retire to consider their verdict but would merely turn towards each other, put their heads together and, more often than not, cheerfully return verdicts of guilty. They readily accepted police evidence, especially when given with the requisite air of seriousness and authority. The business of the Old Bailey was done briskly by four judges enjoying generous holidays, whereas now it requires the attention of twenty-four.

The police investigation into the Towpath murders had not run smoothly. A hand-axe which the prosecution claimed was the murder weapon had been left in the police car which had taken Whiteway to the police station on his arrest for the other lesser offences of assault. Whiteway had pushed the axe out of sight under the seat of the car where it had been found by a police officer. Instead of handing in this important exhibit the police officer who found it blithely took it home and later used it for chopping wood. Eventually it was retrieved. The police officer had the apt name of Cosh; he fainted during my cross-examination.

But the kernel of the prosecution evidence was a statement amounting to a confession, which it was alleged that Whiteway had made at Kingston Police Station. The statement began, 'It's all up. You know bloody well I done it. . . . I bashed her, she went down by the lock. The other screamed out down by the lock. Never saw her till then I didn't. I nipped over and shut her up.' The statement went on, 'Put that bloody chopper away . . . it haunts me.' The statement ended, 'Give it us,' meaning the statement. 'I will sign it.' The police admitted that he had later said, 'So you have done it on me. I shall say it is all lies'; and about the statement, 'You tear that last one up. I did not give it.'

To Arthur Prothero, Whiteway emphatically denied that he had ever said those words or made any such statement. He claimed that he had been tricked into putting his signature on the paper on which the police officer had written the statement. Obviously the statement, if given in evidence and if it was believed that Whiteway had said those words, was damning. If Whiteway had not said those words then the police officers had concocted false evidence. There could be no halfway house; either Whiteway or the police were lying.

The duty of defence counsel, if Whiteway persisted in his version of what had or had not been said in Kingston Police Station, would be to confront the police officer, to face him with the suggestion that he was lying, and to present the jury with a stark choice concerning whom they believed. And I knew that the choice would be between an articulate and poised policeman and an unprepossessing and ill-educated prisoner. What

I, as defending counsel, thought was the truth was not a matter for me. I had a professional duty to perform.

When I received those instructions in the form of the written brief from Arthur Prothero I at once insisted that I should see Whiteway. I had to receive from him, from his own lips, what he had to say about that statement. However improbable any alternative might seem I had to check whether there was any other explanation. For instance, could the police have made a genuine error? Was there some misunderstanding about what Whiteway had said? Or even had Whiteway in his dislike of the police officer said the words as a stupid taunt, words which he had (as the police admitted) shortly thereafter withdrawn? Any of these explanations seemed improbable but I had to hear directly from Whiteway what it was that he said had passed during that interview.

I saw him with Arthur Prothero in one of those bare rooms with a wooden table and chairs which are set aside in prisons for such conferences. Whiteway was a heftily built man with a cleft chin. He rarely looked directly at me when he spoke. I turned straight to the statement, the confession. Had he confessed? No. Had he used any of the words set out in the document? No. Could the police officer have made some error out of confusion over what he was saying? No. Was that his signature on the paper on which the confession was written? Yes. How had he come to sign the document? He had been tricked. How had he been tricked? He had signed thinking the document set out something else. What something else? He did not know, but there were more than two sheets of paper passed to him and when he signed there was a piece of blotting paper covering them. He signed four or five times. He had been shown where to sign.

There was a pause. Then I said to him that I would present to the Court his defence in the terms of what he had told Arthur Prothero and me, but that he would have to go into the witness box and swear on oath that what he said was true. He would then be subject to cross-examination. I said that I must tell him frankly that in my judgment the challenge to the veracity of the police officer was unlikely to prove acceptable to a jury; that I would, as I must, present his defence, his case, as he had instructed; but that he must understand that, if this was not believed, the chance of a verdict of guilty would be increased. He must be prepared for this. Hitherto he had been almost monosyllabic. Now he said, 'Well, then I will hang and go to hell – and when I get there I will meet the policeman.' I left the room.

Arthur Prothero asked me if I would like a junior counsel to help me. I said I would, and he briefed Michael Havers, a few years junior to me in age and call. I told him that Michael too must personally receive from Whiteway's own lips those instructions which must result in direct confrontation with this senior police officer. This Michael did. The instructions were repeated. Later Michael asked me if he, rather than I, could take Whiteway through his evidence. This was unusual but I realized that it would allow Michael's name to appear in the reports of the case. It was odd, but I agreed.

The trial began on 15 September 1953. The judge was Mr Justice Hilbery, an affected man who worried about his vowel sounds and in court often made elaborate play with a cambric handkerchief. He was, however, an experienced criminal judge. I felt sure that he would not fancy the challenge to the police officer. I was right.

The evidence of the schoolgirl was excluded, upon my objections and argument, on a point of law; the bloodstains were investigated; evidence of campers near to the river was probed. Then the moment came for the evidence of Detective Superintendent Hannam. Dapper, grey hair carefully brushed, he gave his evidence with authority in a grave and solemn manner. The cross-examination lasted some two and a half hours. At one stage I invited the witness to sit at a table and demonstrate how the confession came to be written and signed. In the newspapers it was reported that it was a tense scene with people in the crowded court craning forward to watch.

In his summing-up the judge said, 'It is quite impossible without indulging in hyperbole to overstate the gravity of the accusations made about the police officers.' It took the jury less than an hour to convict. On the appeal later in the year the Lord Chief Justice revealed publicly that Whiteway had admitted the attempted rape of the married woman at Windsor and the rape of the fourteen-year-old schoolgirl. Of the words in the statement, 'Put that bloody chopper away ... it haunts me', Lord Goddard said, 'If there was a case of the phrase of bloody Lady Macbeth being brought into real life, this was it.' Whiteway was executed on 22 December 1953.

There was an extraordinary sequel, twenty years later. After Whiteway's conviction in 1953, I wrote a personal letter to Mr Hannam. I had, after all, been obliged as counsel to challenge his integrity. He replied courteously, expressing the view that, if he and I continued respectively to carry out our professional duty, so much the better for all. Fortunately I kept this letter. In 1973, twenty years later almost to the month and when I was Attorney General, Mr Hannam wrote a letter to *The Times*. In this letter he recalled being cross-examined in a case in 1953 and he alleged that in a letter to him after the case counsel had admitted that he had known that the statements which his client had made to the Court were untrue. From the letter Mr Hannam quoted words in inverted commas: 'We knew that they were all untrue but they were my instructions.' The important words were 'knew' and 'my instructions'. The case and the counsel of which and of whom Mr Hannam was writing were easily and speedily identified. The case was the Towpath Murder and the counsel was myself.

The press took over. This letter by Mr Hannam was published on a Friday morning. Here was the Attorney General himself accused of putting before a court untruths of which he was aware, untruths of which he 'knew'. Accordingly: 'THE DAY SIR PETER ADMITTED AN UNTRUTH' (*Evening Standard*): 'LAW CHIEF AND FALSE ATTACK: SENSATION' (*Evening News*). I issued a statement denying that the words quoted by Mr Hannam had been in my letter of September 1953. Mr Hannam curiously replied that I had written him two letters. This was untrue.

All that weekend the storm raged, headlines, photographs. It was certainly good copy: the head of the English Bar accused of knowingly making false accusations and admitting it in his own letter. In a more sober footnote the *Daily Telegraph* wrote that, even if counsel suspects what his client tells him is not true, he is still bound to put to the Court what his client says: if counsel has certain knowledge that the client is not telling the truth it is his duty to return the brief.

That weekend I found among my files Mr Hannam's original reply to the letter which I had written to him in 1953. From what Mr Hannam wrote to me, it was clear that my letter could not have contained the words quoted by him in his letter to *The Times* twenty years later. So I asked him to come and see me, and he did. He admitted that nowhere in my one and only letter to him appeared the words quoted by him. He then wrote a second letter to *The Times*. In it he wrote, 'It is regretted that memory over twenty years allowed me to confuse the contents of two letters I received, one from the prosecution and one from the defence, and it was not in either of these that my final quote actually appeared.' He withdrew the accusation. It was never clear, however, from what came the original quotation which was the basis for the accusation. Anyhow, by Monday it was all over. The storm now subsided as quickly as it had arisen. 'I MADE A MISTAKE, SAYS EX-YARD CHIEF' (*Evening News*); 'EX-DETECTIVE RETRACTS' (*Guardian*); 'EX-CID MAN SAYS SORRY' (*Sun*); 'FALSE DEFENCE BY RAWLINSON CLAIM DROPPED' (*Telegraph*); 'I HAD A LAPSE OF MEMORY' (*Evening Standard*). But it had been rough while it lasted.

Attorney Generals are fair game. If they are to do their job properly they must usually become ogre-figures. But a liar and a cheat was a bit too much. I was very glad indeed that I had kept that letter of twenty years ago. I wondered what might have happened had I not. The truth would have been the same, but its demonstration might have been very much more difficult.

My old friend Rosa Lewis had a saying which came back to me during that weekend. 'No letters, no lawyers; and kiss the baby's bottom.' I ought to have remembered that when I took up my pen and wrote to the police officer after the Towpath murder was over. At least I never did it again.

During the trial I had been insulted in a London club for daring to attack the police; I had received scores of letters, mostly abusive. One noted that I had political ambitions and commented that, if I was as incompetent in politics as I was at the Bar, 'God help the country'. One night during the case, when I was working late into the night in my chambers, there was a knock at the door. I opened it and a middle-aged lady pushed past me and settled down in a chair. She told me that she was from MI5 and that she had vital information about a green bicycle. It took me over an hour to get her out.

Despite all the trauma of this sad, unpleasant case, it was, paradoxically, a professional breakthrough. I had certainly been exposed to an ordeal, but from now on, in legal and even in certain public circles, I had become known. However, I was not unhappy to finish for a time with the Old Bailey, and to return to the quieter civil courts in the Strand, where for the following two weeks I plunged into a long and boring case before an Official Referee who waved no cambric handkerchief and who patiently investigated not confessions to murder but schedules of a builder's omissions, and where I encountered quantity surveyors and not mysterious ladies who late at night claimed to have come from MI5.

Chapter 7
Peter Lorre Intervenes – The Trial of Ruth Ellis

In the eighteen months which followed the Towpath Murder Case and my acquisition of professional notoriety, I was involved in two other important criminal cases, both of which played a part in changing public opinion about the law: one on the law about the private sexual conduct of adult men, the other on the penalty for murder. Further I was elected to Parliament. But by far the most important event for me was that I got married and, like Winston Churchill, lived happily ever after.

It was, as the Duke said of Waterloo, 'a damn close-run thing'. I was a most inappropriate suitor: a cousin, many years older, with three daughters, the eldest of whom was only a few years younger than Elaine. We had met in 1953, when she was en route from the States to finishing school in Switzerland. With her father and stepmother she was making trips around Europe, to London, Rome, Provence and Paris. There I pursued her.

To her family I made a specious excuse that I was in Paris attending some wholly imaginary conference. I was invited to dine. Later Elaine and I escaped, and we climbed the steep steps up to Montmartre. It was, of course, spring. We danced, of course, in the garden of a café under the light of the moon, reinforced however by coloured electric lights, naked bulbs strung on wires. The music was, of course, an accordion. Everything was perfect, except the circumstances surrounding the suitor. But as we wandered down the hill and watched, traditionally, the dawn coming up, not like thunder but slipping up around the dome of the Sacré Coeur, somehow I knew that it would eventually come right.

That winter Elaine was taken to Jamaica, this time by her mother and stepfather. Understandably neither they, nor her father, approved of the suit of her English cousin. The customary pressure had been applied. Before she left for the Caribbean, she told her father that she had now decided to marry a childhood boyfriend, who had just returned to the States from serving in Korea. Her father gravely made a note in his pocket-book. But I had not given up. When Elaine and the family arrived in Jamaica there was a hotel strike. Fortunately for me, the post was still working. I fired off letters, cables, flowers. I did not know of her decision but I was certainly very apprehensive.

Staying at the same time at their hotel, Round Hill, were the cast of a film then being shot on the island. It was *Twenty Thousand Leagues Under The Sea*. Kirk Douglas and Peter Lorre were the stars. Years ago, before the war, I had met Peter Lorre on the film-studio floor when he was playing in Alfred Hitchcock's *The Man Who Knew Too Much* for which my father had written the script. Peter Lorre could not possibly have re-membered the schoolboy who watched the film re-enactment of the Sidney Street siege twenty years earlier. But it is to him that I owe great happiness.

While at the hotel he noticed the lovely but rather sad girl and got to know her. It is sometimes easier to talk with a stranger than with those who are closer and Elaine began to confide in him. She told him that she was torn over what she should do. She knew very well what was sensible and what her family would advise. Peter Lorre asked her to tell him the two stories: that of the affluent American just home from the Korean War who was her contemporary, and that of the older divorcé with three children who was her cousin. When he had heard both stories, for some inspired reason he did the improbable thing and plumped for me.

My flowers and cables kept arriving, brought secretly to Elaine out of sight of her mother and stepfather by grinning hotel staff who overlooked their union principles for the sake of true love. My bombardment went on ceaselessly. But, although I did not know it, the counsel of Peter Lorre had proved decisive. Elaine, however, could not bring herself to face the knowing looks of the hotel staff by openly cabling back a direct answer to my ever more pressing entreaties. So she cabled discreetly: 'Thanks for cable. Letter following.' The disappointed desk clerk sent off her non-committal cable. By now the hotel staff were aroused. They felt it was time that they should take a hand.

In London I was becoming frantic at the uncertainty. So I shot off another cargo of flowers. This time the hotel staff deliberately delivered the flowers to Elaine in the presence of her mother and stepfather. This brilliant stroke brought the crisis to a head, as the hotel staff intended that it should. Shyly, a more explicit cable was despatched. In London I celebrated. In New York, after a telephone call, her father sighed philosophically and crossed out the name of one prospective son-in-law and substituted another.

We were married the following December in Newport, Rhode Island, with the snow thick upon the ground. I hope that Peter Lorre rests in the peace which he so deserves.

The first of the two important criminal cases came in 1954. It was a prosecution which made me personally angry, and that is usually not good for the exercise of professional skill.

A major advantage of the British legal system which divides duties between barrister and solicitor is that the barrister receives instructions from the solicitor. He is thus once removed from the lay client. This is very advantageous, especially in criminal cases. For what the client requires from his advocate, the barrister, is the exercise of judgment. In advocacy, judgment is all, or almost all; and for judgment to be best it must be cool and it must not be warped by emotion. An advocate is engaged in the practice of persuasion and to persuade requires performance. This is why the advocate is so often perceived to have much in common with the actor. As that is so, the barrister should remember Diderot's famous paradox that in order to express emotion with the maximum of effectiveness, the actor must be utterly empty of emotion during his performance.

Modern advocacy eschews any expression of embarrassing emotion. It is over sixty years since the Old Bailey heard anything like Edward Marshall-Hall in his peroration to his speech in the defence of the beautiful Frenchwoman Madame Fahmy, who had shot her Egyptian husband Prince Fahmy Bey in their suite in the Savoy Hotel. Marshall-Hall entreated the jury, 'Open the gate so that this western woman can go, not into the dark night of the desert but back to her friends who love her ...' etc., etc. Nowadays, it has been said, the successful modern advocate must have the style of a chartered accountant who is accustomed to reading the lesson in church.

But in 1954 I and my colleague and friend, Bill Fearnley-Whittingstall, were both angered and resentful over the circumstances surrounding the prosecution of three men of otherwise undoubted quality accused of sex in private with other adult men, two airmen in the RAF who looked browbeaten when they gave their evidence and who were neither seduced nor seductive. The case also involved illegal police searches of premises and a denial of access to lawyers while a statement was obtained in such circumstances that the judge at the trial eventually forbade its use in evidence. The whole prosecution had to me the savour of a witch-hunt.

I defended one of the three accused, who was a journalist. Bill Fearnley-Whittingstall, the dominant jury advocate of the day, defended another, who was a peer; and Harry Hylton Foster, later Speaker of the House of Commons, represented the third, a landowner. Contrary to what some believe, sometimes it is often more difficult for the prominent to receive justice than it is for the humble.

I was still only a junior; the others, including the prosecutor, Khaki Roberts, eight years earlier prominent in the prosecution team at Nuremberg, were all silks. Apparently my defendant selected me because, as he later wrote in a book, 'a few months before Rawlinson had attacked' the police mercilessly – a thing which, he wrote, 'I suspected was "not done" in legal circles.'

The trial was in the Assize Court, the Castle, in Winchester in March 1954. The weather was bleak and cold. The trial was sad and sordid; the witnesses for the prosecution, in contrast to the bearing of the accused, sullen and unappealing. The police irregularities, searches without warrant, were revealed. Diaries, correspondence, address-books had been rifled. The statement extracted from the journalist was excluded. A feature of the trial was the number of gawping spectators, not the greasy mackintosh brigade but the well-to-do and the literary who thronged the court in the Castle. Some came to gloat; others to sympathize. I did, however, feel some sympathy for one woman, a schoolmistress in charge of a party of about a dozen schoolgirls. As she tried to usher her charges into the court, she was confronted by Bill, his black gown flapping like a demon-king in a pantomime. 'Go away,' he roared. 'Go away, you nasty dirty woman. This is no place for children. Take them away, you wretched woman. Take them away.' The poor woman gathered up her chicks and fled in terror down the hill.

The three accused were all convicted. They were sentenced to what in those days were reasonably light terms of imprisonment. The peer said later that prison was little worse than recruit-training in the Guards Depot. But the prosecution and the manner of the investigation left a nasty taste in many mouths. The prosecution seemed to me at the time, as it seems to me today, thirty years later, to have been an act of public cruelty. It contributed to a change in the climate of opinion which, a decade later, led to a change in the law.

Eighteen months later, in June 1955, I was briefed as the junior of three counsel in the defence of Ruth Ellis, who had shot her lover outside the Magdala public house in Hampstead. Her solicitor was John Bickford, a conscientious and kindly man who did all that could be done for her. At the very end she replaced him with another solicitor. I never knew why.

Ruth Ellis was tried for murder on 20 June at the Old Bailey. The jury were out considering their verdict for only a quarter of an hour. Their verdict, their inevitable verdict, was Guilty. The sentence, the inevitable sentence, was death by hanging. Twenty-two days later she was hanged at Holloway Prison. That execution led many to alter their opinion about the propriety of and need for the death penalty. A decade later it was, effectively, abolished.

As the law stood in 1955 there could be no real defence on her behalf to the charge of murder. The leading counsel in our defence team, Melford Stevenson, could do little. Ruth Ellis gave evidence. She spoke of the troubled relationship with her lover and of past quarrels and violence. She told of her feelings over his behaviour during the last few days of his life. He was 'behaving disgustingly'. On Easter Sunday she went up to Hampstead and shot him. After she had given her evidence she returned from the witness box to the dock, looking assured and without regret.

The photographs of Ruth Ellis in the newspapers showed a young woman with bright blonde hair. That was not how she looked when I saw her in a cell in the Old Bailey some weeks before the actual trial. For her appearance at the trial later in June, hairdressing material was sent into the prison and her hair freshly dyed. When I saw her, it was faded. She looked little like her photographs. The occasion when I spoke to her arose after she had been brought from prison to the court to be present when the judge fixed the actual date upon which the trial proper was to begin. John Bickford asked me to see her in the cells after the date of trial had been settled and before she was returned from the Old Bailey to Holloway Prison.

At that time, to go down to the cells, a barrister, provided that he was in robes, could enter the dock in the court and go down the steps inside the dock which lead to the corridors which run beneath the court. There prisoners in custody are kept to await the start of their trial, or the verdict of the jury. The surroundings were grim. The air reflected the tensions and anxieties which were daily experienced in that place, although mostly by persons without merit who had given no mercy and deserved little in return. John Bickford, as the solicitor, could not come the short way through the dock in the court and down the stairs. He had to go out to the side entrance of the main court building, and enter another door and approach along corridors to where Ruth Ellis was waiting. So I arrived in the room well before him.

Ruth Ellis was with a wardress who, on my entering, left us alone. We shook hands, hers a small, limp hand matching the listless face and the hair from which the dye had faded. I explained to her what had been decided by the Court. She had of course been present, but John Bickford had wanted to ensure that she understood what had happened and also give her the opportunity to tell me anything further that she might wish to say. I assumed that the real purpose of my visit was to reassure her that all that could be done would be done to save her from the gallows.

We were seated facing each other across a table. She listened while I repeated that the trial would now begin on 20 June. She looked at me steadily, quite composed but with dull eyes. I asked if she wanted anything. Was there anything that I could do? She flicked her faded hair back with a toss of her head.

'You will make certain, won't you,' she said quietly, 'that I shall be hanged? That is the only way that I can join him.' I caught my breath and said that she must not talk like that. But she shook her head and repeated, 'I want to join him. I want to join him.' Again I said that she must not speak or think like that, but she made a gesture as though to brush me and my words aside. Clearly, she implied, I did not understand.

John Bickford then arrived in the room. She stood up. She said she wanted nothing. She made it clear that she wanted to say no more. She wanted to return to Holloway. A little while later I shook her hand and left her with Bickford. I climbed up the steep stairs into the large dock of No. 1 Court where a trial was being heard. As I appeared as though from the floor and moved to the door of the dock and was let out by the warder, the judge glanced up and then back to his notes. The traffic of counsel between court and the cells was quite usual. But I felt greatly disturbed.

On the morning of the day when she was hanged, 12 July 1955, I could think only of what she had said to me in that bleak room under the dock of No. 1 Court at the Old Bailey.

Chapter 8
MP – The Suez Crisis and the House of Commons

After our wedding in Newport in December 1954, Elaine and I travelled to New York and then boarded the *Queen Mary*, en route to St Moritz via Cherbourg on our honeymoon. We spent New Year's Eve of 1954 on board ship in mid-Atlantic. I am not sure who could have been driving the ship during that evening of celebration for the whole crew seemed to join the party. We took the tender in Cherbourg and the train across France to Switzerland. In St Moritz the sun shone and we skied and crunched through the snow in the starlight between restaurant and hotel.

After a few days I received an unexpected cable. Would I return within three days and face the Selection Committee of the Epsom Conservative Association, who were seeking a candidate to succeed their present selection, Sir David Maxwell Fyfe, the political friend into whose ribs Harold Macmillan would slip the dagger seven years later. But now Sir David had been ennobled and had become Lord Kilmuir and been appointed Lord Chancellor. This appointment caused consternation at Epsom where accordingly they had to seek at short notice another candidate in place of David, who some months earlier had been selected to succeed the sitting member Malcom McCorquodale who was retiring at the next general election. The cable announced that I had been put on the shortlist.

In some trepidation I explained this to Elaine. She claims that at the time she hardly knew the difference between Republican and Democrat, let alone Conservative and Labour, and that she had had no idea that I even wanted to get into Parliament. Hastily I assured her that there was no likelihood of being selected, that I was now very busy at the Bar, but that I wanted to keep my name forward in Conservative circles so that in a few years' time I might have a chance of getting into the House. With grace, little knowing what the next twenty-three years would entail and the countless round of coffee mornings and fêtes and weekend conferences to which I was condemning her, she consented. Anyway, the weather in St Moritz was turning. It began to snow hard. We took the train to London, to our first home.

Three days later we went down to Epsom.

The selection of a candidate in those days was very civilized, or at least it was among the civilized people of Epsom. Each candidate and his wife (there were no women on the list) were taken separately to a different house, kept in ignorance of who were the rivals, and at the due time brought to face the music in the hall where the Selection Committee of about sixty people awaited him. There each candidate separately made his speech, was observed, questioned and led back to the house from which he had been brought to await the verdict. If it was rejection he and his wife were given drinks amid polite expressions of regret and sent on their way. If it was selection, the pair would be brought back to the hall to receive the accolade.

When our turn came we were taken to the hall and on to the platform. When I had told Elaine that there was no likelihood of my being selected, I had overlooked the impression she herself would create. For there she sat, exquisite, a bride. All eyes were upon her. Since I did not at that time care in the least if I were not chosen, I made a rip-roaring speech. Almost before we realized what was happening, we were back again on the platform. I had been selected. Care at once descended like a thunder-cloud upon me and upon my oratory. I stumbled through the thanks and niceties and made pledges for the future. The committee, so recently enthused, looked at each other with some concern. Was this the firebrand they had heard only an hour earlier? But they took comfort at another sight of the bride of the man whom they had chosen. Four months later came the general election. I was an MP.

It was just like going to school, or joining the army. The only people who were agreeable were the messengers in their tailcoats and badges. I went for the first and last time into the Commons gallery of the House of Lords to watch the ceremony of the reading of the Queen's Speech at the Opening of Parliament and to watch the arrival at the bar of the members of the Commons. This, I remembered, was the only part of the ceremony which Queen Victoria enjoyed. They came in, she once said, 'jostling and talking like nothing on earth but a pack of schoolboys or a herd of bullocks'. Nowadays she would have to include schoolgirls and heifers.

In the gallery I met a tall, slim young member as new and shiny as myself. He was Humphrey Atkins. We became and remained firm friends. But there was a lot to learn, not only the geography of that rabbit warren of a Palace of Westminster, but also much of the bowing and nodding, the crossing of lines and the wearing or not wearing of a hat when raising points of order and all the other arcane rules of a highly traditional institution. The Whips, the head prefects, were exceedingly serious, especially the Chief Whip Patrick Buchan-Hepburn, and when I ever sought to go home I found always one of them stationed on the door who told me that I couldn't. Later I found an Old Hand who described a subterranean route down passages and basements which would bring me out on the far side of the door so jealously guarded by the Whip on duty. This I discovered, but I made the error when I emerged of not turning right, which would have taken me out and away, but of turning left; and so I burst in through the door on the inside of which was the guardian figure of the Whip. He looked as surprised as I did. I did not repeat that mistake.

The new boys of 1955 were invited to a reception to meet the Cabinet, of whom only Alec Home made any effort to put us at ease. Then we were summoned to a dinner with the Prime Minister, Anthony Eden. I was put next to him. He told me, although I did not grasp its relevance, that the worst time he had ever had in politics was when there was a local government reorganization which amalgamated Warwick and Leamington, the two halves of his constituency. He brooded moodily over this – as though it still rankled. I, rather surprised, thought about Yalta, or Indo-China, or Western European Union. Suddenly he became very cross. That afternoon at Question Time, Jim Callaghan, then a very minor figure who had just been elected to the Labour front bench, had shouted at the Prime Minister from the far corner of the Opposition front bench. The Prime Minister now recollected this. He bridled. 'He is nothing but a corner boy', he said. 'A corner boy.' The storm then passed as quickly as it had arisen and he smiled his gentle, captivating smile and for the rest of dinner spoke enchantingly about painting and seriously about the trenches in the First World War.

In the House Rab Butler had introduced a second Budget immediately after the election, increasing indirect taxation. I was never captivated by Rab's public image; his private magic, in his nearby house, yes. There he would guffaw and giggle irreverently. I was impressed by Clement Attlee, waspish and effective; and by Nye Bevan. I stood beside the latter at the Speaker's annual reception, and I made some banal remark about what a lesson it was to a newcomer to observe him speaking in the House. He then said very charmingly that he had found it very difficult when he was first a Member until he learned from Lloyd George that it was all a matter of judging the pause – that the effectiveness of any speech in the House turned upon using pauses and judging how long to make them. He told me to try: but I never dared, not consciously that is, for quite a time. Harold Macmillan had been another pupil whom Lloyd George had similarly instructed.

Then there arose the contest for the leadership of the Labour Party upon Attlee's retirement, between Herbert Morrison and Hugh Gaitskell. Morrison had made some appallingly bad speeches from the front bench. He lost the leadership election and he returned to the backbenches where he proceeded to make impressive speeches before he retired to what Disraeli called the Elysian Fields of the Lords and to graze in the pastures of the film industry's Certificate Office, an odd end to a lively political career. But it was a sinecure which he needed.

Meanwhile that summer of 1955 I made my maiden speech on a dull legal subject, restrictive practices and monopolies. When the speech was reported in *The Times* there appeared at the end the flattering word 'Cheers' in brackets. This was due solely to Christopher Soames. As was the custom, I spoke of my constituency Epsom and I included a pleasantry comparing the free and easy audience on the Downs and the unrestricted conditions of Epsom's great race to the restrictive practices imposed upon the lawns of Ascot. Christopher had been dozing and he woke with a start to my reference to racing and the Derby and Ascot. So he gave a great stentorian rumble of 'Hear, Hear', before wandering out of the chamber. Thus my maiden speech earned the accolade of 'Cheers'.

I soon realized that it was not easy to combine a busy law practice with the House. I had to abandon the work which I was then getting at the assize towns and quarter sessions on the Western Circuit. These courts were too far from London to permit me regularly to finish in court and get to the House; and there were always the Whips to encounter if one arrived late or sought to leave early. The luxury of a pair was rarely allowed to a new boy. Although many Members technically had qualifications, they were not barristers of standing and practice. There were some who had abandoned the Bar for the City or for professional politics; there were others who now and then were offered a brief in a convenient London court. But there were only very few of us who were practising seriously. It was a great help when, after four years in the House, I got silk at Easter 1959, because thereafter the cases which I did were fewer in number although greater in matter.

On 26 July 1956, when the courts and Parliament were nearly up, Elaine and I sailed to the States. I had arranged to meet in Newport John

Kennedy, then a senator, and to visit the Democratic Party Convention in Chicago to meet Adlai Stevenson, then the likely Democratic candidate in the presidential election to be held in the autumn of 1956. On the night that we sailed there came the news that President Nasser of Egypt had seized the Suez Canal and all the property of the international Suez Canal Company.

Two years earlier, on 10 October 1954, the British government had entered into an agreement with Egypt to withdraw all British forces from their then base in the Suez Canal zone, which they had occupied since 1936. In the same agreement, Egypt and Britain solemnly agreed to uphold the Convention of 1888 which proclaimed the principle of freedom of navigation of the Suez Canal, the waterway which linked Europe to the oilfields in the Gulf.

Since the Convention of 1888 the Canal had been acknowledged to be an international asset. Its owners were the Suez Canal Company, which was recognized as an international entity, and the navigation and maintenance of the waterway was worked by international pilots and operators. Its importance as the link between east and west had been apparent since its construction. Oil had increased its significance. It was considered by Western Europe (and, so it was then believed, by the United States, which was becoming more and more dependent upon the supply of oil from the Middle East) that international control of the Canal was a vital strategic requirement of the nations of the Western Alliance.

But after the withdrawal of the British troops from the Suez Canal zone in the twenty months following the 1954 agreement, this international asset lay defenceless, an easy prey to any Egyptian government minded to quarrel with the West and prepared to breach the Convention. On 26 July 1956, with the last British soldier finally withdrawn, that was what occurred. The Egyptian government of President Nasser, angered by the withdrawal of American and British aid for their Aswan Dam project, without warning and in breach of the Convention forcibly expropriated the assets and bank balance of the Company, and ordered its international employees henceforth to work upon pain of immediate imprisonment solely to the command of the new masters.

The West reacted vigorously, and at first unitedly. During the following weeks, while Elaine and I were on our visit to the States, meetings were summoned in London of the nations whose ships used the Canal. To Prime Minister Anthony Eden, were the nations to stand aside and permit the successful seizure by force of this strategic international asset, the danger to the West and to international order was clear. He saw the seizure of the

Canal by Nasser as a new test similar to that to which, twenty years earlier, in the face of Hitler's early aggression, the West had failed to respond and which as a result had led the world inexorably down the path into universal war. Rather than run from this challenge, he was prepared in the last resort to fight – as were the French and the Israelis. In November of that year, and in the last resort, that is what they did.

But President Eisenhower, in the middle of his campaign for re-election, his Secretary of State, John Foster Dulles, and his administration were not. On 3 September, the day when Elaine and I returned to London from the States, he informed Anthony Eden that American public opinion over the Suez crisis flatly rejected the use of force. Eden later wrote that he found the message from Eisenhower 'most disturbing'. In the end he was not deterred. But the fighting still lay several weeks ahead.

Meanwhile in the States on 5 August I was at a dinner party with Jack Kennedy. Our host had arranged it so that Jack and I could talk meaningfully about the Middle East crisis. But Jack, whom I had met in London both before the war and after and whom Elaine knew (she had been at his wedding), had different ideas. He said that he would see me in Chicago at the Convention where he was going to challenge Senator Kefauver and run for the vice-presidential nomination. For there was present at the dinner a very pretty girl and our host's desire that Jack would talk politics with a boring MP from London was not shared by Jack. He pursued the pretty girl for the rest of the evening.

A week later I left with Elaine's stepbrother Mathews Dick junior, a staunch Republican, for the Democratic Convention in Chicago. What impressed me about our journey from New England to the Middle West, halfway across the continent, was that Mat never one spent a single dollar. He merely kept producing from his pocket a small piece of plastic card, and with this he obtained our aeroplane tickets, our meals and drinks, and hired the cars. I had never seen this before and I thought that we might end in prison.

In Chicago, at the Cow Palace, with the ever-present stench of meat from the stockyards, Mat and I got our tickets and wandered around the Convention. Mat selected a badge to wear. He chose 'Harry's man is Harriman'. Harry was the ex-President Truman, and Averell Harriman, a rival to Adlai Stevenson for the nomination, was his 'favourite son'. The scenes, now so familiar on television, were to me then extraordinary. We met a real live Tammany Hall boss, Carmen de Sapio, who for some reason seemed to think that Mat, who had never met him before, was a very, very good friend and slapped him warmly on the back and enquired warmly after his family. I managed to get into a meeting in which ex-President Truman was counselling all the Democrat Women running for office on how to get elected. I was allowed in as a visiting parliamentarian and I was the only man present – save for Harry. As far as I could judge his advice to them was to use unscrupulously all the female advantages which the good God had given to them and, if it might help, never hesitate to burst into tears. The modern feminist would have had apoplexy.

Later, when I was talking with Adlai Stevenson, he commented wryly as we looked on the internal television at the scene on the floor of the Convention with its sea of waving banners, bands and long-legged cheer leaders, 'It is not much like your Conservative Party Conference.' More's the pity, I thought, as the bands burst into 'New York, New York', or 'You Come from Rhode Island' or 'San Francisco' as each delegation recorded its vote. After all, I thought, we might have 'On Ilkley Moor', 'The Lincolnshire Poacher' or 'The Old Kent Road'. Then we witnessed Jack's failed challenge to Senator Kefauver, about which Jack nevertheless expressed satisfaction at the support he had attracted. It was his first sortie on to the Convention scene. Four years later he would dominate it.

Mat and I flew east after this inauguration into the extraordinary American political scene. One thing was very clear to me. No one wanted to talk about any crisis in the Middle East, or about Nasser and his seizure of the Suez Canal. They all had far more important fish to fry. For they had an election to win, although how any of them had the idea that they had the remotest chance of defeating Ike I never discovered.

The Suez expedition is in many people's eyes the event which marks the end of the world power of Great Britain. To the new Member of Parliament, first elected fourteen months previously, the drama witnessed from the backbenches in a House almost continuously in session during the autumn of 1956 was immensely exciting and strangely stimulating. Parliament, which hitherto had seemed a staid, school-like institution with all its formal rules and customs, suddenly erupted into a madhouse. The prim countenance of the Mother of Parliaments was transformed into a snarling mask. From 23 October, when Parliament reassembled, and for weeks thereafter, the uproar was unending. This time of national, and for Anthony Eden personal, humiliation made sensational parliamentary theatre. No parliamentarian who did not live through those weeks can really claim to understand the nature of the House of Commons. In few other national assemblies could the leader of a nation be confronted daily, and for weeks on end, by nearly three hundred shouting and jeering political opponents. That was what Anthony Eden had to endure, and to a lesser extent his Foreign Secretary Selwyn Lloyd.

It is a little macabre to write that one had enjoyed it, and that does not convey precisely the reaction of an onlooker-participant who was moved at times by passion comparable to that of those on the Opposition benches. For a government backbencher it was rather like being a spectator with a ring-side seat at a particularly bloody prize fight, in which one's own man was often on the ropes, sometimes driven to the floor but somehow always climbing back on to his feet to carry on the fight, acquiring thereby a dignity which his attackers singularly lacked. The junior backbencher himself was safe from being personally knocked about since he had little opportunity, if any, actually to participate in the fight. He did not have to face that collective hatred which came from an Opposition baying for political blood. To witness at close hand the venom directed at that tall figure standing at the despatch box, outwardly debonair but internally wracked with illness and anxiety, was certainly not an agreeable spectacle. Indeed it was terrible. But it was also very exciting.

At times, such as when Anthony Eden left the Front Bench on his way out of the House, the whole Opposition rose and shouted and catcalled at him. Once only the judicious suspension of the House by Speaker 'Shakes' Morrison thwarted the outbreak of actual violence. On one occasion I caught sight on the Opposition Front Bench of Edith Summerskill, who had been one of Attlee's ministers. She alone seemed not to be carried away. But she was standing, her face set like that of a stern headmistress. One arm was supporting the elbow of the other, which, with hand and finger pointed, she was jerking like a horizontal piston, backwards and forwards, in time to the rhythm of her chant of 'Resign' (in, out, went the arm), 'Resign' (in, out), 'Resign' (in, out). Then, as if she had done her duty, she neatly swept with a hand the rear of her skirt to ensure that the seat would not crease, and sat down. There she sat acidly looking around at her colleagues and at the scene beside and above her, her lips pursed and her brow creased. About her prim ears the crescendo of noise swirled. I could see that she did not altogether approve of what was happening, but that she knew that nothing could halt it and that she felt she could not be excluded. The hooligans, however, had taken over. It was touch and go lest the sittings turned into a major brawl.

On the hooks of each Member in the cloakroom there still hang sword knots made by circlets of pink tape. They are the reminders that Members were required to leave their swords behind before entering the Chamber. On the floor of the House two parallel lines run from the bar in front of each of the opposing front benches until they reach the despatch boxes on the Clerk's table which then serve as the division between government and Opposition. The lines are measured as a sword's length apart. They were useful reminders during those fierce and angry days.

I was in court on some days, and I hurried to the Chamber in the late afternoon. The noise could be heard in the passage ouside the swing doors which open into the Members' Lobby. In the House the benches were packed; on the steps between, Members sat squeezed like sardines. Those unable to find a place stood in a solid phalanx at the bar. It was impossible for anyone to achieve any sense of detachment or to weigh up argument in debate. The passion and the fever swept away all judgment. We were all naked partisans.

For the ministers, the scenes on the floor of the House were followed by further drama in the Party meetings upstairs in the Grand Committee Room. The 1922 Committee was then presided over by John Morrison, large, benign, avuncular, the archetypal Tory squire, the last of that breed to preside over the 1922. In the 1922 and the Foreign Affairs Committee, the Party debate became fiercest after 6 November and the announcement of the ceasefire imposed upon the British expeditionary force. Earlier, when the expedition sailed, Tony Nutting and Edward Boyle had left the government; the former Attorney General, Sir Lionel Heald, peering over his half-moon spectacles, had expressed his unpopular doubts over the international legality of that which Lord Chancellor Kilmuir had sanctioned. But the manner and the brutality of the socialist attacks in the House on Anthony Eden and the verbal brawling and contempt for parliamentary order following the vacillating leadership of Hugh Gaitskell, had closed the Tory ranks. It was only after the ceasefire on 6 November that there arose serious division in the Conservative Party.

Then, at the 1922 Committee, up rose Captain Charles Waterhouse, grey-clipped moustache, former officer in the Life Guards, first elected to the House thirty years earlier. He had opposed the 1954 withdrawal of British troops from the Canal zone under the treaty with Egypt. He supported the expedition which Prime Minister Eden had launched but he now opposed its humiliating withdrawal. To support him there was Hinch, Viscount Hinchingbrooke, handsome, elegant, who sported the extra-tall stiff collars of an earlier age which pushed even nearer to heaven his noble chin; and Julian Amery, with his orotund oratorical periods which caricatured an earlier generation of parliamentarians. They were a stylish and attractive group. But the majority, brilliantly manoeuvred or alternatively cajoled by the Chief Whip Edward Heath with a sensibility for dealing with the Tory Party and its coalition of awkward squads (an art which, alas, he had forgotten a decade and a half later), held firm between the critics of the whole adventure and the critics of the ceasefire. In the 1922 Committee I expressed the unoriginal view that although many might sympathize with the Life Guards Captain, once the ceasefire had been called there was no alternative but to support the government or to plunge the Party into self-destruction. These platitudes caused a few grey heads to nod and the Whip to make a note.

Later I went into an almost suicidal conflict with the BBC on behalf of the government, obtaining and opening an adjournment debate upon their reporting of the crisis. The Labour MP George Wigg effectively turned the tables and stole all the thunder by talking for an hour and a half. The Assistant to the Director General of the BBC and Woodrow Wyatt, then out of Parliament and prominent as a television anchorman, to both of whom I had referred in the debate, complained. I apologized to Woodrow.

From the worm's-eye view of a new backbencher, the Suez affair certainly ensured that life in Parliament could never be the same again. All that followed had to be anti-climax, even those occasions when, many years later, I was obliged to wind up debates and face the hecklings of such as the red-faced Denis Healey, whose thuggery as a politician was matched by his off-stage amiability. During those weeks of Suez, the House, which hitherto had lived up so little to a new boy's expectations, had proved that it was certainly alive and kicking. And how it had kicked!

In December, Anthony Eden, ill and exhausted, had retired to recuperate at Goldeneye in Jamaica. To leave the political field at such a time and to be pictured sunning himself in the Caribbean, however badly he was in need of a rest, was a decision of breath-taking insensitivity. His absence on leave meant that command must invitably pass to other hands. There came to the 1922 Committee to visit the troops an hilarious double act, 'Wab and Hawold', as Bobbety Salisbury described them. Their appearance together was much savoured by the irreverent. Rab Butler, it was generally felt, had had his head well down beneath the parapet during the parliamentary crisis when the shot and shell were at their fiercest, as, many believed, was his wont and as I was to witness in another crisis six years later. Harold Macmillan, it was felt, had like the Grand Old Duke of York marched his men to the top of the hill and then very smartly turned about and marched them down again. But it was also felt that he had at least been in action.

Whimsically Harold mused to the 1922 over the evening of his political days, and of the viscountcy which was the conventional reward for a senior Cabinet Minister and over the Golden Years which lay ahead. He outspoke and outsmarted his colleague on this double bill, and the colleague looked as if he knew it. After this, in the hearts of most of the parliamentary Party, although not expressed to the Lobby correspondents who hung about waiting to ensnare unwary backbenchers and who so wrongly forecast the succession six weeks later, the leadership question had been all but decided. That viscountcy would become an earldom (the traditional reward of Prime Ministers) and would have to be put on ice, the golden years postponed. I was in the West Country in January 1957, engaged as counsel at a public enquiry on the siting in Hardy country of a nuclear reactor, when I received a note that Anthony Eden had resigned. I had no doubt who would succeed him.

The following parliamentary years afforded the connoisseur of advocacy the entertaining spectacle of the ex-Grenadier Etonian Prime Minister knocking the ex-civil servant Wykehamist Leader of the Opposition all over the parliamentary ring and onto the parliamentary ropes. In his winding-up speeches, which by rule commenced sharp at nine-thirty in the evening and had to cease sharp at ten o'clock when the debate concluded, the Prime Minister would pass the first twenty minutes of his speech full of sweet reason and ripe with gravitas, answering the debate, complimenting the contributors, advancing argument in rebuttal. Then in the last few minutes he would change gear and turn the performance into 'knock-about', savagely thwacking the Opposition, piteously stunning the unfortunate Hugh Gaitskell, and rousing his Tory troops to such enthusiasm that even the ranks of Tuscany sitting on the benches opposite could scarce forbear to cheer at these ineffable parliamentary performances.

His recently disconsolate and divided Tory army rallied, and 'Supermac' (as in the Vicky cartoon) flew from his victories in Westminster to captivate and capture the country, winning a place in public affection which neither profligate management of the economy nor 'little local difficulties' nor sordid ministerial scandals would ever diminish.

Chapter 9
Silk – The Libel on General Anders – The Night of the Long Knives, July 1962

At the height of the parliamentary drama and excitements of Suez, Elaine and I moved house, to Chelsea Square, where we remained for fifteen years. In the opinion of a heavily pregnant wife, it was not the smartest of timing.

In retrospect our establishment there seems enormous, for we had two Spanish maids who arrived, disconcertingly, in one of the longest and largest automobiles which I have ever seen. We were relieved to discover that they had been given a lift by a friend who was a chauffeur at an embassy. Of the two, one was round and short; the other tall and thin. Appropriately it was the former who was the cook. Neither spoke a word of English but both laughed a lot. They made the house very happy.

Early in 1957 they were joined by a very formidable nanny. Every day she would push our new-born son, Michael, in his pram up Queen's Gate, heading for the rendezvous in Hyde Park where in those days the rabbits and grand nannies liked to play. She pushed the pram to the park at great pace but usually in the middle of the road, undeterred by the hooting of the traffic. We were, she informed us reproachfully, the only family with whom she had been who had no title. She made clear that she would be obliged if we would keep it quiet that I was in politics. An immense woman with a prominent nose, and by then in her late fifties, she came with us next year on holiday to Newport in the States. She sternly enquired of me whether she would be safe alone in the car in which she was driven to the beach by my father-in-law's black chauffeur, who had known Elaine since childhood. Despite all this nonsense, and beneath the nanny hide, there lurked a generous and kindly woman. She became ill and died a few years later, mourned by titled and untitled alike, and even by that black chauffeur with whom she had become firm friends.

A few doors along from us in the Square lived Rayner Goddard, Lord Chief Justice since 1946. He was driven each morning to the Law Courts in a very antiquated Rolls. I never dared to ask him for a lift; probably he would have cheerfully agreed. On the Bench he was a formidable figure who suffered criminals, foolish witnesses and loquacious counsel equally badly. He was a robust Chief Justice and, he liked to boast, a very good judge – of port, which he enjoyed drinking at the Garrick or in Pratt's. Outwardly stern and forbidding, he was never slow to have second thoughts or to correct his own misjudgments; he aroused great personal affection in those who knew him and hostility in many who did not.

By 1958 he was eighty-one, and in July he tried his last case. I had been briefed as counsel for the defence, and the accused were two remarkable young men, undergraduates at Oxford who had served during their National Service in the Royal Navy. In the Oxford University magazine *Isis*, under the heading 'Frontier Incidents', they had written an account of how British torpedo boats in the Baltic circled and photographed Russian warships in order to provoke radio traffic which could then be monitored. On one occasion, they revealed, the boats had even landed a small party on Russian territory. The article was taken extremely seriously by the authorities, the two undergraduates were interviewed by Special Branch and they were charged with offences under the Official Secrets Act. A Law Officer of the Crown decided to prosecute. It was a grave situation for the two young men, but while awaiting trial at the Old Bailey, they sat for their final exams. One, who later became a professor of sociology, got first-class honours.

I knew that there was no defence in law to the charges but I thought that the most effective way of demonstrating their reason for writing the article, the sincerity of their beliefs, and their surprise that the matter was so serious was for them to tell their story to the Court in their own words. So at the outset I advised them to plead Not Guilty, and then after they had given their evidence to change their plea to Guilty. This was a little unusual but the judge at the trial would then have heard their explanation from their own lips, while they would have made clear that they were not trying to avoid responsibility for what they now accepted amounted to an offence. I told the prosecutor, the Solicitor General Harry Hylton-Foster, what had been decided, and so it was done. After the trial Rayner Goddard wrote to me that he approved the course which had been taken.

In the result and after he had heard all the facts and the explanations, Rayner read the undergraduates a lecture and sentenced them to three months' imprisonment to be served at an open prison, to which he personally arranged that they were immediately sent to ensure that they spent not even a few hours in an ordinary prison. They served one month and then were released. That was the last case Chief Justice Goddard ever tried and I was glad to have been a part of it.

In the past it was the tradition that when the office of Chief Justice became vacant, it was offered to the Attorney General of the day. On 29 July 1958 and when Rayner's resignation was known to be imminent, *The Times* declared in a leader that any appointment to the office of Lord Chief Justice must not be regarded as 'some political plum', an attitude which in the past had led to the selection of some thoroughly bad Chief Justices. The leader was clearly aimed at Reggie Manningham-Buller, who had served as Attorney General since 1954 and who would dearly have liked to have been appointed. Another who also greatly wanted the job was Patrick Devlin, then a High Court judge, a bitter rival of Reggie. The two had crossed swords during the trial of Dr Bodkin Adams (accused of murdering by poison elderly patients) in which the conduct of both Devlin, the judge and Manningham-Buller, the prosecutor, had aroused critical comment in the profession. Patrick Devlin carried on the rivalry beyond the grave in a surprising book which he wrote about that trial after Reggie's death.

In the event neither was appointed, and it was better so. But the faint echoes of that tradition which the rejection in 1958 of Attorney General Manningham-Buller broke, were heard by me as Attorney General in 1971 when upon the retirement of Chief Justice Parker, Prime Minister Heath formally asked me to visit and spoke to me privately to tell me the name of the Chief Justice's successor.

In the spring of 1959, I applied for silk. For those times I was young, not yet forty, and because of our service in war my generation had come to the Bar older than usual. It was the custom then to have to write to every junior counsel on your Circuit senior to yourself in call to the Bar to tell them of your application in case this prompted them also to apply and to advise the Circuit Leader. Mine was Khaki Roberts, and he replied that I was trying to take bread out of his mouth!

Applicants were not told if they were successful, and they had to wait to read the list which was published just before the Easter holiday. On the night before the list was due to be published in 1959, I was in the House of Commons. I received a message to telephone the *Express*. 'Congratulations', said the assistant editor, Willie Crumley. Next day we had a luncheon for a party of friends at a restaurant in Chelsea which went on very late. Then Elaine drove me to the country where we were to spend Easter with my parents. After dinner we played croquet in the dark, sticking candles on the hoops until I was happily led to bed. Nothing in all my official life, past or in the future, ever afforded me so much joy as that Easter news.

Taking silk means that from then on the barrister ranks among the senior counsel in the profession. It is called 'silk' because the QC exchanges the stuff gown of the junior barrister for one of silk, beneath which he wears a swallow-tailed court coat and a waistcoat with cloth-covered buttons. The barrister who has been made a QC moves into the front row in counsels' seats in the court room. The drudgery of the junior barrister of drafting pleadings, the formal legal documents which recite the claims and defences of the parties, ends. The new QC will have fewer but usually 'heavier' and more important cases. He becomes the 'leader' of the team handling the particular piece of litigation, and he is usualy only briefed in cases which require a team of two counsel because of the importance and complexity of the matter under trial. He is brought in because the cause and the client want the experience and skill of senior counsel which he has acquired during his years of experience at the junior Bar.

From time to time some legal academics are awarded silk, as a mark of honour to acknowledge their contribution to learning. In the past, some politicians were made QCs by a friendly Lord Chancellor. They were known as 'artificial silks', since they were rarely if ever in court, had no practice and had been appointed solely because of their position as a minister or MP. That custom has happily ceased.

But the taking of silk is not without its risks, and some who have found great success in the skills of drafting and desk work of the junior barrister find that upon translation to the new role which is principally that of an advocate in major causes, success eludes them, and a handsome income as a junior barrister turns when a silk into penury.

I was lucky and on the very first day after I had been sworn in as a QC I began a substantial defended divorce case involving a well-known person. Most important of all, I had moved chambers – a great stroke of luck – and I joined as the junior silk the chambers of Gerald Gardiner, then a very successful and grand practitioner. It was a small exclusive set, only six barristers strong. When the clients could not afford Gerald, I often got the brief, and at fees negotiated by the clerk, Harold Goodale, on a scale which when I first saw them marked on my briefs made me feel faint. I soon got used to it.

To the outsider, Gerald and I must have seemed rather an odd couple – the staunch socialist and the staunch Tory. We did have in common that we had both been Guardsmen, but that was not generally known of Gerald.

In his youth he had served for a very short time as an ensign in the Coldstream Guards. This was never now mentioned. His interests and affiliations had long since shifted from such elitist circles into other elites of a different but, in their own way, equally exclusive kind, such as the Fabian Society. He was a man of complete integrity, dedicated to such causes as the abolition of capital punishment and, of course, the coming of the socialist millennium. He was a fine advocate with a tall handsome presence and an enormous and lucrative practice. He had been a most successful chairman of the Bar.

When addressing a jury, he told me that he never looked at them as individuals, but fixed his eye just above them so that his imperious glance moved down the line of the seated jury in the jury box just a few inches above each head. Somehow that epitomized his way through life. For Gerald was personally generous but cool. If it ever came to it, I knew that he would be sorry when I was placed in the tumbril but he would reason that, alas, it was for the common good and it was better so. Because he was against capital punishment the tumbril would trundle off to Siberia. I would at least be spared the lamp-post.

At the end of one summer holiday, we were having tea together in his room. He enquired where I had spent my holiday. I said, in Spain. He shook his head reproachfully. 'I could not go there,' he said. 'I would not be happy taking a holiday in a dictatorship run by a general.' I sipped my tea guiltily and asked where he had been. 'In Yugoslavia', he replied, brightening. I thought of Marshal Tito, whom Evelyn Waugh for some reason in 1944 always referred to as she, and buried my nose in my teacup.

Nevertheless in chambers we got on very well, and when after the election in 1974 he left to become a handsome-looking and law-reforming Lord Chancellor in Harold Wilson's Labour government, I as the retiring Solicitor General took over the chambers and his room, and succeeded to the vast eighteenth-century bookcases and other furniture which he let me have on exceedingly generous terms.

So for me the translation from junior to QC had been delightful and exciting. It meant fewer but fatter cases and an end to all the drafting of tedious sets of papers which is the drudgery of the junior barrister. Now it was advocacy in the front row, with a junior sitting behind, a silk gown upon my back, and judges mysteriously more polite.

The next year, in 1960, I did my first libel case as a QC, a case of great interest in which we re-fought in a court room in the Royal Courts of Justice in the Strand some of the battles of two world wars.

In 1946 London had celebrated with a victory parade. As the various formations of British and Allied forces marched or drove through the streets of London on that day of celebrations, one detachment of one of the Allies was ostentatiously absent: the Polish forces, who had been the first to fight the Nazis, were not invited to take part. On the day before that parade Harold Macmillan, who had been Resident Minister at Allied Headquarters in Italy, wrote a letter. In it he said, 'With all the legitimate joy and pride in every British heart will be mingled much sorrow and even shame. My thoughts will be with you and your troops.' That letter was addressed to General Wladyslaw Anders CB, Commander of the Polish II Corps in Italy, Commander-in-Chief of the Polish Forces in the USSR and for a time acting Commander-in-Chief of all the Polish Armed Forces.

Five years earlier, General Anders, then a prisoner of the Russians, had been suddenly led on his crutches from his cell in the Lubianka prison to meet Beria, the notorious head of the NKVD, the Soviet secret police. General Anders had been wounded in the fighting around Warsaw in 1939, and for twenty months had been a prisoner of the Russians invading from the east. During those twenty months of imprisonment, seven of them spent in solitary confinement, he had been starved, beaten and insulted. Suddenly, in the summer of 1941, without socks and still wearing his prison trousers, he was driven to meet Beria and from Beria taken to a flat where the dining-room table was groaning with hors d'oeuvres, salads, meats and bottles of champagne and brandy. Asked what he would like to eat, he called for one scrambled egg, and began immediately the task which Beria had invited him to undertake and for which the Russians had released him – to take command of a Polish army which he was to organize in the Soviet Union now under invasion by the Russians' former ally, Nazi Germany.

Eventually in 1942, after meetings in Moscow with Winston Churchill and Stalin (with whom he dined while awaiting Churchill's arrival) General Anders led the Poles and their families, in all some 115,000 people, out of the Soviet Union and into the British command in the Middle East. From them was formed the famous Polish II Corps whose men fought beside the Allies and who died with such gallantry on the battlefields of Italy.

This story, and more, was told again in February 1960 in a court of the Queen's Bench in the Royal Courts of Justice in the Strand.

At the end of the Second World War, of the 112,000 men then on the strength of General Anders' Polish II Corps (whose casualties had been replaced by reinforcements joining after the end of hostilities) only seven officers and six thousand men of the survivors of the exodus chose to return home to Poland, by then firmly under the domination of the Soviet

Union. The remainder opted for exile in the West. The years of exile passed and, as with all exiles, indeed like the eighteenth-century English and Scots Jacobites, factions sprang up among the Poles. But none so deep and bitter as that between the vast majority of the exiles who rejected the Communists in Warsaw and a few who resented the dynamic leadership of their former General Wladyslaw Anders.

In a Polish paper circulating in London among their community, there was published an article which alleged that General Anders in the war had refused to fight the Germans in defence of Warsaw in 1939; that from his earliest days he had thought of himself more as a German than as a Pole and that he personally had always believed in the victory of Hitler. The article was a vicious attack upon the reputation and credibility of the man who to the thousands in exile and to many in Poland was a great national hero. The authors of this attack and their supporters were sustained by the Communist government in Poland who wished to denigrate the General and the exiles who refused to acknowledge the independence of what they called the puppet Warsaw regime. General Anders at once began an action for libel. He briefed me as his counsel and the court battle began on Tuesday, 9 February 1960.

I had, fortunately, as my junior counsel, one of the exiles, a Pole, George Dobry, who had himself served in the RAF. He is now a judge. In the court room there were set up on easels great maps showing the Pripet marshes and the campaigns in Poland of the First World War; the battle before Warsaw in 1939; the route of the exodus of the Polish Army from Russia which the General had led through Persia into the Middle East; and the battles in the Allied campaign in Italy in the Second World War.

Scores of witnesses were called to give evidence. On behalf of the authors of the libel, there came into the witness box, from Poland itself, Professor Kot, a former ambassador to Moscow and a supporter of the Communist government: and Stanislaw Mikolajczyk, who had been Prime Minister of the government-in-exile during the war, the negotiator with Churchill and Stalin. He had after the war joined the Warsaw government. But he had not flourished there for long and was soon put aside. The Communists, however, now sent him to London to speak against Anders.

I called among other witnesses Count Edward Raczynski, the Polish Ambassador in London at the outbreak of war and later Foreign Minister; the Polish fighting commanders; the British general Beaumont-Nesbitt, who had served at Allied Headquarters in Italy; and Field Marshall Alexander, the Commander-in-Chief in Italy. The Field Marshal's evidence was directed solely to speaking of the loyal and dedicated service which General Anders had given the Allied cause in the war against Hitler and Nazi Germany. It was incontrovertible and, naturally, very impressive. But to the surprise of everyone in court, counsel for the defendants, Neville Faulks QC, rose to cross-examine Lord Alexander. Everyone in court bridled. How could there be question about what the Field Marshal had said? 'I only rise to cross-examine you' said Neville sweetly, 'so that I can tell my grandchildren that I once cross-examined a Field Marshal.' He then sat down.

The most poignant moment in the case was when I asked one of the Polish generals, who had commanded a division in the terrible assault on Monte Cassino where now the Polish graves lie like leaves, if he was not a Companion of the British Distinguished Service Order and the holder of many great Allied orders for gallantry. He replied that he was. When I asked him what he did now, he replied simply, 'I am a waiter'.

The Warsaw government, so anxious to help destroy the reputation of the leader of the London exiles, had freely allowed witnesses to come from Poland but they denied to us facilities or access to people and records. They even produced one witness who claimed to have seen Anders as a young man in 1915 strutting about in German uniform; another said that in 1939 in defence of Warsaw Anders had deliberately disobeyed his orders to fight the Germans. All this evidence was intended to demonstrate that Anders was, at heart, more a German than a Pole, with sympathy for the Nazi cause and a traitor to Poland. Both witnesses were shown to be liars.

The case lasted three weeks. The appearance of surprise witnesses from Warsaw and their sudden production of new documents required anxious and hasty study after the Court had risen and often late into the night. Elaine fed me mugs of thick black coffee as I passed sometimes whole nights poring over maps and notes. I was deeply conscious of all that was at stake, not only personally for the General but for the whole of the brave, exiled community.

During the case Elaine came to listen in court and often she sat beside the General on the benches behind me. At the end as we waited in the corridor for the jury verdict, he offered her one of his long, yellow Russian cigarettes. 'I believe, Madame,' he said, 'that you are more nervous than I.'

I certainly was, since the jury were out considering their verdict for far too long for my peace of mind. Then the jury bailiff, quite irregularly, told me that he had overheard the jury squabbling in the jury room. 'But it's all right,' he said, looking at my anxious face. 'it's only about how much damages to give the General.' In the end they awarded General Anders

£7,000 damages, which in 1960 was a very substantial sum. His reputation as a great and patriotic Pole was vindicated. The black coffee had been worthwhile.

During those years and despite my clash with the BBC over Suez, I began to appear frequently on the radio and television – the latter was more and more assuming political significance. One of the most prestigious programmes of the time was *Free Speech* on Independent Television. It went out first live and then as a recording shortly before and shortly after luncheon on a Sunday. The chairman was the lawyer and author, Edgar Lustgarten. The regular performers were Bob Boothby, Michael Foot, A. J. P. Taylor and Bill Brown. Now and then they rested one of the regular team and brought in an outsider, an amateur. On occasions I was invited.

We met mid-morning in Edgar Lustgarten's chambers in Albany. There we drank champagne. To the newcomer this only increased the apprehension. From Piccadilly we were driven to the studios and launched into the programme. We were all told the first question, but after that it was a free-for-all. It was an alarming experience particularly since the regulars all knew each other so well. But Edgar Lustgarten was an expert and above all a fair chairman, and he played it straight. On *Free Speech* the novice was left to the tender mercies of the regulars and allowed to sink or swim on his own without being half-drowned by the chairman unfairly handing out the more awkward 'feeds'.

After the live transmission the group retired for a very handsome luncheon, during which the recording went out to another part of the country. There was a television set in the room, and as the opening bars of the signature tune blared out, Bob Boothy would take his chair and set it down plumb in front of the set. While the rest of us went on with our luncheon and cowered at the sight and sounds of our performances, Bob Boothby would follow every word avidly, congratulating himself to himself and loudly applauding the points which he had made in the programme. His self-congratulation reverberated around the luncheon room. 'Ah, I was excellent there ... Yes, yes, that's it, that's the point ... Well done, well done ... I dealt with that splendidly....' When it was over he would swing his chair round and eat and drink as energetically and as loudly as he had performed.

Partly because of this broadcasting activity I was elected chairman of the Conservative backbenchers' Broadcasting Committee. At this time a third television channel was to become available, and both the BBC and ITV, who each had only one, desperately wanted the second.

Disraeli said that 'if you want to know what envy is you should live among artists'. For several months I experienced not the envy of artists, but that of television tycoons. I was lunched by Sir Ian Fraser of the Independent Broadcasting Authority and dined by Hugh Carleton Greene, Director General of the BBC. The former was lofty and gave the impression that lunching me was personally distasteful but somebody had told him that he should. The other smiled and smiled, with the eyes narrowing behind the gleaming spectacles while more and more invitations arrived to appear on 'Any Questions'. With Hugh Greene I felt that I was dealing with a Renaissance princeling who held in one hand a bag of gold and in the other a dagger, but meanwhile kept both firmly behind his back.

The BBC was undoubtedly far fleeter of foot in making friends and influencing people than their, at that time, brasher rivals, and they got their second channel. Hugh Greene then led the Corporation into its 'liberation', throwing open the windows of Broadcasting House like Pope John XXIII the windows of the Vatican so that nothing was ever the same again and, some would say, never so good.

On the broader political scene there emerged in the late 1950s and early 1960s a development which, although we did not appreciate it at the time, would irretrievably alter British society and end the hitherto homogeneous character of the people who inhabit these islands. This was the mass immigration from the Caribbean and the Indian sub-continent which came about following the British Nationality Act of 1948, which the Attlee Labour Government had introduced when the Union Jack had been lowered over the Indian Empire. From a wholly unrealistic belief in some future role for the then rapidly disintegrating British Empire, the Act had given, literally to millions, the right of British citizenship and the right if they so wished freely to enter and reside in the already over-crowded British Isles.

At the time of the Act, its authors presumably never believed that many would ever exercise the right to enter and reside in Britain so gratuitously, even irresponsibly, given to them. However, within a few years hundreds of thousands began to arrive, and the situation which had been allowed to develop was suddenly evident to a wider public when there began to appear photographs of the crammed immigrant ships arriving and of the bewildered faces of crowds of new immigrants dispersing into the inner cities.

As an MP for a suburban constituency all that I was aware of at first was the appearance of smiling and friendly black faces among the staff of the several large hospitals in and around Epsom. Then I began to receive letters from constituents: thoughtful, quite reasonable letters enquiring about the desirability of this development. Then questions began to be raised at public and private political meetings. In the House, in conversation with colleagues representing seats in the Midlands and in the cities, it gradually became clear that there was a national groundswell of anxiety. Next, on visits to speak in several constituencies, I encountered the deep unease which many were beginning to feel and to express. The gist of the comments at this time was to question how the newcomers could fit into the social life of their new country and whether they, and especially their children, could be fairly asked to identify with the Britain of history and with the society (with all its faults) in which the questioners had been bred and for which they had so recently fought. Or would that character, they asked, now have to change to accommodate the immigrants, and if so why? A mild-mannered man at one meeting stood and said that the tradition which he and his fellows had learned at school was of Arthur and his knights (did they ever exist?); of Harry at Agincourt, of Nelson at Trafalgar, of the Guards at Waterloo and, more recently, of the Few in the skies above Britain in the blazing summer of 1940. How, he asked, and why should the newcomers identify as a people with that story? I could not answer him. Nor could I answer the question why the people had not been consulted before this change had been allowed to come about.

Soon the questioning began to grow more fierce, as people witnessed the need for different teaching in their children's schools, and some streets began to change character from the cockney or scouse of old to something a little more exotic. But it was always the sheer scale of the immigration rather than its nature which concerned these people and of which at meetings they would complain. Quite suddenly we as MPs became conscious that there had arisen a grave problem, and that it now required law to limit the numbers of those entitled to come in; and, later on, uncharacteristically for the British, law to make people act fairly to the newcomers. But when Rab Butler in 1961 sought to impose the first and modest limitation on the right of entry, Parliament witnessed a passionate onslaught on Rab's Bill by the Leader of the Opposition. Hugh Gaitskell stood at the dispatch-box trembling with genuine emotion as he passionately denounced any attempt to control the influx of immigrants which was arousing concern, if not in him and to his friends, then certainly in the public, who usually lived a lot closer to it all than did the liberal establishment.

The immigration of late 1950s and 1960s inevitably and irreversibly altered the character of British society. It was the most significant political development of my time in public life, of greater significance for the people of Britain even than the European movement. That all in public life over this period were so ignorant of its significance while it was occurring is an indictment which none of us who served in government or Parliament during those years should ever be allowed to forget.

While encountering this new and bewildering political development and in the House supporting Rab Butler from the government back-benches during the various stages in the passage of his Bill, I went in July 1962 to hold my Sessions at Salisbury, where I sat as the Recorder. I was back in London in the first week in July and I was preparing the Horobin case which was due for trial. On my return I did a broadcast and in the following week began a libel action in the High Court in the Strand.

In July London itself is often dusty, and so are political tempers. It is the month for political crisis. Parliamentarians are weary and irritable after long and late sittings on the annual Finance Bill, and the Whips are always anxious to have the House up and away. In 1962 the political commentators were running stories on the poor form which the government was showing. That after five years the Macmillan administration should have run into a bad patch was not unusual for any government, but ministers, most of whom had been in office for eleven consecutive years, were undoubtedly looking stale. The public, it was felt, was growing bored with the old familiar faces. Above all the Prime Minister was losing some of his lustre. There was talk that a younger man was now needed at the helm. It was being hinted that Supermac was finished.

On Friday 13 July the Prime Minister struck. The political dagger was wielded in earnest. Seven of the cabinet were summarily dismissed, including David Kilmuir, the Lord Chancellor. Attorney General Reggie Manningham-Buller, reincarnated as Lord Dilhorne, succeeded him. John Hobson, the Solicitor General, was promoted to Attorney. So there was a vacancy in the office of Solicitor.

The next day Elaine and I went to Epsom so that I could hold my monthly interviews with constituents, or surgery as it is called. A lady was brought in to see me. Wearing my constituency surgery smile and with pen poised ready to record her difficulties with pension or rates, the smile was quickly wiped off my face as she proceeded to give me a graphic and explicit description of the difficulties which she was encountering in managing to hold her water. She was an amiable patient in one of the local mental hospitals who had mistaken mine for a medical surgery and me for the doctor. She was extricated from the room without disaster.

From Epsom we set off to spend the weekend with my parents by the sea in Sussex. I was back in chambers on the Monday, 16 July, and mid-morning Martin Redmayne, the Chief Whip, informed me of the wish of the Prime Minister to see me.

It was just after luncheon that I made my way up from No. 12 King's Bench Walk in the Temple, past El Vino's and into Fleet Street to find the taxi which was to take me to Admiralty House and into a life which thereafter would never be quite the same.

Chapter 10
Solicitor General – The Spy Vassal

When I was seated in the late summer of 1962 behind the large desk in the tall room of the Solicitor General in the Royal Courts of Justice, the words of Prime Minister Macmillan in his elegant lecture to me on the duties of my new office had certainly not faded from my mind. So I sought out the words of Attorney General Sir John Scott at the end of the eighteenth century, when he declared that the Attorney General had it in his power to choose whether he will or will not prosecute and that 'he will act according to his sense of duty ... it is his duty to regulate his judgement by a conscientious pursuance of that which is recommended to him to do'. He went on 'no man ought to be in the office who would hesitate to say, "My conscience must direct me, your judgement shall not direct me."'

The Solicitor General is the second Law Officer of the Crown; the Attorney General is the first, whose duties include the constitutional responsibility for criminal prosecutions. The Solicitor has all the powers of the Attorney to perform the Attorney's duties in his absence.

I knew that, ever since 1924, ministers and particularly prime ministers had been especially wary of becoming, or being seen to become, involved in the exercise by the Attorney General of his constitutional duty alone to decide whether to launch, or desist from launching, a criminal prosecution. For in 1924 the then Prime Minister, Ramsay MacDonald, had played a typically confused part in conversations with the Attorney General, Sir Patrick Hastings, concerning the decision of the latter to withdraw, for perfectly proper reasons, a prosecution for sedition against John Campbell, a Communist and ex-soldier. Of these conversations, which amounted to pressure to prosecute, MacDonald had privately written to the King's Private Secretary in Balmoral, 'I sent for the Attorney General and the Public Prosecutor and gave them a piece of my mind'.

As a result of parliamentary questions about political interference with the duty of the Attorney General in respect of criminal prosecutions and as a result of the debates which followed, the first and minority Labour government had fallen. Ever since then ministers had been taught to be especially careful never to interfere in the Law Officer's responsibility over criminal prosecutions. This part of the Law Officer's duty, it was accepted, was not one in which political colleagues could ever intervene. So it was, I felt, essential, even as the second Law Officer, to know the precedents for the principle that over prosecutions the Law Officer may consult to establish what is or is not the wider public interest, but that the decision is his alone. This study and research was well worth the doing in view of what lay ahead. John Hobson, the Attorney General, found me at my study. He approved. After all, he said, he hunted every Saturday.

I had known John Hobson for many years and liked him immensely. For years we used to have luncheon together with Stormont Mancroft and Harry Hylton-Foster at the same table in the Inner Temple. John had succeeded Anthony Eden in 1957 as the MP for Warwick and Leamington. He had had a substantial practice on the Midland Circuit. He loved all field sports, and he was perhaps happiest on the hill in Scotland. He was thorough and industrious, to the point of driving his juniors and the barristers in the Law Officers' Department almost crazy with his determination to master every single detail of everything put before him, details which his subordinates often felt were irrelevant or, at best, unnecessary. He was engaging, straightforward and of transparent integrity. He was not, however, 'street-wise', which was the quality which, alas, he was going to need.

In September of 1962 I was at work in my lofty room in the Law Courts. All seemed to be going smoothly. I was enjoying the work. Life on the whole seemed rather agreeable. After my dubbing as a knight by the Queen I had appeared as 'Mr Solicitor' in the courts in two cases for the Crown. In the Commons I now sat on the front bench among all the Great Men, and as a Law Officer had attended the Committee stage of some Bill at the urgent entreaty of the very new Parliamentary Secretary to the Ministry of Labour, Willie Whitelaw. I came to explain a point of law, and was respectfully thanked by Willie, and grandly withdrew. Best of all, nearly six years after our son Michael, a daughter had just been born, to the great delight of Elaine and myself and to that of our two Spanish ladies. So that September afternoon I sat feeling pretty complacent. The Attorney General was in his constituency. I was minding the shop. I was certainly not in a mood to anticipate trouble when the Director of Public Prosecutions, Toby

Mathew, was announced. I knew him well, but in my new glory I received him, standing rather grandly in front of the fireplace.

'Sit down, Solicitor', Toby said genially as soon as he had come through the door. He was looking decidedly pleased with himself. 'Sit down. You will need to. We have arrested a spy who is a bugger, and a minister is involved.' I duly sat. My honeymoon in office was over. For this was the start of the Vassall affair, which over the next few months would propel the government into a head-on collision with the press.

The spy, Vassall, was a civil servant in the Admiralty who the following month was to be sentenced to eighteen years' imprisonment. The Minister was the Civil Lord, Tam Galbraith, and his involvement arose simply because Vassall had served in his Private Office as the assistant to Tam's Private Secretary, making travel arrangements and engagements, and Tam had written letters to him about such mundane matters as the office furniture. But Tam had addressed those letters 'My dear Vassall', and the recipient was secretly a spy and a homosexual.

After Vassall's arrest and trial there arose a violent campaign in the press, principally directed at Peter Carrington the First Lord and Tam Galbraith the Civil Lord at the Admiralty. Tam resigned on 8 November. In April 1963 he was totally cleared of any impropriety or negligence. He returned to his office for a short time; but his spirit was broken and his career and indeed his family life were effectively ruined. A wholly innocent man had been destroyed by gossip and rumour. The Prime Minister was much criticized for having accepted his resignation.

These events, this example of an innocent man gravely wronged, had consequences beyond the fate of a falsely accused Civil Lord. They played a significant part and had much influence when, next year, there came the need to form judgments upon the conduct of another more experienced and more robust minister.

Originally, Prime Minister Harold Macmillan had been advised and had agreed that after the conviction of the spy Vassall an enquiry should be conducted within the civil service to examine any security weaknesses which had emerged. But the press was by then busily attacking Lord Carrington, Tam Galbraith, the Ambassador in Moscow where Vassall had served and been seduced, naval security chiefs and civil servants. By November a fierce parliamentary row had broken out. The Opposition, led by George Brown in the Commons, called for the setting up of the cumbersome and massive procedure of a formal enquiry under the Tribunal of Inquiries Act 1921. At first the Prime Minister rejected the demand. But the pressure grew.

On 7 November John Hobson and I were called to Admiralty House to discuss with the Prime Minister whether to accede to the demands of the Opposition to turn the proposed civil service enquiry into a full-scale tribunal. We sat beside the fire, drinking whisky and soda. At the end of our talk, the Prime Minister said, 'Very well, we shall retire. But we shall retire to the thunder of the guns.'

A week later he proposed in the House the motion setting up a tribunal to enquire into the circumstances of the Vassall crimes; into allegations of the existence of another spy in the Admiralty; into allegations reflecting upon the honour and integrity of ministers, naval officers and civil servants; and into any breaches of security or neglect of duty. The tribunal under Lord Radcliffe began its hearings on 21 November 1962. One hundred and forty-two witnesses were heard. It sat in secret for sixteen days and six half-days, and in public for seven days and seven half-days. Its sittings went on well into 1963. It finally reported on 5 April 1963. It wholly cleared Tam Galbraith of all the gossip and refuted the slander about him.

The Attorney General, John Hobson, despite criticism of his personal participation as counsel, played a leading role in the tribunal proceedings. He presented witnesses, made submissions and cross-examined. In the course of the hearings two journalists, Mr Mulholland of the *Daily Mail* and Mr Foster of the *Daily Sketch*, when the authenticity of certain of their reports was probed (some of which included accounts of Vassall's transvestite habits and which were, even at the time, regarded with some scepticism), refused to disclose their sources and eventually were sent to prison for contempt. Thereupon war was declared by the press upon the Macmillan administration.

While the Attorney General went off to his arduous and time-consuming duties with the Radcliffe tribunal, I went to the Old Bailey to prosecute a Miss Barbara Fell for offences against the Official Secrets Act. She was on the staff of the Central Office of Information and she had given documents to which she had access to her lover, a member of the Yugoslav diplomatic staff. They were not all documents of a very high category of secrecy. One was the valedictory despatch of the British Ambassador in Paris, Gladwyn Jebb, written in exquisite limpid prose. During his tour in Paris, he had witnessed the demise of the Fourth Republic with its procession of prime ministers which had been swept aside by General de Gaulle after the referendum which established the new constitution of France. Ambassador Jebb reviewed the political changes and the coming of a new age in French political life. He concluded gracefully, '*Sed in Arcadia vixi.*'

I could not see how this could have greatly harmed British interests or encouraged Marshal Tito. But, understandably, the Foreign Office does not want the despatches even of its most literate ambassadors handed over during pillow-talk sessions to the diplomats of other nations; and there were documents which found their way into the Yugoslav diplomatic pouch more confidential and more secret than the nostalgic report of Sir Gladwyn Jebb.

Twenty-five years later there would probably have been an outcry that there was any prosecution at all. A campaign would have been mounted to show how unimportant were the matters leaked; that the foreign government knew all about them in any event; and that anyway it was the public duty of Crown servants to tell everybody everything. Times were different in 1962. The spirit of iconoclasm, although emerging, had not yet swept away all rules of loyalty and confidentiality in the Crown service. The Official Secrets Act applied, so Miss Fell entered a dignified plea of guilty and was sent to prison.

The turbulent year of 1962 was coming to an end. The Cuban missile crisis had brought the world to the brink of war. The hitherto infallible, unflappable Prime Minister had sacked a third of his Cabinet and was thought to be weakening; Hugh Gaitskell was dying; and a spurious scandal had claimed one innocent minister for a victim.

During the second half of that year, through my appointment to office my personal life had been transformed. I was now to be projected into the eye of a storm.

'All that is left for the Solicitor General in normal times', once said F. E. Smith, Lord Birkenhead, 'is the elucidation of unintelligible legal difficulties in minor and uninteresting Bills.' But in 1963 the times were not normal. A swimming party at Cliveden on 8 June 1961 was to cast its long, dark shadow over the whole of the year which lay ahead.

Chapter 11
The Profumo Affair and the Five Ministers

On Monday 28 January 1963 I was in my room in the Law Courts. The Attorney General was away from chambers, deeply involved in the proceedings of the Radcliffe tribunal which was still enquiring into the circumstances surrounding the activities of the spy Vassall. Once again I was minding the shop at the Law Officers' Department when I received a visitor bearing grave news. The visitor was Billy Rees-Davies, Conservative Member of Parliament for Thanet, who practised at the criminal Bar. He had only one arm and so, of necessity, he wore cloaks. This gave him a raffish air. When he was announced I had a premonition that he was the harbinger of bad news, and I was not wrong.

Billy told me of rumours circulating about the then Secretary of War, Jack Profumo. Not very far away the Attorney General was dealing with rumours and allegations, which were daily being demonstrated as false, about the First Lord of the Admiralty Peter Carrington and Tam Galbraith, the Civil Lord. Here was I now being told of other rumours about another minister.

These rumours about this colleague concerned, Billy Rees-Davies told me, a young girl, Christine Keeler, who was involved in a shooting incident with a West Indian. The man was shortly to stand trial at the Old Bailey. The story of the young girl and her intimate relationship with the West Indian and with the Secretary of State for War was about to be published in a newspaper. The scandal would be immense.

My meeting with Billy Rees-Davies took place at eleven-thirty in the morning. I saw the Attorney General when he returned, weary, from the tribunal at four-thirty in the afternoon, just before I left for a meeting. I told him what Billy Rees-Davies had told me. I saw John again at six, after my meeting. He arranged to see Jack Profumo that night at eleven p.m.

A few days later I went with John to Jack Profumo's room. John told me that Jack Profumo had denied any impropriety with the girl and that the whole story was a malevolent newspaper stunt. Now John wanted me to hear for myself what Profumo had to say. In the Secretary of State's room I listened to Jack's categorical and emphatic denials of any impropriety with the girl, who in 1961 he emphasized, was certainly not a prostitute nor involved in the kind of world into which two years later she had apparently sunk. I asked if the Minister was prepared to issue a writ for slander or libel if opportunity presented itself. I warned him that in any lawsuit a defendant might well seek to prove that he had committed adultery and then his whole life and his conduct would come under close investigation and, when it came to court, under a public searchlight. I said that once he had issued a writ he would have to pursue the case to its end either in settlement and apology, or in the verdict of a jury.

The reply was vehement, a declaration that he would sue anyone who ever published this libel about him. The newspaper, he said, had a note from him to the girl addressed as 'Darling'; but not everyone who called a woman darling (and this was a common form of address in the theatre circles in which he and his wife moved) had committed adultery with her. It must be remembered, he insisted, that when he had met Christine Keeler she was vastly different from what she had apparently become.

It may be, he concluded, that in the present climate of press hostility to the government arising from the Radcliffe tribunal and the imprisonment of the two journalists, he might not at first be believed. But he was determined that he would not be driven out of public life and ruined by lies and gossip of the kind which had so recently destroyed our colleague, Tam Galbraith. He repeated that he had not slept with the girl; that he was being dragged into her present story solely because he was a minister, probably to get money out of him or to make a better story to sell; and that the liars were using elements in the press who were determined to get their own back on the government. He was not going to resign; he would fight to the end. He would be damned if he would tamely let himself be destroyed.

This was certainly articulate and trenchant. But it was, at that time, only words. I had heard similar words from people contemplating the launch of an action for defamation, and some when they learned what it involved I had heard of no more. What I waited to see was whether that fighting talk would be turned into action. For instance, would he really sue? On 3

February Jack Profumo consulted Derek Clogg, a man I knew well and a solicitor in an important firm with great personal experience in matters such as these. Derek Clogg saw John Hobson and told him that he, Derek, had been told by his client to sue and seek injunctions whenever the opportunity presented itself.

The next day, Clogg brought to John Hobson leading counsel whom he had instructed on behalf of Profumo. This was Mark Littman QC. They told John that a solicitor acting on behalf of the girl had made an approach saying that a Sunday newspaper had offered her £1,500 for articles but that she wanted £3,000 (later raised to £5,000) to 'disappear' after the trial of the West Indian at the Old Bailey. Mark Littman and Derek Clogg took the view that this could amount to a blackmailing approach. It seemed to bear out the suspicion of which Jack Profumo had spoken to me a few days earlier. On 5 February, on the instructions of their client and with his authority to say that he was ready to give evidence in any criminal prosecution, Mark Littman and Derek Clogg visited the Director of Public Prosecutions.

This robust reaction, which committed Jack Profumo publicly to give evidence on oath in a court of law, certainly demonstrated that he was prepared to live up to the protestations which he had made to John and me. He was indeed translating his words into actions. He was indeed not going to surrender to threats or gossip and lies nor be driven to political ruin. He was not going to resign. He was going to fight, and he was prepared to fight in public – and to fight on oath.

John had told what he knew to Martin Redmayne, the Chief Whip. There followed discussions between the Chief Whip, the Prime Minister's Principal Private Secretary Tim Bligh, and the Prime Minister himself. The position, then, at that time was that Profumo emphatically denied the rumours. He was advised by a distinguished and experienced solicitor who told us (although he had no obligation to do so) that he himself wholly believed his client. Instructions had been given to issue writs for libel, and the Director of Public Prosecutions had been informed that the Minister would give evidence if any blackmail charges arose.

But my practice at the Bar had made me perhaps more wary in such matters than John. I remained uneasy. I spoke with John. I said that if all was not as it appeared he would be blamed and there would be no mercy. I reminded him that the Conservative Party was in the business of winning and keeping power; it had no scruple in sacrificing any of its servants should interest demand it. John said quietly that there was no alternative. Statements had been made to him on honour. On those assurances of honour, and in the light of the pledges to sue or to prosecute (promises which it seemed were being redeemed), he must support to the hilt. Otherwise he said all confidence in colleagues was finished. There had to be standards of trust between colleagues and this was between him and a life-long friend. Similar words about the need for trust between colleagues were used by the Prime Minister in the House of Commons later in the summer.

I was moved and impressed by John's resolution. But I hoped that some opportunity to demonstrate the truth of what had been protested in private beyond the issue of writs and the notice to the DPP would present itself. On the night of Thursday 21 March that opportunity suddenly arose.

In the House of Commons on that evening, the House was debating the case of the two journalists who had been convicted of contempt of court before the Radcliffe tribunal and had been sent to prison. John and I, the two Law Officers, were both seated on the government Front Bench. George Wigg, Barbara Castle and Richard Crossman spoke from the Labour benches. Each referred to scandal attaching to a government minister. It was clear that they were referring to Jack Profumo. I remember thinking, 'This is Jack's chance. The affair is at last in the open.' John and I both realized that Profumo had now been presented with the opportunity for which he said he had been waiting, the chance publicly to scotch the rumours and nail the lies. We withdrew to a small room behind the Speaker's Chair. With us went Bill Deedes, then a member of the Cabinet who had also been on the Front Bench, although neither before nor after that evening was Bill further involved. John went and fetched Martin Redmayne. We drafted a few non-committal words for the Home Secretary, Henry Brooke, to use in winding up the debate from the government front bench. This he did. The debate ended. It was then eleven at night. Its business finished, the House rose and the Home Secretary went home. But we had work to do.

We knew that to make use of this opportunity it was necessary to act swiftly. The accusations, for that is what they amounted to, had to be rebutted quickly before an eager press took them up and developed the story throughout the weekend. The House was due to sit at eleven o'clock the next morning, Friday. This would be the ideal moment to reply to George Wigg and to refute the gossip.

The Chief Whip spoke to the Prime Minister, who agreed that Profumo could now substantiate the assurances to his colleagues which he had given in private, and that Profumo should make a personal statement in the House to clear his name. Iain Macleod, the Leader of the House, who would be concerned if a personal statement were to be made, joined us. We moved to a larger room. Jack Profumo was telephoned, and John and I suggested that Derek Clogg, Profumo's solicitor, should come since this fortuitous opportunity could be used to rebut all the rumours and allegations. Derek Clogg would be able not only to suggest what he thought should be included but he would also be needed to ensure that the personal statement did not prejudice any of the litigation which had been started on Jack's behalf. So it was essential that he should come with Jack.

I, myself, felt glad that at last the moment of truth had arrived. Any refusal to make the statement would lead over the weekend to exploitation of the story based upon what George Wigg and the others had said under the cloak of parliamentary privilege and which could therefore safely be published in the newspapers. After such comments in the House, the crisis had certainly been brought to the boil. The only explanation for any refusal to answer in public the comments would be that all the protestations made in private had been false. But none of us for one moment expected that there would be any refusal to make a statement. We believed that Jack Profumo would be as eager as we to seize this chance to clear his name. So we waited, relieved, that the climax had arrived.

Jack Profumo and Derek Clogg joined the five of us who were still in the House. The three lawyers then went into another room, and we drafted the statement. Derek Clogg did indeed require that it should be comprehensive so that it met all the known rumours and gossip which had been circulating for so many weeks and he ensured that its terms would not prejudice the litigation that had been launched. I wrote out the draft statement.

We re-joined the others, Martin Redmayne, Iain Macleod, Bill Deedes and Jack Profumo, who had been talking and awaiting our return. I read out what we suggested that the personal statement should include. When I came to the words, 'Miss Keeler and I were on friendly terms', Jack Profumo interjected, 'Do I have to say that? It sounds so awful.'

I thought that he was referring to the wording. The words were certainly trite and stilted, but at the time I could think of none better. I asked how else it could be put. The matter was then discussed. it was agreed that the statement had to cover the accepted fact that Profumo had known the girl two years before but that he emphatically denied any adultery or impropriety. So in the end he accepted the words and shortly thereafter we broke up, the statement settled.

At the time I did not gain any impression of drowsiness; his interjection belied any lack of understanding. There was also plenty of time later that morning to recant if there was to be any recantation, for the statement would not be made until 11 a.m., several hours ahead. I certainly did not expect any as I went home and got into bed at 5 a.m. I rose again at seven-thirty. I did not go to the House, but went early to my work at the Law Courts. There I suddenly began to think about that interjection. Did it mean more than I thought that it had at the time? I waited, for the first time, with some anxiety. Then John told me that the statement had been made as it had been written. I felt ashamed that, for a moment, I had doubted.

On 3 June Jack Profumo made his confession that what he had said to the House on March 22nd was false, and he resigned. On 8 June Stephen Ward, who had seemed to endorse the personal statement of Profumo, was arrested and charged with living on the earnings of prostitutes. A police investigation into his activities with women had started in April, two months earlier. Later commentators have alleged that Henry Brooke had instigated that investigation and the subsequent prosecution. That is untrue, and is a libel upon him and upon Sir Charles Cunningham, the then Permanent Secretary at the Home Office; and upon the Commissioner for the Metropolitan Police; and upon John Hobson, who as Attorney General bore the sole constitutional responsibility for all prosecutions. Neither Henry Brooke nor John was involved, nor were they consulted. Their accusers claim that this investigation and prosecution of Ward was an act of political malice and revenge. That is absurd.

Regarded solely from the point of view of the party political interests, the very last thing that the government wanted after John Profumo's personal statement, which had apparently lanced the boil, was for there then to be staged a sensational trial with massive publicity in which all those matters would be raked over and in which, in particular, all the ladies would star. It was moreover the last thing which suited Jack Profumo himself, who in April was still a member of that government. For over a criminal investigation and prosecution into offences concerning living off the proceeds of prostitution, Ward could get no help from Profumo his friend the Minister, nor indeed from any friend. The matter was now personal to him.

In the spring of 1963 the police were presented with a situation where allegations and accusations and gossip about the behaviour of prominent people and their conduct with women were circulating around London like wildfire. The gossip centred upon Stephen Ward and the pretty girls who seemed to become so conveniently available for his acquaintances. It was impossible for the police to ignore these rumours about Ward or to avoid an investigation. To have done so would have laid them open to the charge that, out of favour to the interests of people in high places, they were failing in their duty. How they conducted that investigation is another matter. But any enquiry into pimping necessarily involved obtaining information from tarts, not always the most reliable of witnesses. Henry Brooke and John Hobson did not seek to call off the police. Neither did they set the police on to Ward. They are both dead and unable to refute these intrinsically silly but nevertheless cruel libels. In fact, I well recollect the concern when the Attorney General realized that a criminal trial lay ahead.

On 13 June I attended the Cabinet with the Attorney General. This was unusual. Either one or other of the Law officers attend to give advice on law, never both. That we were both invited to this Cabinet was upon the suggestion of the Lord Chancellor. For the government was facing a major crisis as much within its own ranks and from its own supporters as from its opponents over the handling of the matter, and both John and I had been much involved.

It was reported that some members of the Cabinet were especially uneasy over the conduct of the five ministers who had sat together when the Profumo statement was prepared, because they had acted deceitfully or incompetently, or both. Resignations were in the wind. It was being said that the five-minister meeting had been some inquisitorial process; that it had been a drum-head court martial which had, in the event, reached the wrong verdict. In fact it had been rather a council of war, to arrange how best to exploit the opportunity which had at last been presented to a colleague to proclaim in public what he had so long protested in private.

It was rumoured that Rab was keeping his head well below the parapet. After all, the position of the Prime Minister had become precarious, and he was then heir apparent. One of the Cabinet who was said to be highly critical was the Minister of Health, Enoch Powell. When I was called to speak by the Prime Minister, I looked down the long table. I remember looking straight into the intense eyes set in the white face of the Minister of Health as he leaned forward the better to hear. They never shifted while I spoke. In the event no minister resigned.

On the day after the Cabinet and three days before the debate on the affair in the House of Commons, I wrote to Martin Redmayne.

> Royal Courts of Justice
> London
>
> 14th June 1963

Dear Martin,

I presume that both you and I will be accused of gullibility over our part in the Profumo deceit. For my part I should like to make plain that in the interviews I had with him in February I pressed him firmly over his story and received clear, categorical and what seemed convincing denials of any guilt whatsoever. I think it should also be remembered that at the time when Profumo said he knew the girl, she had not then taken to drugs and West Indians; and also it should not be forgotten that at the time when rumours were circulating about J. P. the Radcliffe Tribunal was sitting and it was not long after similar rumours had been circulated about another of our colleagues, rumours which we knew to be totally false.

Be that as it may, the object of the statement which I helped to draft was to inform the House and the Country of the truth and to set the record straight. It was made when we knew that Profumo strenuously and vehemently denied all guilt; when the evidence of more than friendship was at best tenuous; and when we knew that Profumo had gone to the considerable length of instructing his Solicitor to approach the D.P.P. with a view to starting blackmail proceedings, and had given this Solicitor instructions to sue for libel or slander even a friend or colleague if the opportunity presented itself.

We were in the event deceived. And so was his Solicitor, Derek Clogg, a man of the highest reputation and great experience. Moreover I think that I have had as much experience of this kind of legal practice as anyone in my profession, and my professional judgement was as completely deceived as was your judgement as a man of the world by what was not only a wicked series of lies, but was also a most brazen and convincing performance which led to the application to the D.P.P. and even an action in the Courts.

I of course regret that we were so totally deceived, but I utterly reject any suggestion that Profumo's claim was one which could have been obviously or readily rejected.

Yours,
Peter

Such was the public mood in those days that on one occasion Martin Redmayne found himself suddenly surrounded by press men as he went to get into his car. 'What's all the fuss about?' he was reported to have said. He was much abused for this. It was used to show his crassness and flippancy, an illustration of how lightly the Chief whip took this grave political crisis. In fact what he had said was 'What's all this about?'

The debate was held on 17 June. Two hours before it began Martin and Oliver Poole, the party Vice-Chairman from Central Office, attended a crisis meeting of the 1922 Committee. Afterwards Martin advised the Prime Minister that the Conservative majority, usually ninety-eight, might well drop to forty but that he hoped for fifty. It was an ugly and an uncomfortable debate. The deceived were well mocked.

One of the current allegations was that the girl had been sharing her favours simultaneously with the Secretary of State for War and a Russian diplomat – in other words, with a Soviet spy. So the issue, the Opposition insisted, was primarily all about security. Ivanov, the Russian diplomat, they insisted, was the key. No question of sex and salacity and the morals of ministers had ever entered the patriotic and pious heads of Opposition MPs. Politically they sought to present the affair solely as a security scandal, and the languid Prime Minister, this Edwardian anachronism in the swinging sixties with his head in the clouds of international affairs and his nose in Trollope, was the quarry.

Harold Macmillan, although under great strain, spoke well. Harold Wilson was skilful and effective. But Iain Macleod, usually a prince of debaters, was not at his best. Martin got a majority of fifty-seven but, as he later said, it was no famous victory. After the debate, bruised and miserable, I drank morosely with my friends Humphrey Atkins and Tony Royle.

From then on, like waiting for Godot, everyone waited for Lord Denning. For Lord Denning had been invited to make a one-man personal enquiry into the whole affair.

Meanwhile, in July, I went off to the Old Bailey to prosecute a man called Martelli on a charge of committing acts preparatory to engaging in spying. He had been found with shoes with hollowed-out heels, the soles swivelling to reveal secret cavities. He had in his possession 'one-time pads', the regular noting-paper for the despatch and receipt of secret messages. In his defence he admitted that he was being pressured by the Soviets to act as a spy but he denied that he had succumbed to the pressure and he swore that he had no intention of using the kit with which he had been supplied. He was acquitted. These were not good days for the Law Officers.

In September Lord Denning reported. In his report one paragraph, and only one, criticized ministers. They had not, he indicated, asked themselves the proper question. The question, he implied, was not whether Mr Profumo had in fact committed adultery; rather the question was, had his conduct been such as to lead ordinary people reasonably to believe that he had committed adultery. He drew an analogy from civil law, that if a man commits adultery his wife may have just cause for leaving him but that it does not depend on his in fact having committed adultery. For if a wife, the analogy went on, reasonably believes that the husband has committed adultery, she has just cause for leaving him. The reason, said Lord Denning, was because his conduct was such as to destroy the confidence and trust which subsists between them. Lord Denning applied this analogy to the situation presented to the ministers.

This analogy surprised some and angered others. Lord Shawcross QC (a former Labour Attorney General) said that he simply did not understand the Denning criticism of ministers on this basis and he said that Lord Denning's analogy was utterly false. The true analogy, said Lord Shawcross, was that of the wife who herself implicitly believed that her husband had not committed adultery although other people thought that he had. Lord Shawcross considered that Ministers, rightly or wrongly, believing that Profumo had been speaking the truth, would have acted wrongly if they had thrown him to the wolves because they thought that a lot of other people thought that he was guilty. Of the 'darling' letter, which the newspaper which held it itself found only 'effusive but not conclusive', Lord Shawcross said that not for a moment would he have drawn an inference of adultery from that letter.

The analogy drawn by Lord Denning and the road in logic which he had followed to indicate that ministers had asked themselves the wrong question greatly angered John Hobson. He claimed that Lord Denning had turned the rule inside out, so that on Lord Denning's thesis people should be condemned and banished if there were reasonable grounds for believing that they had done wrong even if their judges believed that they were innocent. According to John this was bad law and worse morals. Under this odd doctrine, he complained, the enquirer became blameworthy upon the basis that he had failed to act when there were reasonable grounds to believe a person was guilty although the enquirer himself believed that the man was innocent. John Hobson also greatly resented the fact that Lord Denning had never asked him whether he, John, had ever asked himself 'the proper question' and that he had never been given the slightest opportunity to deal with the question for which Lord Denning now blamed him for ignoring.

In fact we had all of us addressed ourselves to Lord Denning's 'correct' question time and time again. But we were presented with a solemn and trenchant denial, and a stubborn refusal to be sacrificed because of appearances. We were acutely conscious, as we were repeatedly reminded during our questioning, of what had happened to an innocent colleague on the strength of some letters, harmless in content but addressed 'My dear Vassall', to a man who later turned out to be a homosexual and a spy. We were presented with resolute action involving the issue of writs and of assurances to the DPP of a readiness to give evidence in a criminal prosecution. So what then to do? Enforce resignation? How? Alternatively, require the dismissal from office of a man who perhaps later, by litigation, might demonstrate his innocence? What justice would that have been? The Prime Minister had already earlier been much criticized for what was said to have been a cowardly acceptance of the resignation of Tam Galbraith. This one was not prepared to resign.

So the correct question was never 'appearance', nor the analogy of the wronged wife. The only courses open were dismissal, because of convictions that this Minister was guilty; or support, either because of confidence in his innocence or, at worst, because the charge was non-proven.

John, as he had told me, was sustained by reliance upon assurance given to him upon honour. For the four years of life remaining to him, he remained glad that despite the cost to himself he had not condemned a friend to ruin on appearances, but rather had relied upon the word of a colleague in difficulty. He did, however, resent the fact that somehow talk about sleeping pills and the pain of a gallant wife had not only aroused sympathy but had switched opprobrium from the deceiver and on to the deceived. So, with due respect for one man's remarkable and selfless twenty-five years of rehabilitation, it is only fair to the memory of others who are dead that errors should be corrected, that absurd accusations should be rebutted, and that the pain of friends of great integrity should be remembered and that their reputations should not be left unchampioned.

But, in believing in Profumo, we had been wrong. So I offered to go. In his autobiography Harold Macmillan wrote, 'Sir Peter Rawlinson who had been specially concerned with Profumo's statement in the House generously offered his resignation, but I was quite unwilling to accept this. I felt that if there was blame in our handling of this difficult situation we must all share it. The major responsibility at any rate lay upon me.'

It was kind of him to describe my offer as 'generous'. It was not meant as a noble gesture. It would have been no great personal sacrifice. I would readily have returned to the Bar, as I finally and happily went a dozen years later. But I did feel that, as we had been wrong, a price ought to be paid, that some head ought to roll. Mine might have taken some of the pressure off John Hobson, whose integrity and sense of right I greatly admired, while one departure might have eased the storm in which the government was then being tossed. But my resignation was refused and I realized that if I insisted my resignation might only help to bring down a Prime Minister whom I greatly admired and whom I had been elected to support and whose then heir apparent and probable successor, Rab Butler, was not, I felt, a man to go tiger-shooting with at a time when political tigers were menacingly on the prowl.

So I stayed on in the room with the high ceiling in the gloomy corridor in the department in the Law Courts. But I had learned the lesson. Of one thing I was thereafter certain. For me, in my political life, never would come again even the faintest hint of 'glad confident morning'.

Chapter 12
A Swearing-in Ceremony – The Government Defeated

During that frantic June of 1963, while the political scene was dominated by the aftermath of the Profumo resignation, I also had my routine duties, handling for the Treasury a mass of amendments to the Finance Bill with which I had been asked to make myself responsible. Reggie Maudling was the Chancellor.

One day I was asked to attend a meeting at the Treasury, at the invitation I was told of the Chancellor. It was to be with him and two of the Treasury 'knights', great civil servants of immense experience and prestige. These mandarins were, I understood, anxious to include in the Finance Bill some abstruse amendments to revenue law. I got myself well briefed on the revenue law by my lawyers and by Reggie Hill, the very experienced Standing Counsel to the Inland Revenue, or Treasury 'devil' as Standing Counsel were called. My task was to explain to the Chancellor the effect on revenue law of the proposed changes.

The meeting was at two-thirty, after luncheon. I dutifully arrived dead on time and I was greeted by the grave mandarins. Then Reggie sauntered in, smoking a large cigar. He was welcoming but seemed rather surprised to see me. The cigar smoke wreathed us in delicious scent. One of the Treasury knights coughed deprecatingly. Then the civil servants explained that they had invited me to attend in order to explain the legal consequences of the amendment which they suggested ought to be included in the Finance Bill. The change, they purred, was technical if a little complicated and, they hastened to add, wholly free from any political consequence. They apologized to the Chancellor for not having given him notice of their proposal but they felt that it would not prove controversial.

It was my turn to feel surprised. I did not then know Whitehall as well as I did later. However, I duly explained the point of law, sticking closely to my brief. Silence fell. Reggie lounged back in his chair and blew a few reflective smoke rings. Then he said, 'No, no, it won't do.' He then gave his reasons. They seemed, to me, excellent. We shuffled out. The mandarins looked thoughtful.

As I was driven away from the Treasury I thought to myself, 'That was a very impressive ministerial performance.' Reggie had been taken, for some reason, unawares. The knights were a formidable pair. Had they planned to 'bounce' the Chancellor? But Reggie had at once grasped the complex point, recognized the implications and rejected their proposal on valid and respectable grounds. 'There', I thought as I travelled back to the Law Courts in my musty Humber, 'is a truly Rolls-Royce brain.' And so it was. That intellect accompanied a generous and likeable personality, with a civilized, irreverent attitude to affairs which later, alas, led him to take less care in some business activities than was altogether wise. To work with him was certainly more agreeable than working with some others.

Another congenial and impressive colleague was Tony Barber, then Financial Secretary to the Treasury. Once I was in the Commons Smoking Room having a quick break before dealing in the Chamber with my next batch of amendments. Suddenly, prior amendments were passed on the nod without debate, and mine unexpectedly came on. I was out of the Chamber having my drink, so Tony nonchalantly took up my papers from where I had left them on my seat on the bench and he was well under way when I puffed in, wiping the froth from my lips.

Part of my duties with this Finance Bill was to move a set of amendments which abolished the controversial property tax, Schedule A. I had spent hours mastering the complex legal machinery involved in this important proposal. I had to prepare myself for the robust debate which would surely arise since although there had been a vociferous public campaign by house-owners to be rid of this tax burden, there were others who felt that it was a just impost upon those owning property and that to abolish it would be favouring the fortunate home-owner too greatly. So I prepared for battle.

However, when I rose to open the debate the clock stood at four o'clock in the morning. Jim Callaghan, who was leading for the Opposition as Shadow Chancellor, thanked me shortly for explaining the provisions and sat down. I waited for the debate, which never began. The House was weary and exhausted. The provisions were approved. I slipped thankfully away.

In such a manner does the British Parliament often make law.

In the autumn had come the end of the reign of Supermac, lying like an old lion on a sick bed in Sister Agnes'. When the 'soundings' were made a few weeks later to find the acceptable successor, I plumped for Quintin Hailsham. Later when I became Attorney General I sometimes winced at his expression to colleagues of his off-the-cuff opinions on questions of law which it was my and not his responsibility to proffer. My advice was given after research by my department and by Treasury counsel. His came off the top of his head. I then used to wonder if it was a sense of foreboding which had led me to support his candidature for the premiership lest he ever became, as he did, Lord Chancellor. In fact I supported him because I admired his intellectual ability, and he certainly had the panache and *brio* which I thought was needed for the premiership. I believed that the job would bring him the judgment which his detractors have always said that he lacked.

I was close to him, in the sense that colleagues in public life are ever close. Later on, in the Shadow Cabinet days when I was responsible for the law and he for Home Affairs, we would sometimes be paired together in debate, he to open for the Opposition, I to wind up. Sometimes such was the quality of his remarkable performance, there was little need for anyone else. On a few occasions no one, I believe, could restore what he had started off so wrong. In the Law Courts when he came back to practise in 1964, his early days were difficult. He had not had the advantage of having been a Law Officer. He had been in political office for many years and he had been forgotten at the Bar. But he clawed his way back into a good practice. Sometimes we were in cases together, allies as counsel for different clients. He was always the mercurial same. Once I even appeared as counsel on his behalf.

Quintin had written an article for *Punch*. Raymond Blackburn complained to the Court of Appeal that the article was prejudicial and a slur upon the Court. Quintin was summoned to appear before the three judges of the Court of Appeal, Tom Denning in the chair. It was all rather absurd, but unpleasant for Quintin who faced the possibility of censure or at worst a fine.

In the end they dismissed the complaint, but not without a few pompous and rather wounding phrases about the chastened Quintin. (Nowadays it is sometimes harder for those of prominence to receive impartial justice because such is the influence and thus the subconscious fear of the organs of the public prints, in word or picture, that courts often feel they must lean over backwards not to be seen to favour prominent persons. This sometimes leads to less than absolute justice. Gone are the days when it was the meek who could not find it; now it is sometimes the grand.) But the pompous phrases of the Court soon bounced off the ebullient Quintin, shortly to be the Lord Chancellor sitting above those critical judges. Perhaps some echo of this incident was the reason for the added spice to debates later in the House of Lords when Tom Denning and Quintin rarely seemed to agree.

After the case, I ran into him with Elaine and my young son in the corridor outside our rooms in the House of Commons. Quintin went down on one knee, stretched wide his arms and bellowed, 'My saviour! My saviour!' 'Is he mad?' my son whispered after we had all parted. 'No,' I replied. 'He is back to his old form.'

He sat on the Woolsack for twelve years in all. This was a long stretch, but then, as he said himself, there was no alternative. He made it possible for my co-religionists not to be excluded from the Lord Chancellorship. He towered intellectually over his whole generation in public life; he suffered grievously by the awful death, which he witnessed, of his wife Mary in a riding accident in Australia, and he found, at last, happiness again which he so richly deserved. He played a unique role in government and the Tory Party for forty years.

But back in 1963 an injudicious appearance at a fringe meeting at Blackpool at the Tory Conference, cradling his new-born daughter, lost him support for the leadership. Alec Home got the succession, Alec who is the only man whom I ever encountered in public life without a spark of vanity or pretension or that streak of unpleasantness which seems essential for those who reach the top of Dizzy's greasy pole.

So the troubled government under its new Prime Minister staggered into 1964, a year in which a general election had to be held. On New Year's Day my second son, Anthony, and I both figured on the same day in the column of *The Times*, which announced that I had become Privy Councillor and that he, more importantly, had arrived. Our family was now complete, although the laughing Spanish maids had gone back to Barcelona and the old Nanny had gone for ever.

The swearing-in ceremony to the Privy Council in January of 1964 proved to be particularly memorable, not because of who was sworn in but because of how they did it. I was teamed up with Lord Merthyr, Chairman of Committees in the House of Lords and President of the Magistrates' Association, and we were both to be sworn in at the same Council. The oath for me as a Catholic was, as is the custom, trimmed to eliminate some gratuitous insults to foreign pontiffs, and Lord Merthyr and I attended at the Privy Council office for the customary rehearsal one hour before the real thing.

A solemn courtier played the role of the Sovereign as Lord Merthyr and

I were taken through the ceremony and taught when to advance, bow, swear the oath, kneel, kiss hands, rise, retire backwards, and so on. Lord Merthyr, while enthusiastic, found the correct sequence of manoeuvres difficult to master. He was for ever either retiring backwards on his knees, or trying to kiss hands standing, which bent him almost double; or he found himself swearing the oath at the wrong time or facing the wrong direction. I feared lest his confusion prove infectious. The solemn courtiers were patient, smiling courteously at the unexpected movements. As time went on, however, they got slightly nettled. The stand-in Sovereign whose hand was being grabbed when he least expected it, grew tetchy. We were due shortly at the Palace. At last a final rehearsal went, approximately, right. So we set off. The courtiers looked relieved to see us go. Only the Clerk to the Council, Godfrey Agnew, and the attendant ministers would actually witness what was to happen. And, of course, the Sovereign.

At the Palace the old theatrical adage that all would be right on the night turned out to be wrong. Lord Merthyr proceeded with an air of quiet confidence to get himself inextricably entangled in the procedure, kissing the oath he was meant to read and reading the hand which he was meant to kiss. Part of the time he seemed to be facing the door. I just went on, leaving him, as it were, kneeling. The line of six attendant Privy councillors, the ministers, began to weave and sway like poplars in a healthy gale; their faces crimsoned in manly efforts to keep them straight. The eyes of the Sovereign gleamed ever brighter. By then Lord Merthyr, himself amused, but for some reason still determinedly fixed on his knees where he had been for what seemed an inordinate length of time, appeared totally disorientated. A firm hand, which was still being feverishly sought for inspection and embrace, at last drew him to his feet. Eventually the ceremony, indisputably more lengthy and elaborate than usual with its extra bobs, surprising about-turns, its advancing and retreating and especially its genuflections, drew, like all good things, to an end. It had been, the old hands present declared, a memorable Council, the best they had ever attended.

The general election came that October. The government, unusually in modern times, went its full legal term. In my constituency, Epsom, we held some twenty public meetings. In 1987 they held two, so much has the style of electioneering altered. I went off to Paddington where, as his one-time Footlights straight-man, I had been asked by Jimmy Edwards to speak in support at his adoption meeting. He was deadly serious but, of course, the audience only longed for his trombone and the rages of his stage headmaster.

The count at Epsom was held on the morning after polling day; so we were able to watch the evening election results on television. There are few activities more exhausting than electioneering, and through that night we lay on cushions, spreadeagled on the floor of our drawing-room, waiting for the screen to tell us where I would be working on the following day. It is a strange sensation, which has happened to me on three occasions, to watch a television screen and know that what it will reveal over the next few hours will determine not only one's employment next day but may alter one's whole life and that of one's family. However, in 1964, the result was so close that it was not until the following afternoon that it became finally settled that the government had been defeated by a whisker and that the age of Harold Wilson had begun.

So with a farewell reception by the Queen (to be repeated a decade later) it was goodbye to the musty old Humber, the drab corridor in the Law Courts, and (the only regret) to Doris Wickens, my private secretary, as in came the two new boys, Elwyn Jones and Dingle Foot.

With great personal excitement, I crossed Fleet Street and took over the chambers in King's Bench Walk from Gerald Gardiner, who had gone to be the new Labour Lord Chancellor. The very day I took over the chambers I received a general retainer from Lord Rothermere and from Associated Newspapers. Within hours I was at work deep in consultation.

So began six exciting and, which was much needed with our growing family, remunerative years back at the Bar.

Chapter 13
King's Bench Walk – Retained by the Daily Mail – The Moonie Libel Case of 1980

Westminster Hall late at night is an eerie and mysterious place. By day it is usually thronged with parties of visiting sightseers and pretty secretaries who scurry through the great hall on their way to their appointments with their demanding bosses. But even then it has a strange brooding atmosphere, its air stale and oppressive. At night it is dimly lit and, when it is empty of people, footsteps echo on the stone-flagged floor beneath the ancient hammer-beam roof as Members, after a late-night sitting, hurry through to New Palace Yard and the car which will take them home.

At such an hour it is not a place in which many care to linger. People who pass through always seem glad to reach the swing doors at the eastern end and to leave it behind them. Most, perhaps unconsciously avoid walking over the brass plaques let into the stone floor, especially those which record where a Sovereign or a canonized Lord Chancellor were sentenced to death. But places which have witnessed scenes of great drama often seem to bear this particular atmosphere, as though the very intensity of such scenes in the past may have somehow imprinted them on the fabric of the structure itself. To some, those scenes may be conjured up. I think of those two mature and respectable ladies, one a don and the other a school mistress, the Misses Moberley and Jourdain, who at the start of this century experienced their great 'adventure' in the grounds of Versailles. I always hoped that it might possibly happen to me and whenever I walked alone very late at night through that place I often experienced a sensation of being watched by the actors in the scenes upon which that roof had once looked down. I liked to imagine that somehow they were still present. But I never encountered any of the great ghosts in Westminster Hall, only that strange, cold, almost threatening atmosphere.

We went to that Hall as a family, with my second and grown-up daughter

Dariel and her boyfriend in the raw, dark days of January 1965, joining the queue of mourners filing past the catafalque which bore the coffin of Winston Churchill. A few days later, I stood in the transept of St Paul's with the sound of the Battle Hymn of the Republic ringing in my ears. Then John Eden and I stood together on the steps outside the Cathedral and watched as Winston Churchill was borne away, and the last great state occasion of the British Empire drew to its close.

That had been a sombre church-going of that time, but others which followed were much happier. Two daughters, Mikaela and Dariel, were soon thereafter married to the sound of trumpets of the Irish Guards Band, and a third, Haidee, a few years later.

But church-going in my own Church had become less meaningful when, after the Vatican Council, came the changes to the liturgy that Catholics had followed for four hundred years. Like the pain inflicted upon so many devout Anglicans by the virtual abandonment in certain parishes of the great language of the Prayer Book, the virtual abolition of the Latin Mass and the introduction of a new and prosaic rite distressed many of the Catholic laity. The Roman Church at that time seemed to have fallen into the hands of iconoclasts who sought to abandon all forms of beauty in the liturgy. Priests, fearful lest they be accused of being out of tune with the new trends in modern life, introduced strange and ridiculous practices either in the pretence that these were authorized by the new dispensation or, alternatively, demonstrating that they did not care a fig if they were not.

All this came hard to the generations who had been bred to the mystery of the Mass, to the doctrine of transubstantiation, to belief in the reality of the bread and wine turned into the actual Body and Blood. Those generations had been taught that ancestors had died for this belief and that it was this doctrine which, rightly or wrongly, differentiated us from other Christian faiths. So the sacrifice of the Mass had always been cloaked in great reverence and mystery. In the past it had been recognized that the fallible laity, without the vocation of the priesthood and the grace of ordination, needed help to sustain their belief in the miracle which was happening under their very nose, and so the least that the priests could do was to surround this extraordinary event with solemnity and dignity. Suddenly it was all changed, as if confidence had been lost in the mystery itself. The laity were confronted with extravagances and excesses by some of the clergy, who seemed desperate to throw their cassocks over their church steeple in order to prove themselves contemporary.

It was a time, admittedly, when all institutions were being ridiculed and all authority questioned. But it came as a shock to those brought up to revere the magisterium of the Roman Church when it was seen that even she was rushing as fast as any to respond to what many at the time recognized were the vagaries of fashion. If her authorities wanted to abandon fish on Friday, well, obedience to that anachronistic rule was always only mildly inconvenient and was generally accepted as just one of those rather agreeable idiosyncrasies of those eccentric Papists. Abandonment of that minor rule might be a pity but it mattered little. However, when they began to mutilate the liturgy of the Mass so that it was turned, in style, into a form of committee meeting presided over by a rather ineffectual chairman and when they began to abandon the great traditions of European ecclesiastical music and introduced inferior strummers on ill-tuned guitars, and when the monks of Downside gave up the plain-chant, then there arose murmurs about *la trahison des clercs*, and some went off and read their missals in private.

Those who lived in London were fortunate to find at the London Oratory in the Brompton Road one Community which, while remaining strictly within the precepts laid down by the Council, refused to abandon all the great styles of the old practice of the faith and remained an oasis for those, and they are not a few, young as well as old, who find the road to the Gate of Heaven easier if it is made a road of beauty. It is after all difficult to think that anyone will mind how the Gate is reached, so long as it is. But for some, that which had been the most significant event in mundane lives, the Mass – whether it had been a great High Mass sung in a cathedral to the music of Haydn, or murmured in the humblest tin church in the smallest village, or whispered to a group on a battlefield gathered round a makeshift altar of ammunition boxes – had then inexcusably been turned into something so ordinary that neglect of attendance brought no sense of guilt.

Slowly, however, some reaction set in and the worst excesses of the 'player priests' were curbed. But it has never wholly regained its old magic. Unbelievably, the new ideas of the iconoclasts had managed to do that which in the days of the religious wars some fought to have done – namely, to lessen the importance of the Mass and so to loosen the great bond which had always bound Roman Catholics together, the bond which meant that wherever a man travelled, in whatsoever place in which he found himself, he would find the Mass with which he was familiar and which he knew, whatever he may have done, gave him the most precious experience in his life. The apologists for change claim that it was for the best that they had, by their changes, revived what would otherwise have died. They cannot ever prove whether the new drove away or retained the worshippers. Perhaps the apologists, who proved to be influential and powerful, are right when they say that the new style is more meaningful for the worshipper of today. But they are wrong when, with much unChristian virulence, they sneer that protest is only the bleat of a generation whose day has passed. At the time in the 1960s when some rejoiced at the new spirit abroad after the Vatican Council, others mourned over the death of the old.

Change of a different order had overtaken the House of Commons. In 1964, after thirteen years of continuous Tory government, the shock of loss of office and of the abrupt reversal of role showed on the faces of the new Opposition. Gone were the official cars, gone too the prospect of that knighthood which came, after twenty years' service on the backbenches, 'with the rations', like some of the decorations in the 1914 war. Now we had to face Harold Wilson at the height of his powers, always deft, sometimes witty and sometimes oleaginous, as he proceeded to debate the daylights out of the former ministers.

It was a noisy House, and one of the noisiest was a Labour newcomer, Robert Maxwell. Soon he became chairman of the committee responsible for the catering and we were introduced to paper napkins and a much reduced wine list. But he never wholly fitted into the parliamentary scene.

Twenty-three years later, one Sunday evening, I was called to the telephone. It was No. 10 Downing Street. This startled me, for it had been made clear to me that I was not on speaking terms with the sitting tenant. But it was only a Secretary, to say that Mr Robert Maxwell wanted to speak to me. He was obviously on closer terms than I with the residents. When we spoke, he asked me to give evidence for him in a libel action which he was then bringing against *Private Eye*. I was even more flabbergasted at this than I had been to receive a telephone call from No. 10, for I could not have spoken with him for twenty years. I politely declined, for I had been counsel against the magazine so often that it would not have been proper to appear against them as a witness. In any event, there was nothing I could usefully say for Cap'n Bob. But I was immensely impressed with his initiative.

In the early parliamentary days of the new Wilson government in 1964, I led for the retentionists in the debate on Sidney Silverman's Bill to abolish capital punishment. I suggested that abolition might well increase the number of professional criminals who henceforward would carry fire-arms. For this I was severely mocked by the liberal establishment. But between 1969 and 1982, offences in which firearms were reported to have been used increased over fourfold.

For a very short time I shadowed Tony Benn, then Anthony Wedgwood Benn, the new Postmaster General, who was at the top of his most exuberant prep-school-master form, according to his own account laying his stamps at the feet of the Queen to persuade her to accept a reduced profile.

Meanwhile at the Bar, briefs had been flowing into King's Bench Walk. Apart from the general retainer from Associated Newspapers, they came for Odham's Press and the *News of the World*; for the actress Leslie Caron; for a co-respondent in a fashionable Gloucestershire divorce; for police authorities facing unwelcome amalgamation; for two Barbadian Bar students (now both distinguished lawyers in their own country) who had been shamefully treated by the police; for a pirate radio station which pumped sweet music into the receptive ears of housewives from an abandoned fort in the Thames Estuary; and for the explorer Sir Ranulph Twistleton-Wykeham-Fiennes, then a young officer who, for a prank and in the name of the preservation of rural England, had bombarded with fire-crackers the Wiltshire village in which a film company were shooting a film starring Rex Harrison, *Dr Doolittle*. The flow of all this legal work made it clear that I had to make a choice. Family obligation and personal preference did not make the decision difficult. An election process for the Tory leadership had recently been established and the election had been held. When Alec went, I left too.

The general retainer for Associated Press introduced me to Denys Walsh, who was not only the legal adviser to Esmond Rothermere but also his personal friend. Denys' firm, Swepstone Walsh, were the solicitors to the Associated Newspapers Group and one morning I found myself flying off with Denys to New York.

The magazine *Newsweek*, owned by the *Washington Post*, had published an article in its editions circulating in Britain, in which it announced the imminent demise of an ailing and failing *Daily Mail* which, it said, would soon be absorbed by its dominant rival, the *Daily Express*. This story was immensely damaging to the *Mail*, and nearly drove Denys, inclined at normal times to the choleric, into an apoplectic fit. First he and I went off to a judge in his home in London to obtain an injunction to stop further circulation of the story; then we set off for the States to try and force *Newsweek* to withdraw the story and to apologize.

We had arranged to meet *Newsweek*'s counsel, William Rogers. He had been Eisenhower's Attorney General and he was shortly to become Nixon's Secretary of State. Rogers did not survive long at State for he had breathing over his shoulder the guttural Henry Kissinger, who eventually succeeded him. After Kissinger had replaced him, Rogers returned to his lucrative law practice in a magnificent suite of offices at the top of the Pan-Am building in New York. It was there, some years earlier, before he had become Secretary of State, that Denys and I went to negotiate with him over our claim that the *Newsweek* publication had gravely damaged the *Daily Mail*, and to demand recompense.

We were accompanied by our American lawyer, who was the son of Mr Justice Jackson, the principal American prosecutor at the War Crimes Tribunal at Nuremberg. Mr Justice Jackson was a distinguished jurist but his practice of the law had never given him reason to learn to cross-examine a witness and he was disastrously bested by Hermann Göring, from whom he had actually sought the protection of the tribunal! It took David Maxwell Fyfe as the counsel from the Old World to redress the failure of counsel from the New and to deal effectively in cross-examination with the formidable Reichsmarschall of Nazi Germany.

So there were three of us as we soared up in a high-speed elevator to the offices of William Rogers. Denys was already at his most pugnacious. Earlier he had passed an hour dialling in the hotel seeking sausages and had succeeded only in obtaining a very pretty Puerto Rican maid who spoke no English and only laughed hysterically when confronted by an English gentleman deprived of his breakfast. Denys' choler nearly proved fatal when Rogers, genuinely affronted by our claim, which was unknown to American law, greeted us with the words, 'Well, well! Have suit, will travel!' This pleasantry, which gravely increased Denys' blood pressure, cost Rogers' client dear, for with the increase of the blood pressure went an increase in the demand for damages which we eventually wrung from the *Washington Post*. For the publication was in England and English law applied.

When the time came for the *Newsweek* negotiation to be continued in London, William Rogers had gone to the State Department and a rather portly partner of his had taken over. Denys Walsh and I stood waiting for him in my room in King's Bench Walk, standing together by the window which overlooked the gardens of the Inner Temple. Across the river upstream in the distance could be seen the towers of Westminster. It was a singularly beautiful view, which, save for my six years across the road as a Law Officer, I enjoyed for over twenty years. But to reach the room, fifty or sixty stone steps had to be mounted, for it was on the second floor of the early-nineteenth-century building and there was no lift. As the American lawyer was shown into the room, he collapsed into an armchair, puffing like a grampus. 'I get the technique,' he said between gasps. 'I am not saying one word for at least five minutes.'

Eventually the case was settled with an apology in court, the complete withdrawal of the *Newsweek* story, and the payment of a very hefty sum by the proprietors, the *Washington Post*. It had been vital to the future existence of the *Daily Mail* that the story that it was ripe for take-over and absorption into the Express Group should be emphatically killed. Denys, who was intensely loyal to Esmond Rothermere and to Associated, was greatly relieved.

It was in that same room in King's Bench Walk in 1980, fifteen years later, that I first was told about another crucial case in which the *Daily Mail* was involved, and soon almost every inch of floor-space in my room was covered by scores of files and bundles of documents and copies of a black, leather-bound book which had the appearance of a Bible. It bore on its front cover a strange device picked out in gold accompanied by the book's title: *Divine Principle*. Inside the cover was a picture of the head and shoulders of a handsome young man in a dark robe with a white border. Beneath the photograph was the name of the young man: Sun Myung Moon. The photograph had been taken many years previously before the sitter had grown middle-aged and bald.

As I contemplated the mass of material which almost swamped my room in this critical libel action which had been launched against the newspaper, I remembered Denys and our trip to New York in 1966 to try and save the *Mail* from what had then been a very serious threat to its future. When I examined that photograph of Sun Myung Moon the circumstances and the health of the *Mail* as a flourishing newspaper were very different from those when Denys and I had negotiated with William Rogers and his portly partner. It was also a different kind of crisis which Denys' old clients faced in 1980, a threat to reputation as well as pocket, and he would have relished the battle. But Denys would not be there, for it was fought several years after he had died and I had left government, had ceased to be a Law Officer and was no longer in the House of Commons. It was by far the most important case that I was ever to do for Denys' clients, whom he had always served with such great devotion.

On Denys' death his son Brian and his partner carried on the business of his firm, the partner looking after the litigation, especially the defamation work, for Associated Press. His name was Brotherton, and he was universally known as 'Tubby', the nickname which he had acquired during the war as a young flyer in the RAF. It fitted him and, the older he grew, it fitted the better. For he was short and very round. He was also very shrewd, and immensely experienced in representing the interests of newspapers. His skill in negotiating settlements in libel cases was legendary.

As I had a general retainer from Associated, we were working together during these years on all the important cases in which their newspapers were concerned. In June 1980 Tubby came to see me about the libel action launched against the *Daily Mail* by a man called Denis Orme, who styled himself the director in Great Britain of a sect or cult calling itself the Unification Church and the Holy Spirit Association for the Unification of World Christianity. The headquarters of this organization were in the United States; its founder was a South Korean, Sun Myung Moon, whom the members of the cult regarded as the Messiah. He subsequently went to prison in the States for tax offences.

The organization, known universally as the Moonies, was immensely wealthy, raising vast sums from begging in the streets all over the world by an army of young men and women who, as soon as they had been recruited or lured into the 'Church' were at once set to work at this profitable activity. As a result of the great sums of money which were collected by the personable young beggars, the directors of this successful enterprise had prudently and skilfully diversified the profits and had built up a vast financial and commercial empire, investing in publications, newspapers, restaurants, films, fishing fleets, manufacturing and other lucrative concerns. Moonie business was big business indeed. Its fulcrum, perhaps, still lay in South Korea, the country of origin of its founder. There it had substantial factories engaged in the profitable manufacture of parts for weapons of war, an improbable activity for a movement whose head was the 'Messiah'.

But its prosperity depended upon the provision of the cheap, almost slave, labour for its street-begging programme which in turn depended upon the recruitment of young people whom its smiling young activists approached directly on the streets or at bus or railway stations and per-suaded to pass some time with them at their country camps, usually in attractive but conveniently isolated locations. There, in rustic surroundings and accompanied at first by the music of guitars and of song around camp fires, they were indoctrinated with ever increasing pressure and ever mounting pace into the strange beliefs and practices of the cult. Once in the camps, few ever came out – save for those who suddenly came to their senses, sometimes only after many years, or those whom their families managed to rescue. Usually those seduced into joining the sect were young people of high educational attainment who abandoned their academic studies, and above all their families, to follow their unlikely 'Messiah'. Clad in smart suits, they began their service by begging in the Californian streets, and they were ultimately rewarded by an arranged marriage to a spouse selected for them by the 'Messiah', usually of another race, whom they wed in vast mass ceremonies and from whom they were immediately separated.

It was in May 1978 that the local English director of the Unification Church, Denis Orme, and Mose Irwin Durst, the director in North California, had issued their writ against the *Mail* for libel in an article which the newspaper had published and which told two stories of two families, English and American, whose daughter and son respectively had become enmeshed with the Moonies. The article had borne the headline, 'THE CHURCH THAT BREAKS UP FAMILIES', and had described the 'Church' as 'sinister' and told of the brain-washing of young people.

David English was the editor of the *Daily Mail*, and from the statements and information which his reporters had gathered, he was satisfied that what his newspaper had published about the Moonies was true. Under the chairmanship of Vere Harmsworth, now Lord Rothermere, who had succeeded his father Esmond (who had first retained me as the group's leading counsel back in 1964), and with a chief executive of business and commercial genius, Mick Shields, David English had transformed the *Daily Mail* out of all recognition from the time when Denys Walsh and I had flown to New York to negotiate with William Rogers over the *Newsweek* story. By now it was a lively, attractive newspaper under dynamic editorial and business leadership.

This leadership was now faced with the need to make an important decision in the matter of the case of *Orme and Durst* v. *Associated Newspaper Group Limited.* The decision involved principle and practical business judgment, whether the newspaper ought meekly to surrender to what was believed to be a false claim out of consideration of cost and convenience. Many matters had to be taken into account. The plaintiffs, Orme and Durst, would have behind them the immense resources of this basically US but also worldwide organization. Probably these plaintiffs, if sensibly advised, would be content with some modest damages given perhaps to charity, an apology and the withdrawal of the allegation. The matter could then be settled at little cost and with no waste of editorial and management time.

Alternatively, to fight the action and prove that the comments in the article were true would involve a massive assembly of witnesses from all over the world, and the expenditure of a great deal of money and management effort. Moreover great risk was involved. The damages could be immense were the newspaper to lose, and the costs must be enormous. As with all litigation and especially with libel actions, there can never be any certainty of success. Witnesses whose statements read excellently often do not measure up in the court room to what they have written in the calm of an office. They don't always, as the lawyers say, 'come up to proof'. Others, even if they stick to what they have written or have told the solicitors and even if perfectly genuine, out of sheer stage-fright sometimes haplessly convey an air of shiftiness. Still others, who lived outside the jurisdiction of the English Court, could not be compelled to attend the trial to give evidence. This was an important factor for in this case there would necessarily be many of those.

The issue, then, would turn upon which set of witnesses who actually appeared before the Court the jury would believe, because it was quite certain that the Moonies would bring to court, as in the end they did, battalions of well-scrubbed Moonies to tell the world how good and noble were the principles which directed and guided their movement and how false and wicked was the story printed about them. The military-style discipline of their organization would make quite certain that their witnesses would come, as indeed they eventually did, from the ends of the earth.

My task at this stage was to express an opinion; David English had to take a decision. I had to point out the risks, but I advised that if the *Mail* did decide to fight and to stand to their guns, I believed that we had a reasonable chance of success. But Associated had to be aware that even a Committee of the US Congress had failed to demonstrate exactly what these people were up to, and the Moonies, with their credibility at stake, would spare neither effort nor money in order to win. The battle would be long and hard and it would take an immense effort to marshal and present the evidence properly to expose this extraordinary organization.

David English and the Associated management decided that in the interests of truth and of the distraught families who had been so wracked by the loss of their children to what the article had called the 'sinister' oganization, the *Mail* would fight. It was a courageous decision.

So the task for the solicitors now began of interviewing, taking proofs and assembling the evidence of potential witnesses, many of whom lived in the States or in South America or in the East or in Europe. The *Mail* assigned staff to help Tubby Brotherton in this mammoth operation. Vast files of documents were built up as we scoured through all the writings of the 'Messiah' and his lieutenants. The business and corporate affairs of the captive companies in which the proceeds of the street-begging had been invested were analysed. Psychologists and psychiatrists were sought for their advice and if possible their agreement to come to London to testify at the trial. For it would be necessary to show to the jury the effect of the methods used to recruit and then indoctrinate and then retain the young people who had been sucked into the organization, and to explain how there had been achieved the bitter alienation from their families whereby the Moonie neophytes became convinced that hitherto loved parents were now evil, creatures of the devil. Theologians had to be canvassed so that they might come and tell the jury that a faith which elevated the South Korean into the Messiah and denigrated Jesus Christ could hardly rank as a Christian church.

All this demanded a supreme effort from Tubby Brotherton. He and his staff not only had to locate and interview the potential witnesses, but later had to arrange their arrival in London in good time for me to call them in court in some logical order so as to present a comprehensive case which the jury could easily understand. Some of the witnesses whom we particularly needed to produce would come only if they could fly Concorde and be put up at a suitable hotel. One, who was dramatically to produce an automatic infantry weapon, for which the factories of the Rev. Moon in Korea manufactured the barrel, had to be flown from South America.

Tubby's health was not good before this enormous task began. The labour and the strain involved in assembling the evidence and later shepherding the witnesses to court told upon him. He, sadly, did not long survive the end of this great case; he sickened and finally died shortly thereafter. His clients, as they readily acknowledged, owed him a great deal.

Throughout the summer of 1980 my room in King's Bench Walk was filled with hundreds of files of witnesses' statements, company reports and transcripts of 'sermons' of the Rev. Moon, of which we acquired a great number. For it was the habit of the 'Messiah' whenever on a visit to his various headquarters, such as the London house at Lancaster Gate, to summon the faithful around him in the small hours of the morning and lecture them for hours on end. There would pour from him in a stream from his lips and into the ears of his enraptured if weary disciples the peculiar theology of his Holy Spirit Association, mingled with his idio-syncratic views on world politics and his exhortations on the need to destroy world Communism in Korea and elsewhere. Some of the magic for the disciples may have been lost by the need to have the sacred words translated. On the other hand, that may have enhanced it. At the end of these mystical sessions, the 'Messiah' would retire and shortly thereafter fly away back to the Holy Mother (his second wife) and his mansion in New England. The records of these 'sermons' were to prove useful in the probe into the claim of the cult that it was 'Christian'.

All through the summer months I and my two juniors, Richard Rampton and Edward Garnier, read our way through the mass of matter which Tubby and the *Mail* had assembled. Then on Monday 6 October 1980, we entered Court No. 7 of the Queen's Bench Division of the High Court in the Law Courts in the Strand and began the longest libel action with a jury that had ever been heard.

My opponent, counsel for Orme and Durst, was Geoffrey Shaw. The judge was my old opponent of many previous cases in his days as a barrister, James Comyn. He presided over the trial until its conclusion on 31 March 1981 with good humour and courtesy, and his agreeable personality did much to cool the high feelings which fierce argument over deeply felt religious beliefs and the passionate expressions of pain of parents torn from and insulted by their children inevitably engendered. But the real heroes and heroines were the jury.

Before they were empanelled they were warned of the marathon nature of the trial but all agreed to serve and we only lost one whose livelihood required him to retire after three months. So we ended the trial with eleven. After a week of being together, we all got to know each other and each other's habits very well indeed. On 19 December we all wished each other a happy Christmas and we reassembled on 15 January, which allowed me earlier in that month to appear in the Court of Appeal for Jimmy Goldsmith in his successful defence in a libel action which a *Private Eye* journalist, Michael Gillard, had brought against him and which earlier in the summer we had persuaded a jury to dismiss.

Well over a hundred witnesses were called in the Moonie trial, of whom seventy-seven gave evidence for Denis Orme. Mose Durst did not appear. Regularly I invited the plaintiff Denis Orme and his counsel to produce in court as a witness the 'Messiah' himself so that the jury could see and hear him for themselves. Almost every day I said that the *Daily Mail* would willingly provide the 'Messiah', the Holy Mother and all the little Moons with return passages on the Concorde and a suite at the Savoy in exchange for the chance of having His Reverence cross-examined. But answer, and Rev. Moon, came there none.

My final speech lasted six hours, spread over two days. The jury retired at 3.15 p.m. on 30 March 1981, spent what I expect was an agreeable

My grandfather, Sir Henry Mulleneux Grayson, being knighted in 1916 by George V

My brother Michael on leave in England with my father, mother and myself in early 1940

Pilot Officer Michael Rawlinson, killed in action in May 1940 over France

Lt.-Col. A. R. Rawlinson OBE, my father, drawn by a German prisoner-of-war in 1944

(*Above*) Rosa Lewis in her hotel, The Cavendish, in 1950, two years before she died

(*Above right*) In 1960 I represented General Wladyslaw Anders when he sued for libel. Here he is at the Cenotaph in Whitehall in 1949

Conservative candidate in Hackney South, 1951

The Solicitor General in 1964 with Harold
Macmillan, who had resigned as Prime Minister a
year earlier

(*Left*) The new Solicitor General, July 1962

(*Below*) *Daily Express* sketch of the meeting of the
ministers at the centre of the Profumo affair on the
night of 31st March 1963 in the House of Commons
Left to right: P. R. (Solicitor General), John
Profumo (Secretary for War), William Deedes
(Minister Without Portfolio), Iain Macleod (Leader
of the House), William Redmayne (Chief Whip) and
John Hobson (Attorney General)

Elaine on her way to a ball in 1968

Elaine after the ball

Return as a Law Officer: Attorney General, 1970

Westminster Hall, July 1971. From the left: P. R. (Attorney General), John Mitchell (US Attorney General), Warren Burger (Chief Justice, USA), Quintin Hailsham (Lord Chancellor) and Selwyn Lloyd (Speaker of the House of Commons)

(*Above left*) Leila Khaled, who tried to hijack an El Al plane in September 1970, was detained in London and later released. (*Above right*) Arthur Hosein. With his brother he kidnapped Mrs McKay by mistake for Mrs Rupert Murdoch. They were convicted of Mrs McKay's murder

Dawson's Field, Jordan, September 1970. BOAC and Swissair planes, which had been hijacked after Leila Khaled was held in London, being dynamited by Palestinian guerrillas

(*Above left*) On my way to the Rudi Dutschke Tribunal in December 1970 with Treasury Counsel Gordon Slynn (later a judge at the Court of Justice, EEC) and the Legal Secretary Tony Hetherington (later DPP). (*Above right*) IRA attack on London: the devastation outside the Old Bailey, March 1973

Ted Heath with Elaine and our family – Angela, Michael and Anthony – in 1974

Introduced into the House of Lords in 1978
by Quintin Hailsham and Peter Carrington

Back at King's Bench Walk and Chairman
of the Bar, 1975

1983: Elaine and Geoffrey Howe, formerly my Solicitor General and now Foreign Secretary

Anthony Fanshawe (formerly Sir Anthony Royle MP, and Vice Chairman of the Conservative Party) Shirley Fanshawe, Elaine and P. R.

In Provence. Left to right: Elaine, Humphrey Colnbrook (formerly Sir Humphrey Atkins MP and Chief Whip), Avril Webster, Mathews Dick, Maisie Dick, Margaret Colnbrook, P. R.

The Interior Designer – helped by Sam, the youngest son of my eldest daughter, Mikaela Irwin

eaving White's with Rex Harrison (Ian ilmour appearing through the door)

Painting in Tuscany

1985. The end of the road – and the wig

evening together at an hotel, and at 2.10 p.m. on 31 March filed into the court to deliver their verdict. It was the 105th day of sittings and five months since we had all come into court to start this marathon trial.

However confident one feels as counsel, and sometimes however pessimistic, this is always a heart-stopping moment. I personally never used to look at the jury as they returned to court. It used to be said that in a criminal trial, if the jury looked at the accused it meant that they had decided to acquit him. I am not certain that is always true. At the trial at Winchester of the Price sisters and their comrades in the IRA active service unit responsible for the bombing of the Old Bailey and the War Office in 1973, they looked directly at the prisoners and they did not look kindly. In any event when the Moonie jury came back, I looked down at my clasped hands on the desk in front of me and thought only of the weeks and months of effort, of cross-examination of seventy-seven witnesses and the examination in chief of over thirty; of the arguments on law (during the trial we had been several times to the Court of Appeal for rulings on the law); and finally of the hours of final submissions to the jury. All that had been the fruit of many other hours of reading and preparation, often into the small hours of the morning. It had been an effort and a strain. But, I thought to myself, I would rather be doing this than anything else on earth.

The jury foreman was now on his feet and reading from the paper which he held in his hand. Judgment for the defendants. We had won! But the foreman had not finished. The jury wished to add a rider. It urged 'that the tax status of the Unification church should be investigated by the Inland Revenue on the grounds that it is a political organization'. That it was a political organization was what we had been claiming throughout the trial. Then the jury added a second rider, expressing their deep compassion for the young idealistic members of the organization.

This was total victory for the *Daily Mail* and a complete justification of the courageous decision to defend the libel action. When I had returned to my room in King's Bench Walk after leaving court, I thought about Denys Walsh and how proud he would have been of the contribution which his partner Tubby and his firm had made to a really famous and significant victory for the British press.

Seven years later, in February 1988, the government announced that it would not or could not proceed to strike this cult out of is charitable status. That jury in 1980–81 had spent five months daily listening to the evidence. It heard over one hundred witnesses. It had seen and heard from the 'Church's' officers and from its disciples. It had seen and heard from those who had fled from it and from experts on theology. It had seen and heard from heart-broken parents. It was in a unique position to know what the so-called Unification Church really was. The verdict of that jury had been unequivocally that the cult was 'a political organization'.

Why, then, should it have continued to enjoy its tax-advantageous charitable status over all those years? If the charity law was incapable of distinguishing between a truly religious group and a political organization, then there had been seven years during which the law could have been changed. That the government announced in 1988 that it was impotent to deal with this scandal was a wanton neglect of the interests of decent people gravely damaged by this cult, which the *Mail* had branded as sinister, an opinion which the verdict of that jury had so emphatically sustained.

Chapter 14
The D-Notice Affair and Harold Wilson

On Friday evening of 24 February 1967 I went to the Hilton Hotel in Park Lane to make an after-dinner speech at a Metropolitan Police CID dinner. Harry Secombe was one of the principal guests. I made my speech and then off we all trooped into the bar. I had a fearsome weekend of work ahead, so after a decent interval I started to make my apologies and discreetly to slip away. But I was being observed. Suddenly there was a bellow from the then Mr Secombe, who was standing rigidly to attention. 'Fall out the officers.' I slunk away, highly disconcerted.

It was lucky that I did slink, for the weekend work was to be more fearsome than I expected. On the Saturday afternoon I was making notes for a criminal appeal for the following week; then reading the papers in a Monopolies Commission remit on behalf of the glass manufacturers Pilkingtons; and then those in a libel action on behalf of the *Daily Telegraph*. The doorbell rang. Cursing I went down and opened it – to find on the doorstep the legal manager and the editor of the *Daily Express*. My weekend's work was to be dramatically enlarged.

When I saw who my visitors were I suspected almost at once what it might be about. An edition of the newspaper published four days earlier was put into my hands. The story began, 'CABLE VETTING SENSATION.... Security check on private messages out of Britain.... With telephone-tapping in the news – a new controversy which will be a parliamentary flash-point is revealed today ... by Chapman Pincher.' I was then told the story.

On 16 February a young man, Robert Lawson, later described as rather scruffy, had called upon the *Express* defence correspondent Harry (Chapman) Pincher. He told Harry that for at least two years a van from the Ministry of Defence had regularly collected copies of all overseas cables from the offices of Cable and Wireless and from the General Post Office and taken them to the Ministry for inspection. It was, said Lawson, a regular practice. The routine nature of this clandestine examination of overseas messages at once intrigued Harry Pincher. He began to make enquiries.

As soon as Harry Pincher came on the telephone, alarm bells began ringing in the Ministry of Defence. Although the story was denied, Harry gained the impression that there was substance in Robert Lawson's story. The question then arose: was this wholesale vetting of overseas cables just routine snooping by government into the affairs of private citizens? Or was this collection and inspection of the cables part of an operation directed to identifying the activities of a spy? If it were the latter, then publicly to report what was going on would be potentially damaging to national security and the story would fall within the Defence Notice or 'D-Notice' procedure.

The D-Notice procedure was a typically British *ad hoc* arrangement whereby a Committee of officers of the Ministry of Defence and journalists (who were in the majority) issued warnings to editors to avoid printing stories about particularly sensitive subjects which could prove damaging to the security or safety of the state. The Committee was called the Services, Press and Broadcasting Committee. Its notices were purely advisory. They had no force in law; the ultimate decision to print or to spike after warning from the Committee that a D-Notice applied to the proposed story still remained with the individual editor. But the system had proved serviceable and was honoured by the press. It was of course a compromise system which sought to balance the public interest in free speech and the public interest in state security. It had worked well for twenty years, and in a somewhat different form for thirty years prior to that. It was based entirely upon mutual trust – that the journalists would not seek to endanger the state, and that the Ministry officials would not seek to muzzle the press in reporting government activities by spurious claims about state security.

The Secretary of the committee was a colourful character with a handle-bar moustache called Colonel Sammy Lohan. At the end of this particular story he was to meet with shabby treatment at the hands of a civil service board who, in what was described as an 'opaquely worded' report, neither condemned nor cleared him. But the story of the incident was also to end with a vindicated newspaper and a resentful government, not best pleased with its advisers and thus not averse to trying to shift responsibility.

Between the visit of Robert Lawson to the *Daily Express* with his disclosures on 16 February and the publication of the story on 21 February, there had been much activity by Harry Pincher in his attempts to discover whether the story did breach security interests; and by the government, including the ebullient Foreign Secretary George Brown, to stop the publication. For the editor, Derek Marks, there was only one issue: was the story covered by a D-Notice issued by the committee? If it was, he would not print. If it was not, and the procedure was being used to cover up what was politically embarrassing to the government, he would. After conferring with Harry Pincher he decided to print.

On the afternoon of the publication of the story, Prime Minister Wilson in the House of Commons accused the *Express* of publishing a 'sensationalized and inaccurate story' which, he added, was a 'clear breach of two D-Notices'. The next day Harry Pincher in the *Express* rebutted Harold Wilson's accusations and denied that there had been any 'breach of D-Notices'.

Ted Heath and the Opposition now entered into the row between the government and the newspaper. Wilson agreed to make another statement on the Wednesday 22 February. In this second statement he shifted his ground. Now he claimed that the story was a breach of the 'D-Notice convention'. By Friday 24 February other daily newspapers and the weeklies, even the *New Statesman*, joined in the row. None supported the government. Lee Howard, editor of the *Daily Mirror*, a newspaper which generally supported Harold Wilson, resigned from the Services, Press and Broadcasting Committee, expressing the view that he knew of no D-Notice which could have any direct bearing on Harry Pincher's story. That evening Ted Heath sent by hand a letter to the Prime Minister calling for an immediate independent enquiry. Harold Wilson agreed and he set up an enquiry by a committee of Privy Councillors with, inevitably, Lord Radcliffe in the chair. The Opposition selected Selwyn Lloyd as their nominee on the enquiry and over the weekend the government nominated Emanuel Shinwell. These three would now look into the whole affair and report.

It was on this business that my work was interrupted on that Saturday evening. I was instructed to advise and to represent Derek Marks the editor, Harry Pincher, Sir Max Aitken and the *Express* in the proceedings which were to follow.

For the next two weeks we set to work preparing in great detail for the hearings. We went over each step in the story, every meeting, every discussion between the visit of Robert Lawson to the *Express* on Thursday 16 February and the final publication of the story on the night of 20 February. Derek Marks disliked Harold Wilson. I do not know how or why that had come about, but it was personal dislike. But, added to the personal sentiment, Derek bitterly resented that he and his proprietor, former RAF Group Captain Max Aitken DSO, DFC, should be accused by Harold Wilson of deliberately endangering or compromising the security of the country. It was desperately important to Derek, therefore, that his decision to print should not be impugned and that he should be vindicated.

So we toiled away with great thoroughness. Each of the principals whom I was to represent came to King's Bench Walk, and we went through their accounts with laborious attention to every detail. Even happy-go-lucky Max spent hours with me and Andrew Edwards, the *Express*'s able and experienced legal manager. Admittedly it had been difficult to corral Max, but when we got him we kept him. For he played an important part in the story, since on the night when the story was being printed he had spoken with the Foreign Secretary when he and Derek Marks were together at the Garrick Club at a dinner in honour of Trevor Evans of the *Express*, who had recently been knighted.

In a last-hour attempt to stop the story, George Brown the Foreign Secretary had telephoned the *Express* and asked to speak personally to Max. The *Express* exchange asked George Brown to hold on and put a call through to the Garrick. At the club Max was told Mr George Brown wished to speak to him, so he went downstairs to the telephone box. There he found the telephone on the hook so he dialled the *Express* and was put through by the operator there to the Foreign Secretary.

When this incident was investigated by the Radcliffe committee at the hearings, the evidence of George Brown and Max Aitken conflicted. The former said that when he was speaking on the telephone Max had said, 'I have Derek Marks by my side'. Max denied this and the inherent implausibility that Max had ever said this was demonstrated in my cross-examination of George Brown when it was explained that Max was speaking from a Garrick Club telephone box, which was thin, whereas Derek Marks was immensely fat. George Brown was not amused. He insisted that he thought Max was speaking from his office in the *Express*. After our exchanges over this were completed, I then said, before turning to another matter, 'Very well.' George said testily, 'It's no good saying very well. What else could it mean?' I repeated the words 'Very well', and went on to the next part of my cross-examination.

George claimed that, after he had spoken, Max had replied, 'I will kill the story.' Max, in his evidence, said that he personally had known nothing about the cable-vetting story before that moment and that what he had said to George was: 'If we are running a story under D-Notice, we will take it out.' George Brown told the Committee that he just did not believe that Max knew nothing of the story. What with the crowd in the telephone box and despite 'Very well', the suspicion arose that perhaps on that evening the Foreign Secretary had been dining rather well. In support of the stand of the *Express*, Lee Howard of the *Mirror*, Edward Pickering of IPC and Maurice Green of the *Telegraph* all gave evidence.

While we had taken immense pains to prepare for the hearing and present to the tribunal evidence and argument, the government either from idleness or arrogance took none. They were not even represented. So I, on behalf of the *Express*, had a clear field and no competition. Half a dozen years later, when I was Attorney General and Harold Wilson was Leader of the Opposition, we were serving together on the Committee of Privileges of the House of Commons. He confessed to me then that he had made a grave error in not having a Law Officer at the Committee hearings to present the Government's case.

In any event, they paid the penalty, for when the Committee reported in May they found that the article, contrary to Harold Wilson's description of it in the House, was not inaccurate; that it would not be right to say it amounted to a breach of the D-Notices; and that there was no evidence that the decision to publish was taken with a deliberate intention of evading or defying the D-notice procedure. This was total victory for the *Express*, and the vindication which Derek Marks had so anxiously sought. Harry Pincher had written the story, but it was Derek who had decided to publish and who bore the responsibility. He was entitled to his gratification, which he expressed, typically, in a gargantuan luncheon at the Savoy, from which, exhilarated, I tottered back to the Temple.

The government snarled at its defeat, but then it compounded its earlier mistakes by a final act of real political folly.

Only a year earlier Harold Wilson had been swept back into power with a vastly increased majority. Having won against Alec Home by the shortest of short heads in the election of 1964, he had skilfully manipulated the economy and manoeuvred his government through its early months until he called an election in 1966 and overwhelmingly defeated the new Tory leader, Edward Heath. He was on the crest of his political wave. He dominated the House of Commons, and he was getting a good press. On the public stage he was caustic and clever, and in debate he was agile. While in private he was kindly and sensitive, in later years he appeared to become totally self-obsessed.

Prime Ministers are not alone in this. Louis Mountbatten rarely seemed able, whatever the subject, to exclude his personal reminiscences, which he projected into the most irrelevant conversation.

In December of 1963 we travelled up to Cambridge together by train to dine at our old college, Christ's, where I had to speak. Lord Mountbatten was then Chief of Defence Staff. I was Solicitor General. It was a month before I was sworn in to the Privy Council and so I was not yet bound by the Privy Councillor's oath of secrecy. I had been told of my impending appointment but I doubt if the Chief of Staff knew that. Privy Councillor or not it did not deter him from taking me into his confidence. He invited me to share his reserved compartment on the train and during the journey he at once proceeded to discuss and dissect the details of the government defence policy. I sat in silence, goggling.

The train was crowded; people were standing in the corridor outside the compartment which was marked with its official 'Reserved' labels. The blinds were also drawn. Suddenly the door slid open and, presumably out of desperation over the condition of their poor feet, two middle-aged and extremely stout ladies staggered into the reserved compartment and without a word flopped down on to the empty seats. Their unexpected intrusion disturbed the flow of the Admiral of the Fleet not a whit. The secrets, the weaponry, the statistics, the reflections on strategy, the criticisms of allies and the shortcomings of ministers, all poured out uninterrupted – save for some diversions by way of reminiscences of a Supreme Commander or of a Viceroy of India.

The two women at first regarded him balefully, irritated apparently by the uninterrupted noise of his speech. Then they appeared to grow fascinated by the flow of fact and figure, laced with well-known names, which came from the gentleman in the corner. The journey went on until at Cambridge without a glance at our companions and still talking, the Admiral swept out. I followed, praying that the women were not spies. I was rather reassured when, as I banged the carriage door, I saw them looking at each other and wagging their heads, settling down, at last, for a little peace and quiet.

In 1967, before the D-Notice affair, Harold Wilson had been riding high. The only cross which he had to bear appeared to be his eccentric Foreign Secretary; and that was a burden of which he was soon to be relieved. At any rate such, at that time, was his confidence that he decided to deal with the singular rebuff which had been administered to him personally at the hands of the D-Notice Committee of Enquiry which he had himself appointed, by blunt defiance of its conclusions. He produced a White Paper in reply. In it, and in statements in the House, he maintained his attack on the *Express* which the Radcliffe Committee had so categorically rejected.

The whole of the press was outraged. Cartoons appeared depicting the Prime Minister as a small boy rejecting the umpire. In the words of James Margach, the much respected political commentator of the *Sunday Times*, Harold Wilson could claim a unique achievement: 'He has united the entire British Press in a single popular front.'

There was still to come the debate in the Commons. When it came the Prime Minister demonstrated once again his deftness in debate. Having been counsel at the hearing I could not join in. I sat listening, and I heard the two Privy Councillors Selwyn Lloyd and Emanuel Shinwell. Soon it became clear that the government tactic was to shift the attack on to the person of Colonel Lohan, the secretary of the Committee with whom Harry Pincher had lunched during those days before the story was printed. The last words in the debate were those of Harold Wilson and he slipped the stiletto between the ribs of the unhappy Colonel, the civil servant who could not defend himself. 'I was asked', said Wilson, 'if Colonel Lohan had been given full positive vetting. The answer is that he was not.' And he sat down, leaving an unjustified but sinister smear over the head of the wretched Colonel. It was, some would have it, a masterly performance. It was also an unpleasant one.

In the House of Lords, the government found it less easy. Lord Radcliffe, with the asperity and precision of a lifetime of cool advocacy, delicately demolished the government's case. Colonel Lohan, he said, had been presented to his Committee by the government itself as a witness to be relied upon. Cyril Radcliffe went on to wonder how the government could 'reject' a report of a committee which they had themselves set up. It was open for them to disagree with the report, but they could not reject it. The report was a fact, and he ended by musing about the government's wisdom.

From that moment on the glitter began to fall away from Harold Wilson. He had been taken up as the new-style man, light years away from Harold Macmillan and his friends in their knickerbockers on a grouse moor. His was a 'flat 'at', not a deerstalker. He was the contemporary man for the contemporary swinging, not yet sleazy, sixties. But now he had alienated those who had promoted him: he had done it quite unnecessarily, and after the D-Notice affair things for him were never again the same.

Chapter 15
'Lord Rothermere's Witch Doctor Extraordinary'

In December of 1967 Sir John Hobson, the former Attorney General, sickened and died. For three years, since the electoral defeat in 1964, he had borne the burden of advising the Opposition on matters of law. He had been tireless in drafting amendments to government Bills and in advising colleagues in their task of shadowing ministers. With my growing family he had encouraged me to go back to full-time practice at the Bar, taking upon himself single-handed the duty of Law Adviser to the Shadow Cabinet. It was as though he was seeking to exorcise the responsibility which he always felt that he bore for the decline and fall of the Macmillan/Home administration.

Then, in 1967, he told me that he had had enough and that he wanted to leave the House and to seek apointment to the judicial Bench, for which he was well qualified. But Gerald Gardiner, the Labour Lord Chancellor, jibbed. In former days a Law Officer who left politics could anticipate appointment at least to the Court of Appeal. In modern times Jack Simon, a former Tory Solicitor General, had been appointed President of the Probate, Divorce and Admiralty Division; Lynn Ungoed-Thomas, a former Labour Solicitor General, to the Chancery Bench. The experience gained in serving as a Law Officer provides a unique and intensive legal education, and John in intellect and character was eminently qualified for the Bench. But the offer did not come. Gerald Gardiner, who had never served in the House of Commons, had scruples against the appointment of former Members of Parliament. Terence Donovan had been a Labour member of Parliament and a silk specializing in revenue law. He was appointed from the Labour benches in Parliament straight to the High Court Bench, and he became one of the most distinguished judges of the day. He progressed through the Court of Appeal to become a Lord of Appeal in Ordinary in the House of Lords. He told me that he had found his experience in the House of Commons of great help in his judicial work. A leavening of judges with such practical experience can strengthen the Bench.

When after 1970 the Tories returned to office and during the days before the troubles with the unions when it appeared that we might remain in office for a second term, my predecessor as Attorney General, Elwyn Jones, seemed dispirited and uncertain of what the future held for him. I actively promoted his appointment to the Court of Appeal. I believed that the judiciary would be strengthened if men of Elwyn's tradition and experience in the Labour movement could be recruited to the Bench. But it never came about, and only a few years later there, seated in full magnificence upon the Woolsack, was the temporarily dispirited Elwyn.

In that year, 1967, when he sought to leave politics to become a judge, John, tired, almost drained by effort and still haunted by the betrayal of four years earlier and his sensitivity over the electoral defeat, unexpectedly died. I mourned him deeply.

Two days later I was summoned by Willie Whitelaw, with an invitation from Ted. Thirty months previously, Willie had unexpectedly been appointed Chief Whip. To the surprise of those who did not know him but not to those who did, he was an immediate success. He had the qualities which made for a great Chief Whip and it was during these years in the Sixties that he acquired the skills and techniques of political management, of which he became the outstanding practitioner of his day. For twenty years he reigned supreme as the Tory Mr Fix-it. This led then and later to the suspicion by some that behind that bluff and beguiling front lurked a modern Tory 'Trimmer'. Undoubtedly many, in the political sense, soon came to fear his geniality; but of his political acumen and shrewdness none had any doubt. He had even then the disconcerting habit of never looking at the person with whom he was talking but over their shoulder, as if someone rather more important or interesting was standing just behind or approaching round the corner and that this required Willie to keep talking but to look elsewhere. There was an altogether elusive quality about him which belied his appearance and which, with his sometimes rather eliptical use of words, made him despite his bluff 'bonhomie' difficult to pin down. He was certainly a formidable customer. He had quickly acquired great influence in the Party and this increased remorselessly as the years passed. His prestige and reputation was not diminished by a sombre period as the first Northern Ireland Secretary nor by a later rather flat stint as Home Secretary. He appropriately reached his apogee in his final office as a masterly Leader of the House of Lords, where the old gentlemen loved him to distraction.

So at Ted's request I returned to the Front Bench and took on the role of legal adviser to the Shadow Cabinet in succession to John. For the next three years I attended the Shadow Cabinet and teamed with Quintin, the shadow Home Secretary, in debates in the House and led the Tory lawyers in opposition. Oddly enough we, the legal team, were the only group to inflict a defeat upon the Wilson government on the floor of the House during all that Parliament. We did it by one vote, on the report stage on an Administration of Justice Bill. Despite my ironical demands, the government strangely declined to resign (amid cries of 'Shame, shame!') and life went on exactly as it had before.

Much parliamentary activity, inevitably, seems like a game, like the children's game of 'French and English', only played by grown-ups who get more cross. For there are the enemies, the allies, the leaders, the footsoldiers and the sudden mutinies. The whole scene is delightfully lubricated by the constant political 'coffee housing', the gossip about who is on the way up and who down, for in politics somebody always is. And after years of service in the House, there is often earned the soubriquet of 'a good House of Commons man'. Translated that also often means an inordinate bore, who either never made it or who had passed it and still lumbers around, staying on because he has nowhere else to go.

In times not long past, the House of Commons was sustained and given ballast by having a majority among its ranks drawn from two outwardly very different but inherently very similar groups. Both were very English and both shared a sincere love of country. These groups were the knights of the shires, mostly from the south and west; and the genuine trade unionists, mostly from the north. They faced each other as political opponents across the Chamber, and drank together in the bars. Between them flitted, like exotic tropical birds, the career Members on the make. The two main groups regarded these rather condescendingly, sometimes with a certain grudging affection, sometimes with undisguised contempt, as they discussed their points as they would judge horses or greyhounds. But now the knights and the real unionists are mostly gone – to be succeeded by corporate financiers and polytechnic lecturers. The House and the country are the poorer for it.

Newspaper men often complain about the harshness of the English libel laws. At the Bar I have appeared for practically every daily newspaper and sometimes against them. It was Arnold Goodman, not the most reactionary

of sages, who pointed out that you can with safety print what you like –
so long as it is true. To that, some will reply, 'But it is often impossible to
prove the truth.' The answer is, 'Well then, if you cannot prove that what
you print is true, you print only rumour.'

But in 1968 I had the experience of myself being defamed as a result of
a libel action in which I had been professionally engaged. In October 1967
I had appeared as counsel for the *Evening News*, which was defending a
claim for libel in respect of a story which the newspaper had published
about the practice of witchcraft in, of all unlikely places, suburban Surrey.
The news report described strange scenes and ceremonies taking place in
a wood, whose trees were hung with sinister masks and inscriptions. A
reporter had crept undetected through the undergrowth and watched the
unusual goings-on. The newspaper then published the story. The two
elderly principals in the scenes, a man and his sister, thereupon sued for
libel. The newspaper, in defence, claimed that the account given was true.

The action was tried before a jury, with Melford Stevenson as the judge,
in October of 1967. I cross-examined the man and his sister. During the
questioning of the sister, she fixed me with a baleful, intense hypnotic
glare. Coincidentally, I presume coincidentally, my reading glasses, which
I was holding in my hands, suddenly snapped! I bravely persevered with
my cross-examination while my clerk hurriedly brought me from chambers
my spare spectacles. Later, for the defence, the reporter eyewitness gave
evidence of what he had seen and, after a trial lasting four days, the jury
returned a verdict in favour of the *Evening News*. I went off about my
business, less one pair of expensive spectacles.

Seven months later an extraordinary document began to be circulated.
It had been sent to practically every Member of the House of Commons;
all the local councillors in my constituency; and to most of the judges
throughout the United Kingdom and, I later learned, throughout the
Commonwealth. The document took the form of a folded printed pamphlet.
On the cover there was written, 'An open letter to The Witches Advocate'.
Beneath these words was a large photograph of my face beneath my full-
bottomed wig; and perched upon and above my wig, at a rather racy angle,
a large black pointed witch's hat with a sinister white star in its centre.
Underneath was printed 'Sir Peter Rawlinson, Privy Councillor, Queens
Counsel, Member of Parliament' – and then, 'Witch Doctor Extraordinary
to Lord Rothermere'.

So far so good. I was not sure whether those words were a libel on me
or Esmond Rothermere. But inside came the text of the open letter
addressed to the 'Witch Doctor Extraordinary'. The letter referred to the

case in October 1967, accused me of perpetrating 'the schoolboy trick of reading documents out of context' and included the, fortunately false, accusation (which gravely offended my clerk!) that I had offered to defend the case for Lord Rothermere without a fee. There then came some spirited abuse of Mr Justice Melford Stevenson, attributing to both him and myself intimate knowledge and belief in witchcraft, mutual Catholic connections and paranoid schizophrenia. All this was harmless nonsense except perhaps for the libel about the fee.

However, the author then turned to print a very nasty libel involving my eldest married daughter by my first marriage, Mikaela, and my four-year-old younger son, Anthony, by my second. It was because of this part of what would otherwise have been a routine but elaborate circular of abuse, which it is not uncommon to receive, that I became inundated with scores of kindly but embarrassed letters from many of the thousands of people to whom the pamphlet had been circulated. More than two years later, when I was Attorney General, the Chief Justice of New Zealand took me aside at a Commonwealth Law Conference and apologetically thrust the witch doctor pamphlet into my hands. To such distant lands had the libel found its way.

It was because of this slur on my daughter that in 1968 I had to stop the unpleasantness, and so I became a plaintiff in a libel action. After several months I finally obtained an injunction, and the eccentric gentleman was silenced. This was all I wanted. The man was a bankrupt, although he had found the not unsubstantial means to print and post. I traced the probable source of the unpleasant libel about my daughter to the entry of the date of her marriage in *Debrett*, which they had got wrong. The author of the pamphlet must have seen this and upon this founded his nasty allegation that my son was my grandson whom I had taken into my care. The man's resentment at losing his claim against the *Evening News* had driven him to extraordinary lengths in searching out the addresses of the prominent people in whose eyes he sought to damage me and my family in the pursuit of revenge.

So when it is said that our libel laws are too harsh and that people are over-sensitive and over-react when they are defamed because readers pay little heed and soon forget, I remember my own minor action for defamation in which the numbers to whom the libel was published only amounted to thousands and not the millions of readers of a newspaper. I remember the scores of personal letters which I was obliged to write in reply and explanation. I look at the file, which I still have, of correspondence with my lawyers trying to silence the libeller, and I think of the time and money expended and the sense of anger. So I can understand the feelings of a person libelled.

I also remember those spectacles which so unexpectedly snapped in half under the wild, witchlike stare from the witness box. Altogether that was an expensive brief – for me.

Chapter 16
'Selsdon Man' – Election Victory, 1970

I burn easily in the sun, and get bored. To the worshipper, lying like a salamander, a restless companion is intolerable. The devotions are desecrated, the stillness disturbed.

One clear morning in 1957 in Sitges, just south of Barcelona and then still a sleepy little port with one hotel and one place to dance among the tamarisks above the sea, Elaine suddenly stormed off, silently and alone. When she came back, she seemed to be carrying what looked like a suitcase. She handed it to me. 'There,' she said, 'now go off and paint.' So wherever we were on holiday I began painting *en plein air*. I could not draw. I could not mix colour and I still find it very difficult. But it took me out of sight and earshot of the salamanders, gave them peace and me total preoccupation and enjoyment. Peter Thorneycroft, a watercolourist of distinction, notes in his book *The Amateur* how the holiday painter has to acquire sufficiently thick a skin to tolerate the ubiquitous onlooker peering over the shoulder and the uninvited and often, at least for my efforts, wounding criticisms. I have sat perched on my stool before my easel overlooking the Atlantic on the Ocean Drive at Newport, Rhode Island, and endured the tourist buses actually halting to allow the tourists to troop across the rocks to inspect the artist at work on his canvas. They did not linger. Or at the little village of Grimaud in the hills above Ste Maxime, where I would set up and start to paint in early morning before the village came to life and before the sun grew hot. Gradually doors would open, children would appear, and the old men would emerge rubbing the sleep from their eyes to squat on their doorsteps, breaking their fast on baguettes and swills of Provençal wine. One summer I became so much a part of the scenery that I was accepted almost as a convenience. A woman from the house nearby where I was painting asked me to answer her telephone while she went to market. Others followed suit. They never received many messages, for their conscripted 'answer machine' was not very fluent and necessarily terse.

I liked painting *en plein air* in Italy as I could not understand the comments of the onlookers, although the cluck and the hiss of pained breath drawn between the teeth usually conveyed sufficiently what the onlooker felt. But I did not mind. The sheer joy and utter absorption of just trying to paint is sufficient; the pride when something appeared to approximate to what was intended repaid hours of frustration and failure. As for the onlooker critics, the comfort was to tell oneself that they could do no better and probably far worse.

The game of golf has always irritated me. This is, I know, an irrational attitude, similar to the phobia of my father who, if he saw people sitting at a card table, say at a dinner party, had an almost irresistible desire to go and tip over the table. But I could understand that, however unskilled the golfer, the intense concentration required in the effort to propel that wretched little ball along grass paths in approximately a straight line and force it down a minute hole in the ground, provides total recreation or relaxation. Everything presumably is driven out of mind in the fierce struggle to control the flight of that white-wrapped gutta-percha sphere.

My painting was the same. Nothing else comes to mind; hours pass as I work on, comforted by the Mozart or Haydn on the small tape at my feet, surrounded by an enchanted haze of blue tobacco smoke. And whatever may finally emerge on to the canvas, at least the places where one is sitting are usually of breathtaking beauty.

Although those years in the late 1960s were so intensely busy and the times in retrospect now so sleazy, it was, for us, an exciting decade. Ahead lay the years and exhausting preoccupations of office. Opposition in politics is easy; just complain as colourfully as possible, and then propose alternatives in fine-sounding generalities. During those years of private practice at the Bar, banks, film companies, casinos and the newspapers were my principal clients.

I was married to one whom the newspapers described as 'the most beautiful MP's wife'. On holidays we took the children to the States, travelling at least one way on the now extinct transatlantic liners when, for five days, life stood still, measured only by the times for vast meals and games of 'housey-housey' or gambling on wooden horses moved by the purser towards the winning-post according to the turn of a wheel. Or we went to Bembridge, where a colony of friends with children of the same age as ours were established in holiday houses; or best of all to the south of France, where on birthday parties the clown Quoin-Quoin on his single-wheel bicycle spun around the children on the terrace of the villa.

Each week I attended the Shadow Cabinet and sat between Robert Carr and Margaret Thatcher. On the whole it was then quite a formidable political group. Until April 1968, there had been at least three Crown Princes: Reggie Maudling, Iain Macleod, who had returned to the apex of Tory politics, and Enoch Powell. Quintin Hailsham had faded. And in the system of Cabinet government the presence of real alternatives concentrates the mind of any leader wonderfully.

Then, after 20 April 1968, the three Crown Princes were reduced to two. Enoch's speech about immigration at the Midland Hotel, Birmingham, signalled the end of his romantic love-affair with the Tory Party. The alienation could perhaps have been avoided. If it had, with the sudden death of Iain Macleod in 1970, the effective political demise of Reggie Maudling in 1972 and the loss of confidence in the leadership of Ted Heath in 1974, Enoch must surely have become the leader and later Prime Minister. The economic policies now labelled as Thatcherism in essence evolved inevitably from the national mood after the experience of 1974–8 and although implemented by the indomitable will of Margaret Thatcher they would then have borne the imprint of Enoch Powell's romantic vision of Toryism. If he could have remained in that Shadow Cabinet, I do not believe that either the European or the Northen Ireland issue would have driven him out. In politics so often it is the clash of personalities which decides events. The personal quarrel and the personal resentment so often fashion the political stance; and this is when the hidden daggers become unsheathed. But Enoch was truly the lost leader.

From the end of 1967, when I succeeded John Hobson, I was of that Shadow Cabinet but not in it. I was, in a sense, an observer. Because I clearly did not seek political as opposed to legal office, I became the repository of the confidences of many colleagues who would never have entrusted them to others. The others were all competitors. There are no friends at that level of politics. There are only disciples, or rivals.

On 10 October 1969, at the traditional dinner which is given for the Shadow Cabinet at the Party Conference at Brighton, hosted by the Mayor, Elaine and I were seated at one of the tables amid those whom Ted Heath called 'the senior colleagues'. Ted, as Leader, made the speech of thanks in reply to the Mayor's toast. As he always did on such occasions, Ted made a particularly felicitous speech, as always without a single note. In the next few years I heard him make many such in Downing Street. To those who have heard only his 'plummy', rather turgid official speeches, they would come as a surprise. These were always graceful, witty – and short. This was one such.

While he spoke I studied the faces of his rivals, the 'senior colleagues', the political 'friends', watching in vain for signs of pleasure that the Leader was performing with such skill. None came. It was seven years since I had first joined the front bench so I suppose that I should not have been surprised. But I was. I should have learned from my time in the Macmillan government when Rab was outwardly the heir apparent. Little love was lost between those two 'friends' and when the time for succession arrived Harold made sure that Rab did not inherit. But it was only at that dinner that I fully came to appreciate the brutal reality of the nature of personal relationships amid life at the top in politics. Ted had lost one election and his place on the throne remained uneasy. I could see that each of the 'senior colleagues', if the opportunity ever presented itself, would readily unsheath the dagger – in the interests, of course, of the Party and the Country.

The 1969 Brighton Conference was exciting. An election was probable before another conference would be held. My role was to reply for the platform to the Law and Order debate, an annual purgatory. Then there was the round of Area receptions, the special fringe groups, the parties given by the BBC and ITV. In the Party generally there was the feeling that we were on the march. The atmosphere was encapsulated early next year in a Central Office pamphlet, *The Tories Are Coming*. But the focus of attention by the commentators remained upon the performance of Ted Heath. Were he to lose once again to Harold Wilson, his days would be numbered and many in private still had reservations.

At the Bar, the end of the year for me was filled by appearing for the defence at Lewes of a parliamentary Labour candidate accused of rape. It ended in his acquittal. It is often sensible in a jury trial where the central figure has known political affiliations to instruct as counsel someone with the opposite political allegiance: thus there is neutralized any inclination for prejudice in any member of the jury. But sometimes in some litigation this is not so acceptable.

In 1983, presumably because they thought that I was best suited for the task, I was instructed by a well-known firm of solicitors very experienced in the field of law in issue, to represent the *Guardian* newspaper in proceedings brought against them by the Secretary of State over the return of some documents which had been handed to them by a civil servant, a Miss Sarah Tisdall. We failed at first instance before the Chancery judge and again before the Court of Appeal. The *Guardian* then published a letter from an obscure circuit judge which in effect said that their failure served them right for having hired an establishment lawyer. The implication was that I had not tried! I was then sacked by the paper. The solicitors were embarrassed and apologetic. I thought that it might be fun to sue a judge but instead I wrote him a fierce letter. He hastily and penitently wrote a grovelling apology. The *Guardian* with their new counsel still lost in their final appeal in the House of Lords. When I heard the result I confess that I was not heartbroken. It is never fun to be sacked.

On 30 January 1970, the Opposition Shadow Cabinet held a weekend conference at the Selsdon Park Hotel in Sanderstead in the suburbs of London. The purpose of the meeting was to settle and then publish the policies and tactics on which the Tories would fight the General Election which was expected some time during that year. At the end of the weekend a communiqué was issued announcing the fruits of our deliberations. As a result there was born into the political world a creature whom the liberal establishment at once christened 'Selsdon Man', a low-browed, hirsute creature, much mocked by their scribes for wanting to bash the unions and protect old ladies being mugged and even to lower taxes. As the election demonstrated a few months later, however, 'Selsdon Man' was not so unlovely to the voters as the clever critics would have had the world believe.

The last time I had been at the Selsdon Park Hotel had been during the war, nearly thirty years before. The 1st Battalion Irish Guards was then stationed in and around Sanderstead for the southern defence of London. It was during the time when London was still under night attack from the air. On each Saturday evening, despite the bombing and the noise of the anti-aircraft guns, there used to be a dance. Those of us who were off duty would make up parties and, rather grandly dressed in our blue patrols, would arrive with wives and girlfriends to dine and dance.

To one of these parties a fellow officer, Douggie Gilliat, had brought his wife to spend the night at the hotel. After the dancing she had gone up to bed. Douggie remained with some of us downstairs drinking. Eventually, and rather guiltily, he went upstairs to join her in their room, undressed in the dark and slipped into bed beside her. Or so he thought. The hotel suddenly rang with the sound of piercing screams and a bewildered Douggie, in his shirt-tails with his uniform over his arm, scuttled along the corridor to the screams of an outraged elderly female whose innocent bed Douggie in his cups had unexpectedly invaded. He disappeared out of sight in search of his lawful bed, accompanied now not only by the yells of outrage but also by the halloo-ing of his comrades-in-arms. As I drove up that Friday evening in January 1970 to attend the conference, I felt it unlikely that Margaret Thatcher, the only woman among us, would suffer a similar mishap.

The policies announced at Selsdon Park were now those on which the coming election would be fought by the Tories, and the scoffers were so vociferous that their chorus probably encouraged Harold Wilson to go to the country that summer. In May I went to spend a few days with a friend, Arthur Unwin, in his house on Ibiza and while I was there the election was announced. I hurried home. The electoral portents had looked favourable to Harold Wilson. He and his colleagues were confident. The Shadow Cabinet which met on 27 May were not.

When the campaign began I was obliged to go on speaking tours in many parts of the country, and so for periods I was away from Epsom, where Elaine was left to carry the flag, which she did with enormous success. I began to feel that I might do better to stay away for longer! My first outside engagement was to take part in a television debate in Norwich with Richard Crossman, the first of two which we did together during that election. We travelled together by train in a civilized fashion, sharing a compartment and discussing the probable outcome. Richard Crossman was as indiscreet and engaging as ever. He did not give us a chance. The next week we debated on *This Week*. He still did not give us a chance.

I went up to Derby to do a short Midlands tour. Unlike Richard Crossman, the local agents were confident. But when the Shadow Cabinet met in Ted's chambers in Albany on 7 June on the first Sunday of the campaign, the faces were long. Ted was very quiet. Only Iain Mcleod exuded confidence. 'We shall win', he said. The colleagues looked sceptical. It was arranged that we should all meet again on the following Sunday, four days before the poll. That next week I did a tour of the West Country and another of East Anglia. Again the local agents were encouraging. So were my constituency canvassers. I looked forward to more cheerful faces on the next Sunday meeting in Albany. But there was no meeting. It was cancelled.

I did two more television broadcasts. I saw some friends, candidates in London constituencies. It was rumoured that a putsch was being prepared. Ted would have to go. The significant figure in all their gossip was, of course, Willie. Then I went up to Rugby. The message there was the same as on my other tours. All was going well, they said, and they asked why everyone in London was so jumpy. I had eve-of-poll meetings in Harrow and Uxbridge and on polling day toured the polling stations in my Epsom constituency. At lunchtime, the London *Evening Standard* poll was encouraging. During my tour, I was tracked down by my clerk from the

Temple. I had been offered a substantial brief for the following week. I declined, telling him cheerfully that I would be in government next week. My clerk snorted.

That evening for the second, but not the last, time in my life I sat before a television screen and learned that my immediate future was going to be gravely altered. We had won. Derek Marks, the Editor of the *Express*, gloated at the sight next day of the furniture van removing the Wilson belongings from No. 10.

After my count, which was always held on the morning after the main results had come through, I sped back to London, did an ITN interview, went to Max Aitken's election lunch at the Dorchester and then on to the BBC to be interviewed by Robin Day, who was winding up his marathon election programme. I left the studio with Reggie Maudling, who gave me a lift back home to Chelsea Square. 'Now', he said gloomily, 'our troubles begin. We shall be seeing a lot of each other.' And we did.

That was on the Friday. It was not until the following Tuesday, after I had spent the weekend with my parents by the sea, that I received my third and last invitation from my third and last Prime Minister to join his administration. There was no graceful lecture on the historical role of the Law Officers. It came in a brisk, businesslike telephone call. Would I please take the post of Attorney General and move into the Law Officers' Department that same morning. I would and I did.

Shortly thereafter Tony Hetherington, the Legal Secretary at the Law Officers' Department, arrived at my house, not in a musty old Humber but in a sleek new limousine, and took me to the Law Courts. I already knew most of the staff, which was not very difficult, for there were only Tony and four other lawyers and a small back-up team. Then I was joined, to my great delight, by Geoffrey Howe, who Ted had told me on the telephone was to be my Solicitor General. But he had also added the ominous words that Geoffrey would be needed for immediate duties over the trade union legislation which was to be a first and prime task which the new government was to tackle.

On the following morning I was sworn in before Quintin Hailsham, the new Lord Chancellor, and attended the first Cabinet of the new administration. Gone, I noticed, were all the ashtrays into which Harold Macmillan used elegantly to tap the ash of his cigar and Harold Wilson, presumably, the dottle of his pipe. I duly warned my bank manager of my reduced circumstances and settled in for nearly four gruelling and not very jolly years.

PART TWO

Chapter 17
Attorney General

'Patronage Secretary, guard the door.' It was the government dinner at Admiralty House on the eve of the Opening of Parliament in 1962. The Chief Whip, Martin Redmayne DSO, every inch the former brigadier, made his way in his tailcoat and white tie to the end of the room and stood, sentinel, with his back to the door. The Prime Minister, looking more like Arthur Balfour than ever, languidly signalled to the Secretary to the Cabinet, Sir Norman Brooke, to read the Queen's Speech.

In 1970 we came to Downing Street in black ties. We climbed the staircase passing the prints or photographs of former incumbents. Harold Wilson, I noted, was not yet hung. The Patronage Secretary now was Francis Pym. In the drawing-room I encountered Burke Trend, the then Secretary to the Cabinet. 'You must tell me, Peter,' he said, looking around somewhat fastidiously, 'who all these people are.' I did.

Burke never appeared to be at ease with Ted, who found more empathy with that other mandarin, William Armstrong, then head of the civil service. Indeed, towards the end of the life of his administration Ted was criticized for having elevated the latter almost into the role of Deputy Prime Minister. But the administration by then had lost its two principal political heavyweights, with whom it had begun its life. The first had gone very soon indeed in the first weeks of the new Parliament, when the true heir apparent, Iain Macleod, had suddenly died one month after taking office. It was said, and it was true, that right from the start we had lost our trumpet. The government was badly maimed. Two years later Reggie Maudling was forced into resignation.

When I took over the Attorney's chair I decided that, far more often than my immediate predecessor as Attorney General, I was going to lead for the Crown in court, not only in those cases in which in the past it had been customary for the Attorney General to appear as counsel, but in all those in which I believed it to be appropriate. Apart from the fact that I enjoyed being in Court and came fresh from substantial practice, I had been taught that it was the duty of the senior Law Officer whenever possible to represent the Crown in litigation in which the Crown had a major interest. This was not confined to criminal prosecutions (although during the next few years I appeared personally to prosecute on every circuit, save the Welsh – I did not dare to do so there!). I appeared in much civil litigation and appellate proceedings. This policy, I knew, would not prove popular with political colleagues, especially with No. 10, for it meant that when in Court the Attorney was unavailable to attend for consultation or for Cabinet or Cabinet committees. But, while the system still existed in which the Attorney General was the first Counsel to the Crown as well as legal adviser to the Cabinet, I considered that the first duty was that of Counsel. The lesson given me across that long table in Admiralty House on that June afternoon by the first Prime Minister whom I served remained in my mind.

What is certain is that an Attorney General, in his traditional role and by reason of his duty as prosecutor and guardian of the public interest, has under the old dispensation to fulfil a task which, in popular sentiment, must appear remarkably unsympathetic. Even over criminal prosecutions it is noticeable how often the public feel outrage at the time when the crime is committed, but by the time of the trial have shifted their sympathy so that the figure in the dock becomes the hunted and the prosecutor becomes the hunter. Again, as guardian of the public interest, the Attorney General may have to interfere or intervene over a publication or a broadcast. So the media do not love him. Historically he is always the villain whom the public, and now the media, love to hiss.

Even among his own colleagues he has to play the restraining role, guarding against the legislative abuse of power, reviewing and sometimes advising against the pet proposals of ministers on the grounds of their dubious legality. He is the person who is always making difficulties, and since often the legal objections may be abstruse, being based upon complex considerations of law difficult for a layman to grasp and certainly impossible comprehensively to explain in the short time permitted to any item in the agenda of a Cabinet, he is regarded warily by his colleagues.

So the Attorney General becomes, to friend and foe alike, the bogeyman, a popular target for popular commentators. What is absolutely certain is that an Attorney General who becomes popular will not be doing responsibly that which his office demands.

It is said that of all members of the government it is the Foreign Secretary and the Attorney General who bear the greatest burden of business. Those prime ministers whose publicity machine likes to portray them as workaholics existing on a few short hours of sleep and a dry biscuit should remember that Harold Macmillan gave the game away when he ensured that he was discovered curled up in a corner with Trollope. On the other hand in all government business there are some elements of law upon which ministers may require advice, and they keep the Attorney General busy. Apart from the requirement as Counsel to the Cabinet to advise the Cabinet and ministers and to represent the Crown in court, there is the added responsibility for all criminal prosecutions and the requirement to be ready to intervene as the guardian of the public interest.

The Foreign Secretary has at his command a great Department of State with all the resources of such a department at his disposal and he can call on the help of numbers of highly trained specialists to provide minutes or draft statements or speeches. The Attorney General in my day had a private secretary who took his dictation and kept his diary; a driver; and a staff of four qualified lawyers. Through this minute team poured the unending flow of requests for opinion and advice. Of the greatest importance and aid were, of course, the three Treasury 'devils', practising members of the Bar in common law, Chancery and Revenue, all counsel of great quality and ability with chambers in the Temple who devote their time, principally although not exclusively, to Treasury work. With the Attorney General, there is his deputy, the Solicitor General, a Queen's Counsel and a member of the government and of the House of Commons, who by law can exercise all the Attorney's statutory and constitutional duties.

In Geoffrey Howe I had a Solicitor General of distinction. I had known him at the Bar and during his brief earlier time in the Commons between 1964 and 1966. He was a good lawyer with a keen intellect, a man of great industry with a very engaging personality. I valued his ability and political good sense, and he had a quirky sense of humour not immediately apparent from his rather portly Jeeves-like bearing. At that time he smoked cigarettes like a chimney. In order to cut down he ceased to carry them. Instead he would, when in my room, empty the box on my table which I, who did not smoke cigarettes, kept for visitors, and smoke away like a truant schoolboy.

But the Prime Minister, as PMs do, had other plans. Almost immediately, certainly in our first few months, Geoffrey was seconded almost entirely to the Ministry of Labour to mastermind the government's industrial relations legislation. When that was on the statute-book, he went off in our second year together to play the same role in charge of the legislation arising from our accession to the European Economic Community. I was, to a great extent, deprived of the vital assistance of an able and energetic Solicitor General.

When Winston Churchill in 1951 was forming his peacetime administration, he appointed his two foremost lawyers, David Maxwell Fyfe and Walter Monckton, to the Home Office and to the Ministry of Labour respectively. For the two Law Officer posts he sent the patent lawyer Lionel Heald to become Attorney and the then little-regarded (by the Bar) Reggie Manningham-Buller to be Solicitor. He is said to have remarked that David and Walter should always be able to cast an eye and lend a hand if it became necessary.

The story is unlikely to be true, for Winston had known and loved F. E. Smith, who had served in both Law Officer posts and he knew the pressure of work in both. Moreover Prime Ministers, necessarily, have much occasion to work intimately with the Attorney General, usually in the most sensitive aspects of the affairs of their administration. I did so with Ted Heath. It was therefore a considerable imposition to have the Solicitor General levered out of his true role and given other duties. It increased enormously the burden, which in April 1972 was compounded by the extra responsibilities of becoming the first English Attorney General of Northern Ireland. But that lay ahead.

The civil servant barrister, head of the small official team, was Tony Hetherington, with whom I had worked in 1962. Later, after I had left office, he became Director of Public Prosecutions. The appointment of a civil service lawyer to that post is not advisable, and his successor was recruited from the independent Bar. But Tony was unique. He had, above all else, a great fund of common sense, a steady nerve and the facility of handling the great mandarins with whom, when he was Legal Secretary to the Law Officers and much junior in rank, he often had to deal. For all the great men, like Burke Trend, Secretary of the Cabinet, Philip Allen of the Home Office, and the heads of the Security Services, were at some time or another clients of the Law officers.

So it was Tony who on the morning of 23 June 1979 had said goodbye to Elwyn Jones and then set off to welcome me and collect me from my home in Chelsea Square to escort me to the Department, in the same tradition of the civil service as four years later Robert Armstrong, then

Principal Private Secretary to the Prime Minister, bowed from the steps in Downing Street as a disconsolate Ted Heath drove away and, a little later, bowed again, in greeting the surprised Harold Wilson.

As I entered the Attorney's room in the Law Courts on that summer morning, the whole place looked very drab. I had got used to my room in King's Bench Walk. It was then that I decided to try and brighten it up and to start a picture collection. I had a search made for pictures and prints of predecessors back to William de Lodington, who in 1399 received a patent as 'King's Attorney in the Common Bench and all other places' and who may be regarded as the first appointment as an Attorney General for the Crown. The collection of pictures was hung along the long dark corridor of the Law officers' Department in the Law courts in the Strand which I now had christened 'the Attorney General's chambers'. In the rooms of the Attorney and the Solicitor's personal assistants or private secretaries, we hung photographs of the recent holders of the offices. At least the pictures and prints made the place more interesting, while the villainous visages of most of our predecessors showed the visitor what to expect.

After a few weeks I decided to give up all drink. I feared that the pressure might make for too much dependence. Then after some months I went back to drinking wine save in the gruesome weeks of Lent, and lived happily and reasonably dependent ever after.

Chapter 18
The Kidnap of Mrs McKay – A Bomb at Home

'On the evening of 29 December last,' I said, 'Mrs McKay disappeared from her home at 20 Arthur Road, Wimbledon.' I paused. 'She has never been seen again.'

I was back in No. 1 Court at the Old Bailey, where I had been so often before. I had been in office for three months. With those words I began, on 14 September 1970, the prosecution of two brothers from Trinidad for the kidnap and murder of Mrs Alick McKay. The elder, Arthur Hosein, was the most evil man I ever encountered in a criminal court. It was my first case as Attorney General.

Mrs McKay had been kidnapped from her home in mistake for Anna Murdoch, wife of Rupert Murdoch, then the chairman of the News of the World Organization, now of News International. Her family received telephone calls from the kidnappers. They demanded a million pounds ransom and called themselves 'Maffia M3'. Two days after the kidnap there came a pathetic, chilling note written in Mrs McKay's handwriting slanting across the page: 'Alick darling, I am blindfold and cold. Please do something and get me home. Please co-operate or I cannot keep going. I think of you all constantly and have kept calm so far. What have I done to deserve this treatment?' Alick McKay never did get her home. No trace of her has ever been found.

Telephone messages from the kidnappers fixed meeting places to deliver the ransom in suitcases. Police were there, disguised. A car cruised around where the suitcases holding the ransom had been placed on the orders of the kidnappers. But the suitcases were not collected. The car drove away. The demands for ransom and telephone calls to the family continued. Then the car seen near the ransom suitcases was traced to Arthur Hosein, who lived at that time with his brother Nizam on Rooks Farm in Hertfordshire, guarded by Alsatian dogs. The police came to the farm. The pathetic letter from the blindfolded Mrs McKay was found to bear Arthur Hosein's palm print. The brothers were arrested and the demands for ransom ceased. To the police, Nizam said, 'Oh my God, what have I done?'

Before the change of government, Elwyn Jones had decided that he ought to prosecute in this, the first modern case of true criminal kidnap in Britain. In the days of capital punishment the Attorney General, by custom and to mark the peculiarly deliberate and cruel nature of the crime, always prosecuted in cases of murder by poison. In my tour of office I extended that, where possible, to the murder of police officers. The Hosein case, although neither murder by poison nor murder of a police officer, was a horrible and vicious crime. The fear was lest it become a precedent, and introduce into the UK kidnap for gain so prevalent in parts of Italy and the United States. I was sure that Elwyn had been right to decide to have the senior Law Officer of the Crown lead the prosecution, and I took it on.

The trial lasted from 14 September to 6 October. My opening speech lasted five and a half hours. There was no body which could be examined from which the cause and time of death could be deduced. The evidence that Mrs McKay was dead was circumstantial. There was little doubt, on the evidence, that the Hosein brothers had kidnapped her and had held her at some time at the remote Rooks farm. After the arrest of the Hoseins, all pleas from Mrs McKay, all messages from the kidnappers, had ceased. It was the belief of the Crown that she had probably died from exposure one December day or night soon after she had been taken, probably not more than forty-eight hours after the kidnap on 29 December. Horrible as it was to accept, local rumour had it that her body had been devoured by pigs on the isolated farm.

However ugly or brutal the facts and circumstances under examination in a trial, the process of the English criminal court requires that it should be conducted in a matter-of-fact style. Words describing deeds of great inhumanity are used clinically. However dramatic the scene may have been, however bloody the crime, the form and mode and the words used are designed to excise passion and emotion. Sometimes it becomes necessary to quote the actual language used by the actors in the real-life drama. These real words explode like grenades on the lips of judge or lawyer as they are recited in the accents of club or academe, when they seem to acquire an extra nastiness. Then the process returns to the remorseless cool expression of the language of the court. So usually even the worst and most terrible crime assumes an ordinariness as the clinical process proceeds.

But in the trial of the Hosein brothers, a perpetual chill hung over the court. From the elder brother, Arthur Hosein, there exuded a malevolence almost physical in its force. No trial has in my experience equalled the atmosphere which then prevailed. It reached its climax when the dapper figure of Arthur went to the witness box and told his story, denying any complicity in the kidnap and murder. He accused his brother and co-defendant of lying, the police of brutality. He shouted at me during my cross-examination, and abused the judge. He held out his hands to the jury, declaring, 'These hands are artistic, not destructive. I believe in the preservation of man. That is what I am living for.' Describing himself as a 'fashion designer, cutter', dressed in black suit, white shirt spotted with polka dots and bow-tie, he conveyed an impression of villainy such as I have never encountered. When the jury convicted both the brothers of murder and kidnap, Arthur Hosein shouted at the judge, accusing him of partiality. 'From the moment I mentioned Robert Maxwell', he shouted at Mr Justice Sebag Shaw, 'I knew you were a Jew.... You have denied me justice.' There was no one in that court who did not feel that they were in the presence of evil.

The same month of September 1970, during which I prosecuted the evil Arthur Hosein for the kidnap and murder of Mrs McKay, brought with it personal and public crises.

From 23 June when we had come into office and throughout the summer, there had been the customary 'shaking-down' necessary for any new administration. In particular there had been the industrial troubles endemic at that time, requiring emergency provisions to be prepared and implemented. In the five weeks until the end of July, I attended nine Cabinets. That was the month in which Iain Macleod died, and the young administration seemed to shudder like a ship suddenly struck by a giant wave. It had lost the leading debater in the House of Commons – and Enoch, there was no Enoch, the figure who ought to have succeeded him. He was glowering on the backbenches, alienated, resentful at what he took to be betrayal by his Party colleagues for whom, he claimed, he had personally delivered in the general election the vital West Midland vote. There was now only Reggie Maudling as an alternative Prime Minister.

In August I had gone on a holiday (I would have no other for three years) to Antibes, to a villa which we had booked earlier in the year long before the election. It was a shuttered, ochre, mid-nineteenth-century house, up a lane and well back from the sea. It had a front garden with gravel paths encircling formal but neglected flowerbeds, admirable for children's terrifying bicycle races. We were joined by John and Belinda Eden and their family. Close by were Elaine's mother and her stepfather. They had come from the States and had rented a neighbouring villa. Suddenly, after a week, Elaine's stepfather was taken terribly ill and was removed to a nursing home in Antibes. The doctors seemed mystified and uncertain what to prescribe. He became weaker and he was clearly dying. I had to leave for London. A little later Elaine sent home the children with Minda, the round, kindly Portuguese who looked after our house now and then, and who had come to France with us on holiday. Elaine remained. Fortunately she had with her Luis, her brother, and soon her stepbrother Mat Dick junior arrived to take charge.

Back in London in the first week in September as I left our house in London in the early morning my driver, Albert Morley, who had come to collect me to take me to work, pointed silently to the front door. Somebody had been abroad the night before. Wide strips of heavy black tape had been stuck to the door. The strips formed a black cross. I peeled them off. Fortunately Elaine was still in France with her mother and her dying stepfather, and the children were not yet about. A few nights later a bomb was planted against that front door. For some miraculous reason the acid failed to cut through the wire which was meant to trigger the explosion. Instead the device flared, badly burning and scorching the door. There was enough explosive in the device had it detonated to have blown through the door and killed anyone behind it in the hall. We were very lucky.

It was the work of a small group of terrorists. Earlier the home of Sir John Waldron, the Metropolitan Police Commissioner, had been attacked. That attack too, had not caused much damage. But four months later in January 1971 the same group effectively exploded a bomb which ripped through the kitchen of the home of the then Minister of Labour, Robert Carr, causing extensive damage. By then the technique of the group of terrorists in activating an explosive device had improved.

The attack on my home in September 1970 was not at the time publicized. The police had come, and there then began the routine protection which was later to be massively increased when I figured on an IRA death list. The bomb attack on my home was not announced at the time and it only became known publicly late in January 1971, after the attack on Robert Carr, when a letter, 'Communiqué No. 5 from the Angry Brigade', a small anarchist group, was handed in to Fleet Street. It stated, 'We have started the fight back and the war will be won by the organised working class with bombs. We attack property not people. Carr, Rawlinson and Waldron would all be dead if we had wished.' In fact Robert and his wife had only narrowly escaped death. If the device at my home had worked as it had been intended that it should, I or my children might easily have died. In November 1971 two men, found in a flat which held a veritable arsenal of guns and explosives and describing themselves as revolutionaries and anarchists, were brought to trial for conspiring to cause explosions.

In 1970 the use of bombs and attempts to assassinate public figures was a new, or rather a newly revived, feature in public life. When I had been a Law Officer in the early 1960s, only the Prime Minister and the Home Secretary were thought to require personal protection, and that protection was fairly perfunctory. By 1974, when I left office, I had an armed personal-protection police officer with me wherever I went. At houses which I visited, he came and sat in the hall; in restaurants at the nearby table. Only in White's was he prepared to allow me on my own. I persuaded him that no terrorists would dare to penetrate those portals! My home in Sussex was bordered by a ray-protective system; eight armed police were stationed in the barn. All who approached were stopped and investigated. In the Temple another armed officer stood guard outside our flat. On one occasion this policeman on guard burst into the bedroom, revolver in hand 'Get down! Get down!' he shouted. That was not very necessary as we were in bed. 'They are here', he said. 'They are on the roof.' What was on the roof was a cat which had triggered the alarm. Silly as it seems now, it was not altogether agreeable at the time.

Another Special Branch officer accompanied Elaine. One son at Downside, Michael, had his room equipped with a special lock and a panic-button. He enjoyed the excitement. Another son, Anthony, at his pre-paratory school, was not allowed outside the grounds; the police watched the school gate. I felt sorry for any Evelyn Waugh-like prep-school masters who to their horror suddenly found themselves projected into a world of terrorists and real danger: they could hardly have bargained for that when they had signed on to teach grubby little boys. But the one to whom the whole matter caused real anxiety was our ten-year-old daughter, Angela. She would telephone from her convent boarding school to enquire if we were still alive. So we took her away and she went as a day-girl to another convent in Midhurst and her mother spent much time with her. But she suffered.

These were the consequences which modern public service imposed upon a family. The children of those in public life always do suffer. They read and hear and are teased about the criticisms of their fathers (or, nowadays, of their mothers); of how foolish, or dishonest, or ugly, or ludicrous are those whom the child loves and admires. My eldest son did not suffer at all from the fear of kidnap or assassination against which the ever constant armed police guard was designed to guard. That was all rather fun. But he did suffer from the many attacks in the press which schoolfriends were always eager to let Michael see. It cannot be expected that journalists should cease to attack a political figure just to avoid wounding his family. But the public figure has to calculate whether the glittering prizes are worth the pain which a public career can inflict upon his family. Perhaps that is why politicians, or I suppose all performers of any kind, have to grow an extra and toughened layer of skin. No wonder their children, as often as not, suffer and flinch.

The reality of physical danger took me back to my army days. It was an odd sensation to live like this amid the ordinariness of daily life; to go, for instance, to the Chichester theatre for a concert and to see that the whole of the back row had been cleared for us, and we sat there, isolated. When the drums crashed out and the cymbals banged, it was hard not to think of an Alfred Hitchcock movie when the muzzle of the assassin's rifle pokes through the curtain and at the moment of the musical crescendo, the shot is fired! But generally the people we were with were more alarmed than we. Those who lived up our lane in Sussex or beside us in London were at first resentful at this sudden intrusion of danger; but then they became rather grateful for the police presence which at least ensured that their houses were not robbed nor their cars vandalized.

We ourselves were fatalistic. We knew very well that those against whom I was being protected would, or rather could if they so wished, somehow or somewhere find an opportunity. I was most scared when an old Irish Guardsman, an RUC police officer, was driving me to the airport at Aldergrove, Belfast and the car broke down in the midst of nowhere. He pulled out his gun and was ready for the honour of the regiment to die in the ditch with me. But it was by my protector that I was alarmed. And I was certainly alarmed once in Strasbourg where I arrived for a hearing of the European Human Rights Commission. A French police car and a large motorcycle escort were to take me to where I was staying. We set off, the Ambassador at my side, at breathtaking speed. The police motorcyclists were around the car and ahead of it. The motorcyclists in the van of the procession when they came to a crossroad skidded to a halt and waited in the centre of the crossing, their white-gloved hands raised in the halt sign. The oncoming traffic, brakes squealing, was forced to stop in its tracks. Then our convoy thundered up and past, lights flashing, sirens hooting as we swept through the busy traffic of the city. It was an ashen-faced Attorney

General and Ambassador who clambered out of the car at the end of that drive.

At that time in the early 1970s, this was all very novel. For the first time there had arisen serious risk of assassination. A decade and more later, such are the times, it has become an accepted part of life – in Germany, in France, in Italy, in Brighton. Now former Secretaries of State have to retain their bodyguards and their homes are defended like fortresses. For ourselves, when I left government, I wanted the bodyguard presence no more: the price paid by a growing family was too high. So the guards went. Then, after a few months they suddenly came back. Finally they went for good. While with us they were very friendly. One Christmas we all played hockey with walking sticks and a tennis ball, the family against the force. One, a former confectioner, baked Elaine a cake for her birthday with yellow roses, her favourite flowers. My Special Branch officer energetically helped me saw fallen trees at weekends. Once, when I was gardening at my home in my overalls and an old hat, one of the new patrol of the Sussex police arrested me as a suspicious person. We were all good friends, and they were sensitive about the intrusion which they had to inflict on the family.

But there remained for me always the image of the small, drained face of our ten-year-old daughter. Have you really the right, I asked myself, to impose this? For what? Service to the country? These questions were not an inconsiderable factor in my decision when the time came to leave.

Chapter 19
Leila Khaled and the Hijack

On 7 September 1970 the bomb was planted against our front door. In France on 10 September, after a month of painful illness, Elaine's stepfather died. She came home, exhausted and sorrowing, two days later. The Hosein trial began on 14 September and went on for the next three weeks.

A week before the start of that trial, on 6 September, a young Arab girl and her male companion attempted to hijack an Israeli El Al airliner bound for New York out of Amsterdam. The hijackers kicked at the flight cabin door and shots were fired in the plane, which was immediately put into a steep dive. An El Al steward was wounded, the male hijacker was killed, and the girl overpowered. The aeroplane made an unscheduled landing at Heathrow. The girl and the body of the dead man were removed from the aircraft, which then took off and flew on.

The girl, Leila Khaled, was held under the Aliens Order, and the police began enquiries to compile their report to me. To launch a prosecution under British law it had to be established that the attack on the aircraft had taken place when the aircraft was over British land, not over the sea but the actual land. If the girl had been overpowered and the fight on the aircraft was over before the aircraft crossed the British coast the British courts would have no jurisdiction. Under the Tokyo Convention Act of 1967, Israel, in whose aircraft flying the Israeli flag the attack had been launched, had jurisdiction. Israel sought the extradition of the girl. This could be refused if the offence was of a 'political' character, but in the event the Israeli government did not persist in their application.

The El Al aircraft had departed as swiftly and as suddenly as it had arrived. The police had to make such enquiries as they could to determine where exactly the aircraft was during the attack and before the girl had been overpowered. The records of the conversations between the pilot and the ground control were studied and checked. The first message from the Captain reporting trouble on the aircraft stated categorically that he was 'south of Clacton' and that the hijack had begun a few seconds before 12.43 p.m., the time when the aircraft was about to cross the English coast. Both of the hijackers had been very swiftly overcome. The maximum error in the bearings could be between two or three miles. On 10 September the first and preliminary police report was brought to me.

Meanwhile on the afternoon of 9 September a BOAC VC–10, under the British flag on a flight from Bombay to London with fifty-three passengers including women and children, was hijacked. It was taken to Dawson's Field in Jordan, in which country civil war was raging. At the same time other hijackers were busy. A Swissair DC–8 and a TWA 707 joined the VC–10 in the desert. The crews and passengers were held hostage, sixty-five of them British. Among the demands made by the hijackers was the release of Leila Khaled. They threatened to destroy the VC–10 and kill the hostages unless she was immediately freed. An international negotiation began to secure the release of all the hostages of the various nationalities who were held in the desert.

The decision whether to prosecute Leila Khaled was for me, and for me alone. Critics have subsequently tried to blame Ted Heath for what ultimately happened. They have accused him of being weak and soft on terrorism because, in the end, the girl was not prosecuted but deported and flown out of the country. That criticism is unfair. He played no part in the decision. He personally was not consulted. He was informed. He brought no pressure upon me one way or the other. He knew and respected the constitutional position. The decision had to be mine. And so it was.

On 10 September I discussed the preliminary police report with the Assistant Director of Public Prosecutions and the police. I needed further information, and more enquiries were set in hand. What was needed was proof beyond reasonable doubt of the exact location of the aircraft during the few seconds of the attack on the aircraft which was concluded when the girl was overpowered. But when considering the grant of his *fiat* or leave to prosecute, an Attorney General may, indeed he must, take into account the public interest arising out of instituting or refusing to institute a prosecution. He is entitled to consult whomsoever he wishes. I knew of course of the hijacking of the aircraft in Jordan and of reports of the demands for the release of Leila Khaled and the threat to murder the British hostages. In order to receive his official opinion I wrote to the Foreign Secretary enquiring what would be the effect upon the progress of the negotiations in Jordan to secure the release of all the hostages were

Leila Khaled to be prosecuted. Alec Douglas-Home replied that he would give me his answer the next day, 11 September. So I awaited that opinion and the answers to the questions which I had posed to the police.

The next day I heard from Alec. He gave his opinion, after contact with officials in Jordan where the fighting was continuing, that a charge at this juncture would increase the danger to the hostages. I had heard no more from the police, and indeed it was not until 25 September that I received their definitive report. Accordingly I deferred any decision over whether to prosecute. On 12 September the Embassy at Amman informed the Foreign Office that unless it was announced that Leila Khaled was to be released, the Embassy and is staff would be attacked. I made it known that, at this time, I was not ordering that the girl should be charged but that this decision related only to the circumstances prevailing at this date. I still had not had the report from the police.

On 14 September I began the prosecution of the Hosein brothers at the Old Bailey and it was there, on the 18th, that I heard further from Alec, in reply to another enquiry from me, that he was still of the opinion that a charge would increase the danger to the lives of the hostages, of whom by now only six British still remained in the hands of the hijackers. The others had been successfully negotiated into freedom.

When the definitive police report reached me a week later, I discussed it with the police and with the Director of Public Prosecutions, Norman Skelhorn. He had succeeded Toby Mathew in 1964. We had been silks together on the Western Circuit. His role was to express his opinion whether there was sufficient evidence to give a reasonable chance of a conviction were Leila Khaled to be charged. There was some suggestion that some of the crew of the El Al aircraft might return for any trial, but, whether they would or not, the crucial issue was the evidence of the precise location of the aircraft. The statements in the police report therefore concentrated upon the interpretation of radar signals, the flight plot of the aircraft, and the recorded messages from the flight-deck. Norman expressed his view that there was sufficient evidence to launch a prosecution.

But I was troubled. This was no ordinary case, in which, if the prosecution failed, all that it meant was that some person, at worst a scoundrel, might go free. Here the launching of the prosecution itself could cost innocent lives. What if it did, and then the prosecution failed on a technicality? The first message from the Captain about the hijack put his position as 'south of Clacton'. That must have put him over the sea and not over land when the hijack began. The Captain had immediately put the aircraft into a steep dive and in seconds it was all over. One hijacker had immediately been shot by the security guard and the girl was thrown off balance and was swiftly overcome. For the Captain to have sent that first 'south of Clacton' message meant that when he sent it he knew that an attempted hijack had begun. So the hijack must have begun before the aircraft crossed the coast. Moreover, radar bearings were capable of error. The issue was critical. Could I be certain that it could be proved beyond reasonable doubt that when the girl was overpowered the aircraft was not 'south of Clacton' but had actually crossed over the English coast?

In my opinion defence counsel, properly instructed, might be able, quite scrupulously, to arouse sufficient doubt. If so, the English Court had no jurisdiction and the girl would have to be released. What then of the hostages? What if they had been murdered when the prosecution was announced? How would that seem to the bereaved or to the public if people had died and then the prosecution failed? In the result I was satisfied that I would not take the risk of the failure of the prosecution in a case where the actual incidence of bringing a prosecution could bring in its train the death of others. I made a final enquiry of the Foreign Office in case the pressure by the hijackers holding the hostages had eased. I received the same reply as that which I had been given earlier.

On 27 September I made my decision. I had very well in mind the effect then and for the future of letting this hijacker go free. But I had to make a judgment. At 4.15 that afternoon at No. 10 I informed the Prime Minister and his colleagues that I did not intend to prefer charges and prosecute Leila Khaled. On 30 September the last British hostages were freed in Jordan, and she was flown out of the country. The decision, right or wrong, was mine alone.

A hijack, a murder trial, a bomb at my house and a death in the family – September 1970 was a month to be remembered.

Chapter 20
Some Foreigners

A part of the life of Attorney, like that of all ministers, involves inter-government traffic with international opposite numbers. This is often intrinsically entertaining but is also often distracting and time-consuming, especially when it involves trips away from the daily grind of the office in the law courts.

One such was a Commonwealth Law Officers' Conference, slotted into a more general Law Conference, which was held in India and which the Lord Chancellor Quintin Hailsham and I had to attend in New Delhi in 1971. It was all cheerfully and agreeably chaotic, and the chaos began when the bags of Michael de Winton, the official who was accompanying me, were sent on to Bangkok, and he accordingly lost a great deal of face, which the loan of my shirts (they were far too tight for him) only served to exaggerate. During this visit Ted Heath came to Delhi to confer with Mrs Gandhi prior to their both making their way east to the Commonwealth Prime Ministers' Conference meeting in Singapore.

One evening Quintin and I were bidden to the High Commission to a dinner for the two Prime Ministers. We were advised to come early if we wanted a drink since not even in Embassies was liquor served when the Indian Premier was present. Indira Gandhi sat as sour as ever until, after dinner, Quintin begain to reminisce about his father and electioneering long ago. Her face suddenly lit up and she began lovingly and humorously to speak about her father and of his early days in the Congress movement and of trials and imprisonment. She spoke gaily and without bitterness, linking India and her father to her British hosts as though we were all part of the same family, some of whom however had not behaved quite as well as she would have wished. Years later I represented her in a libel action which was eventually settled, and I was glad to have witnessed the more jolly side to her virago image.

The following day there was a great luncheon on the lawn of Lutyens' Viceregal Lodge, now the presidential palace. I was seated opposite the Indian Chief of Staff who, with his bristling moustache and clipped speech, was the very model of a modern major-general. Behind us as we sat at the long tables stood the Presidential Guard, the Household troops in their blue patrols and turbans. In honour of the visiting Prime Minister, the toast to the Queen was proposed. As we all stood, the band struck up 'God Save the Queen'.

I looked across the table at the General in his khaki uniform and red tabs and beyond him at the Household troops and beyond them to the carefully tended English gardens. One hundred years earlier Sir Christopher Rawlinson had been Chief Justice at Madras; thirty years later the young Rudyard Kipling, who had fed my brother and me with tea-cakes and had given us tin soldiers, was scribbling in Lahore in the offices of the *Civil and Military Gazette*; twenty years later still General Lord Rawlinson, a namesake who looked far less a general than my luncheon companion, had been Commander-in-Chief and had died in the house nearby which had been taken over by Pandit Nehru and was now a national shrine.

As the notes of the anthem faded and we drank the toast from our glasses of orange juice, the Raj seemed strangely close. I thought about that curious (love–hate) relationship which the Empire still seemed to inspire. Earlier I had crossed swords, quite jovially, with John Turner, then the Canadian Attorney General, and I reflected upon the proprietary right to attack us which Commonwealth ministers often assumed, and their propensity to get upset if we appeared to react. Admittedly whenever an outsider attempted to join in, it was made clear that the quarrel was nothing to do with them. Once in Australia when I was the victim an American chipped in. To his consternation he was at one rounded upon. Not for him the privilege of Pommie-bashing. That was a family sport. But at Commonwealth Conferences some of the chips on shoulders became a little tedious.

The most controversial Commonwealth Attorney General of my time was Lionel Murphy, the Australian Attorney General in Gough Whitlam's administration. Later he was appointed to the Australian High Court. That great Chief Justice, Sir Owen Dixon, must have turned in his grave when the maverick Murphy joined the Court over which Sir Owen had presided for so many years with such grace and distinction – especially when Mr Justice Murphy was later convicted of attempting to pervert the course of justice. The conviction was overturned on appeal, but the Chief Justice Sir Harry Gibbs protested upon Murphy's return to the Bench.

When he was Attorney General, Lionel Murphy had come to London with Australia's federal Prime Minister, Gough Whitlam, who was seeking an amendment to the Australian constitution to alter the relationship between the federal government and the Australian states, most of whose premiers were however of the same political party as Whitlam and Murphy but were vehemently opposed to any change. The state premiers came to protest to Alec Douglas-Home, who had been deputed to handle the problem on behalf of the British government. Alec had brought me into the negotiations.

The position of the British government was simply that anything required by way of amending legislation in the United Kingdom would immediately be presented to the United Kingdom Parliament once the Australians gave us their agreed recommendation. This at that time they failed to do. Later John Turner of Canada came on a similar mission in respect of Canada and the provinces. For a time, we became pig-in-the-middle in what were wholly Australian and Canadian internal squabbles until a few years later both governments resolved their constitutional differences with their states or provinces and both presented recommendations to amend the Acts which had originally established their respective constitutions. The Westminster amending legislation was thereupon duly enacted.

Sadly, both Canada and Australia abolished appeals to the Judicial Committee of the Privy Council and only a few minor Commonwealth nations retain the use of its appellate jurisdiction. Reggie Dilhorne, when he was Lord Chancellor, had sought to establish a peripatetic Judicial Committee manned by Commonwealth judges which would sit to hear appeals in the country of origin of the appeal and would be presided over by a judge of that country assisted by other Commonwealth judges. This would have established a supreme Commonwealth court of great distinction which would have contributed greatly to the prestige of the common law and provided a practical bond of real significance for an organization whose relevance and unity are rapidly fading. But it was not to be, and nationalistic pride prevented the inception of a common judicial link.

When Lionel Murphy was in London with Gough Whitlam, I gave a dinner party for him at Admiralty House. It was intended to be a social occasion to give him a chance during his visit to meet some of the natives other than politicians. So I invited judges and businessmen and actors, hoping to provide him with an agreeable evening as a break from his official duties. Murphy arrived at Admiralty House late and tight. At the end of the dinner I proposed the health of Australia and of her Attorney General, expressed the affection and admiration of all of us present for his great country, etc., etc. Murphy then lurched to his feet and launched into a slurred but offensive attack on British colonialism, the British government and the British people. The Acting High Commissioner buried his head in his hands. Murphy swayed and wobbled and at intervals gobbled from his glass until he finally collapsed back into his chair. Shortly thereafter he got to his feet and swayed away into the night. Someone bundled him into his car.

I did not see him again for five years, when I was in Australia lecturing to some of the universities upon the life of Thomas More. At a dinner in Sydney where I was speaking, Lionel Murphy, by then Mr Justice Murphy of the great Australian High Court, loomed up. He greeted me like a long-lost brother, slept noisily throughout my lecture and, when it was over, warmly congratulated me on its perception and insight. He might have been a rather splendid, iconoclastic character out of a novel by Evelyn Waugh, but he lacked charm and his fall was regretted neither by his former ministerial colleagues nor by the judges of the distinguished court of which he was briefly a member.

Another Attorney General of my time, an equally controversial character, was John Mitchell of the United States. He came to London in the summer of 1971 when the American Bar held their annual conference there. He was accompanied by his wife Martha, who became famous in the States as 'Martha the Mouth', because from it there came even then dire hints of what the Nixon administration was up to. Her warnings were at the time taken as the ramblings of a tired and over-emotional lady, but they were in fact the first hints of what was later unearthed after the break-in of 'the plumbers' at Watergate. She turned out to be the incoherent Cassandra who even in 1971 was warning that all would end in ashes, as indeed it eventually did for herself, her husband and her President. Elaine had the difficult task of looking after her in London.

The ABA conference began with a great ceremonial assembly in Westminster Hall, with the English, at the request of the Americans, dressed in all the legal finery of their quaint wigs and robes. Quintin as Lord Chancellor was the first to welcome the guests and in doing so he proclaimed his kinship with them through his American mother. I followed him and spoke of my American wife. I claimed superiority since my affiliation had come through the successful prosecution of a suit. My colleagues winced but the visitors purred.

There followed two weeks of meetings, speeches and receptions. I had to host a major reception at Lancaster House, receiving the guests at the top of the great staircase, up which, as one of the guests, skipped George Brown doing a jig to the music of the Irish Guards Band which was playing in the hall. One gushing American lady declared to Elaine that she just loved our house and enquired if we also had anywhere in the country. Elaine gravely and truthfully replied that we had a house in Sussex.

Then I hosted a dinner for all the past and present Law Officers of the Crown and of the Republic. We sat everyone at round tables. At mine I had, of course, Martha on my right. As soon as we sat down she grabbed my right hand and held it in a grip of iron. I was obliged to cut and eat everything with my left, a practice to which I was not accustomed, while she muttered darkly that she ought to tell all. I did not know at the time what she meant, although like all the world I did later. She only let go her grip when I had to get up to make my speech. After dinner she wandered off and climbed the great staircase and got lost in the darkened upstairs rooms. John Mitchell went after her like a retriever, calling out, 'Mother, where are you, mother?' Eventually he caught her and brought her back. She was very tight and he was very gentle.

John and Martha were certainly an odd couple. When the Conference ended she wept on Elaine's shoulder. We were never quite sure why. After he had resigned as Attorney General to become chairman of the committee to re-elect Richard Nixon, his immediate successor while on a visit to England called on me at the Law Courts. Subsequently both these United States Attorneys General were indicted.

Two years later I was invited to address the ABA Conference in Washington. I had been asked to speak about the duties of an Attorney General, but the Watergate hearings had begun in the Congress and I swiftly changed my subject to something less sensitive. I talked with Elliott Richardson, an Attorney General with very different standards from those of his immediate predecessors and at the time a very troubled man. He took me to the offices of the then recently appointed Special Prosecutor, Archie Cox, whom I had last met when Bobby Kennedy was the United States Attorney General. They were literally a fortress guarded by security men and with elaborate electrical surveillance and admission controls. The Special Prosecutor was taking no chances from 'plumbers', the unlawful White House burglars.

Then I met Robert Bork, the Solicitor General who, on Elliott's refusal to act upon Nixon's instructions and on his subsequent resignation, was obliged, at Elliott's request, to remain in office and to sack Archie Cox.

When I first saw him I thought I was in the presence of some eccentric revolutionary. He had a straggly red beard and a deceptively casual manner which concealed his remarkable intellect. It is an odd constitutional system which allows a group led by men of the quality of Senators Kennedy and Biden to block the Supreme Court from acquiring a jurist of such eminence as Robert Bork. Of the three Kennedys whom I met, Jack, Bobby and Edward, Edward was obviously and patently vastly inferior.

Many years later, I was walking through Georgetown with Mat Dick. I noticed a short, hunched figure, pipe in mouth, come out of a house and scurry off down a side-road. It was John Mitchell, not long released from prison. I called after him. He turned and stared at me. Then he abruptly disappeared into the crowds on Massachusetts Avenue.

Chapter 21
Negotiation with Ian Smith

On a wet Sunday afternoon in November 1971 I reported to the Alcock and Brown VIP lounge at London Airport. Soon there ambled into the lounge the ample and significant figure of Arnold Goodman. A little later Alec and Elizabeth Douglas-Home and Denis Greenhill, the Permanent Under-Secretary at the Foreign Office, entered in a swirl of official ceremony. Then we all walked across the tarmac and boarded the special VC-10 which was to take us to Salisbury in Rhodesia. The first official negotiation with Ian Smith since Harold Wilson's abortive attempts six years earlier had begun.

For several months Arnold had been flitting around Southern Africa as our unofficial undercover emissary. He could never be inconspicuous, nor had he been. On occasion he had been seen there in the company of Max Aitken. During these very unsecret trips Arnold had done the groundwork which now permitted a full-scale attempt to settle the dispute and bring Rhodesia back to international respectability. It was on this quest that we took off into a cold night of November rain.

As we were voyaging to an international 'pariah', we were not permitted to overfly certain countries. So the flight, including a fuel stop at Bahrain, was to take eighteen hours. We were due to land at Salisbury at two o'clock the following afternoon. The aircraft was set up to provide a conference cabin in the stern, which could be converted into a dining table. We were accompanied by a group of specialist advisers. We settled down to work around the conference table. Then it was cleared and we dined. After dinner Alec and Elizabeth disappeared into the sternmost cabin, which had been fitted with bunks. The crew began to lay two mattresses on either side of the deck in the narrow waist of the aircraft. Arnold and I were ushered to the mattresses. I watched in trepidation as the vast bulk of Lord

Goodman disappeared beneath the blankets on the port side of the deck and I prayed that the pilot had a steady hand and would have no need suddenly to bank. If he did, I was done for. But the night was calm and I survived, uncrushed.

Before we left London the Foreign Office had advised that a light, tropical suit would be required, adding a trifle condescendingly that an allowance would be provided to finance its provision. So a smart tropical suit had been miraculously built for me within a few days and now lay to hand ready for our arrival. When we were still a few hours from our scheduled landing, the Old Africa Hands on board knowingly warned us of what to expect when we landed and emerged into the stiflingly blinding heat of southern Africa.

On the tarmac as we came in to land the welcoming party was huddled under umbrellas. It was bitterly cold. We came down the steps briskly and walked to the waiting cars. Alec and I were driven to Marimba House, the residence of the British High Commissioner, which had stood empty since the unilateral declaration of independence. Fortunately we were met with blazing fires. I changed, and put my new suit at the bottom of my suitcase. Within two hours of landing we set off, shivering with cold, to the first plenary session.

The two teams sat, as is customary, facing each other across a long table in the Cabinet office of the Salisbury government. Alec was flanked by Arnold and myself, with Denis beside Arnold. Ian Smith had beside him Jack Howman, the Minister for Foreign Affairs, who seemed rather jolly in the style of the secretary of a golf-club; and Desmond Lardner-Burke, the Minister of Justice and of Law and Order, who sat silent and grim. Ian Smith in greeting was brusque, with an air of self-confidence which later in the week I came to suspect was much assumed. He seemed at this first meeting determined to demonstrate that he was not to be overborne whatever the cunning and tricks which he now had to encounter. I glanced down the table at that formidable duo, Arnold and Denis, and I understood what he must have felt. They were so very, very reasonable; and, behind the scenes, so very, very funny. For my part I assumed an expression of what I hoped was inscrutable craftiness as I backed up my leader.

To rebut the assumption that these negotiations were merely a show and that Her Majesty's government had come to Salisbury to settle in order to escape from tiresome domestic political problems with their supporters, the government had made plain that it was firmly locked into the five principles which had been first promulgated by Alec himself in 1964 when he was Prime Minister. They remained the prerequisites for any settlement.

The five principles were: unimpeded progress towards majority rule; guarantees against retrogressive amendment of the constitution; immediate improvement in the political status of the African population; progress towards ending racial discrimination; and the basis for a settlement leading to recognition of independence must be acceptable to the people of Rhodesia as a whole.

In the event, it was this last on which the settlement foundered. For it was the effective rejection of the terms by the inhabitants of Rhodesia which led to the escalating bush war after the withdrawal of Portugal from her colonies, and finally to the birth of Zimbabwe. Yet that the terms of the settlement would be acceptable to the African population Ian Smith at that time was supremely confident. Later he blamed their rejection on the delay by HMG in establishing the commission and in getting down to work. But when the judge, Lord Pearce, and his commissioners took the terms to the people it became apparent that Ian Smith did not really know the people of the country for which he held so passionate an affection. He had become the victim of his own propaganda, so certain was he that the salaried chiefs and the black MPs indirectly elected by the tribal electoral colleges really represented the majority opinion. They did not.

As the week of negotiation passed, my initial reservations about Ian Smith, arising from his original attitude and bearing, altered. It was impossible not to acknowledge his stubborn courage and his personal integrity, while at the same time one was astounded at his refusal to look beyond the frontiers of his beleaguered state to appreciate that there existed a world outside which fiercely rejected his patriarchal politics and racial policies. He would heed no warning about the rumblings of change in Lisbon which might bring the neighbouring Portuguese colonial regimes tumbling down. He could not perceive that in the modern world paternal minority government was unacceptable, even if the alternative ultimately might prove to be corrupt and repressive and tribal. There was a rugged integrity in his simplistic stand. He certainly towered in personality over all others whom I met during that week of meetings. The only African of authority seemed to be the bulky Joshua Nkomo, the Matabele leader, who was being held in custody by the Smith government. He was later brought from detention to Marimba and talked to Alec as I sat with them among the oleanders in the garden of Marimba House. He, and not Robert Mugabe, was then seen as the significant leader of the Africans in Rhodesia.

After the first plenary session we had gone back to Marimba to dine. Denis and Arnold and the others who were quartered in Meikle's Hotel, ten minutes drive from the residence, joined us. We were all tired and rather disconsolate. The discredited Old Africa Hands wagged their heads and muttered that the weather was quite unlike what they had ever experienced before, but no one listened now. I reflected that the only use I could find for my new suit might be at some distant date in the Palm Beach Casino in Cannes. We all trooped, shivering, to bed.

So began seven hectic days of plenary sessions and private meetings between Alec and Ian Smith, as well as meetings with countless groups of representative opinion, black and white, who flocked to Marimba House. To receive most of the delegations, I accompanied Alec. The black Africans generally seemed desperately anxious that Alec should effect some settlement. There was, at that time, no belief that there was any alternative to negotiating an agreement with the all-powerful Smith government, and they felt that any agreement even if not perfect would at least make for some improvement in their lot. I, however, met a Jesuit Father. From him, and from him alone, I received just a faint hint that there might after all be an alternative to settlement and to signatures and to pieces of embossed paper, an alternative which lurked in secret in armed camps deep in the bush. As ever with Jesuits, it is usually wise to listen very carefully. But in the main all others pressed for a settlement with Smith.

I was invited to meet the Bar. This was arranged as a non-political occasion, a visit from the head of the English Bar to fellow professionals. The Rhodesian Bar was at that time multi-racial. All shared the library, from which they worked. All were colleagues and equal adversaries in court. I spent most of my short visit in conversation with two black barristers. I learned that under the Land Tenure Act, black professional men had to obtain a permit to practise in a designated European district and that, after court, the black and white left their common library and went to their homes in the segregated districts. So much, I thought, for what Ian Smith so complacently called his 'meritocrat society'. Thereafter I pressed the Rhodesians on this. It became a feature in arguments, illustrating the invalidity of any claim that conditions depended solely upon achievement and qualification.

The weather had changed. It had now grown muggy, with fine periods interspersed with thunder and showers. The cold and the wood fires had gone. One afternoon I was due to meet and listen to representations from a Chief Tangwena. The Chief when he arrived was old and rather dazed. He was accompanied by two or three very sharp young men. At the time of his visit Marimba was a hive of activity, with streams of visitors coming and going. Each room was filled with deputations and lobbies. As the sun was shining, I suggested to the Chief that we should sit and talk outside.

The interpreter conveyed the old Chief's agreement. So we filed out into the garden, took some chairs from under a tree in front of the house and sat in a semi-circle in the sunshine on the lawn by the oleanders. There were about four or five in the Chief's party; with me were two of our party from London. Black and white seats were thus lowered on to the chairs, visitors and hosts alike. But those chairs later led to trouble back home.

The Chief's story was sad and it was told dramatically. He and his people were being compulsorily moved off their tribal lands. The police had come and tried to drive them away, burning their huts. Through his interpreter the Chief said that he was old and soon to die. But if he were to die in land other than that of his ancestors, his spirit could never join theirs and would be condemned to wander restless among alien ghosts. He asked that the Great Mother, the Queen, should protect him and his tribe and should punish the evildoers who sought to drive him from the lands of his ancestors. He acted out his death and the flight of his spirit. His words were interpreted by the sharp young men, whom Ian Smith would, I suppose, have called agitators. In view of what was later made of this incident, he might have been right.

The expulsion of the Chief and his people from their tribal lands arose from the operation of the much hated Land Tenure Act. I had been pressing the amendment of this Act on behalf of the professional men and for the abolition of permits. Now here was vivid illustration of the need for further amendment of the Act to give protection to Africans with established rights from eviction from their homes unless it was justified in the public interest. The visit of the old Chief had been well worthwhile.

We heard the Chief and his young men out and we then walked with him to his car. I was not conscious that anyone had been or felt insulted. Nor was I conscious that the seat of my pants was damp. Two days later, back in London, a newspaper carried a feature article on the negotiations in Salisbury. It reported that on my visit to the Bar I had pointedly ignored and refused to speak to any of the black barristers, and that I had deliberately insulted Chief Tangwena by obliging an old man and his entourage to sit on chairs swimming with rainwater. It was not only the Rhodesian Front, a group of peculiarly unlovely and hard-faced men whom we had seen earlier in the week, who were up to tricks.

Towards the end of the week it appeared that the negotiation was failing. Ian Smith began to bluster. Alec remained firm. On the Friday night we settled down to draft terms of settlement. Next morning there was deadlock again. That night I dined with Denis and Arnold in their hotel. We were eyed suspiciously by the white diners. Arnold and Denis had by this time developed between them a kind of sophisticated patter-act, and our table became rather noisy with laughter. The suspicious looks turned into glares. It was as though we were laughing in church.

On the Sunday, after Mass in the Catholic cathedral and then lunch with Sir Roy Welensky, former Prime Minister of the Federation of Rhodesia and Nyasaland, I was driven for an hour or two into the country, my first and only chance to see something of it; for it had been arranged that I was to fly back on the Monday night to report to the Cabinet. But if the deadlock continued, the whole delegation would leave. The VC-10 and its crew were told to stand by, a traditional diplomatic move which concentrates wonderfully the minds of international negotiators.

By Monday we had reached the definite drafting stage of a settlement and therefore I alone was to return to the UK 'to fulfil', as the official explanation had it, 'an urgent engagement in London', which a British source said 'was not connected with the Rhodesian issue'. My return was of course to report to the Cabinet, although it did coincide with an urgent but private engagement. This was our removal from Chelsea Square, where we had lived for fifteen years, into the Temple prior to occupying our recently acquired house in Sussex which was then under the builders. But such is the language, economical with the truth, that diplomatic negotiation often demands. I flew back overnight and went straight to Downing Street. There I telephoned to Alec in Salisbury to get the latest news of the negotiations. Then I reported to the Cabinet. As a result a further cable was sent to Salisbury.

The next day we moved house. Even if I was not very helpful, I was at least there. It marked for us the end of an era. From that house Elaine had gone to bear all our children. It had witnessed the salad days of our marriage. It was suggested in the press that we had moved because of the bomb attack, which had only recently been made public. But in fact we had decided that our family had now reached an age when they would be better in the country. The dangers which we feared came rather from our nearness to the liberalized King's Road than from the terrorists.

On 1 December the House debated the proposals for the Rhodesian settlement which Alec had brought back from Salisbury. Under the first of the five principles, the settlement provided fresh enfranchisement based upon income and education qualifications; under the second, guarantee against retrogressive amendments to the constitution with a blocking mechanism of elected Africans; under the third, a large increase in the African electorate and an immediate increase in the number of African MPs; under the fourth, progress towards ending racial discrimination, a justiciable

Declaration of Rights with review by an independent commission agreed with HMG; and under the fifth, a test of acceptability of the proposals by the Rhodesian people as a whole by a commission under the judge Lord Pearce to canvass thoroughly and impartially the views of all sections of Rhodesian opinion. Only if the Commission were satisfied that the proposals were acceptable to the Rhodesian people as a whole would the Rhodesian government proceed to amend the constitution and HMG proceed to its new legislation.

The Foreign Secretary presented the proposals which had been set out in a White Paper. I was to wind up the debate. This last speaker has to speak for the last thirty minutes of the debate, no more and no less. If he speaks for less, that would let in an Opposition speaker and for the government the debate would have been mishandled, to the chagrin and resentment of government supporters and with much loss of governmental face. If he speaks for more, then the motion is lost and the resentment of colleagues is even greater. The Chief Whip usually takes up station on the bench to pull the coat-tails of the final speaker to get him down, if necessary in mid-sentence, just as the clock begins to strike. The absolute requirement to keep rigidly to the half-hour time span contributes to making the 'wind-up' the most difficult of all parliamentary speeches. The House is often noisy at the end of a debate, certainly of a major one, with the Opposition baying for government blood. In a debate on such a controversial subject, passions would be running exceedingly high, the noise and the interruptions and the attempts to disrupt would obviously be immense.

Years before, when about to rise to wind up another debate, I had said ruefully to Iain Macleod: 'What if I run out of things to say?' 'Just keep talking', he advised cheerfully. The trick is to have prepared, and to keep rigidly separate and sacred, the notes for the last five minutes of the speech. These must be put on one side and however great the temptation they must never be touched until those last few minutes. So if the Minister winding up runs out of real matter before the moment arises when he can take up the notes of his final argument, he just has to follow the advice of Iain Macleod – to keep talking, but not by using what he has prepared for those final minutes.

Winding up, then, a fierce debate is always a hair-raising experience, far more difficult to handle than any address in court or from a platform or any after-dinner speech. In front of the Speaker sit, or loll, rows of shouting unfriendly representatives of the people, eager to throw the speaker off his stride, to trap him into loss of temper, or to frighten him into indiscretion. Behind him are his ministerial colleagues, often nervous lest their man fail them. Behind them sit the backbenchers ready to cheer success but merciless in their silence in the event of failure. Harold Macmillan, even in the full flower of his debating glory, used to confess that he felt physically sick from apprehension before winding up a controversial debate in the House of Commons. I certainly did on that evening.

Because of its importance the hours for this debate had been extended by one hour. So I rose to wind up at 10.30 p.m. precisely. Eleven o'clock sharp marked the finish. The interruptions soon began. They are usually to be welcomed because they fill in time and at least make certain that the speaker will have no shortage of prepared material. The danger is that they throw the speaker wholly out of his stride.

Like a batsman whose innings has at last begun, the apprehension of the speaker subsides, or at least reduces, when he gets to his feet and is off. On this evening Denis Healey, of course, began the interruptions; then Sam Silkin; then Elwyn Jones, while the bearded, erstwhile actor (and private good sort) Andrew Faulds began, as usual, to shout. The House erupted. The noise rose before me like the physical force of a gale of wind. It was this phenomenon of sheer noise which Alec Home said that he had forgotten when in 1963 he had renounced his peerage and returned to the Commons, leaving behind him the genteel debating proprieties of the Lords. The Opposition was certainly noisy on this evening. But the interruptions carried me along. At last the final five minutes had arrived. I was home.

I picked up my carefully husbanded last sheaf of notes. 'It would', I bellowed in conclusion, 'be criminal irresponsibility not to give all who honestly and sincerely want to assist the people of Rhodesia a chance to make up their own minds. If they reject the proposals, so be it. But it would be criminal irresponsibility not to give the people of Rhodesia, all the people of Rhodesia, the opportunity to express their views.' It was eleven o'clock precisely, and I sat down to what *The Times* described as 'loud Opposition cries of "Shame"'.

In the event, the people of Rhodesia did reject our proposals. Between our ministerial visit and the arrival of the Commission, many had been at work in the townships and in the tribal lands. Ian Smith said the Commission had been too long delayed. Be that right or wrong, there was not by then sufficient support for the proposals and they fell by default.

But it had been a remarkable effort by Alec. The collapse of Portuguese colonial rule (hinted at by the clever Jesuit father), the unification of the armed groups fighting in the bush and the generous material support which they began to receive brought down the Smith regime eight years later and ushered in Robert Mugabe. A transition might have come about peacefully, with less bloodshed and less tribal strife if in those eight years the proposals in Alec's statement had been fairly and honestly operated and the movement to majority rule had been permitted to evolve from an enlarged franchise in faithful compliance with the new constitutional rules. But for that to have been allowed to happen would have depended upon the fair implementation of the new rules evolved in this negotiation between Alec and Ian Smith. Some are certain that the white Rhodesia Front would never have permitted the new rules to operate. If that had been so it would have been without the consent of Ian Smith. To what he had agreed and signed I believe that his stubborn spirit would have kept him true.

After the debate, weary and exhausted, but mightily relieved, I met Elaine in my room in the Commons. Before the ordeal she had sent to my room a note with a single rose. I kept it as a memento of participating in a failure, a footnote in history, an effort not without merit but one which events overtook and which is now forgotten.

Chapter 22
Police Protection – The Rolls-Royce Affair

An ordinary day began each morning at about eight-thirty. After November 1971, all I had to do was to cross Fleet Street to the Law Courts from our flat in the Temple. We had moved there when we bought a farmhouse in Sussex from the family estate of John Wyndham, whom I had known slightly when he was in the Private Office of Harold Macmillan. Alas, soon after we bought the house he became very ill and was nursed to the end by his wife, the remarkable and beautiful Pamela. He died in 1972.

Douglaslake was a farmhouse with a Georgian elevation, largely built in stone, part brick, part weather-tiled. It was a scheduled building, surrounded by out-buildings including three barns, a granary and a half-timbered bakehouse and copper house. We restored it, and we made a garden. I used to dig up old bottles and eighteenth-century clay pipes and once unearthed a George III penny. We put a crescent-shaped swimming-pool between the barns. Early on Monday mornings in summer I could swim naked in the pool waiting for Albert and the car to take me to London. Elaine could not, since the place was crawling with police.

That may have been one of the reasons why we were never very happy there. There was too much disruption of normal life. One Christmas night the children's acting was interrupted by my speaking at length on a telephone link to the Prime Minister and Home Secretary. Next morning, Boxing Day, a helicopter landed on the field opposite and took me to Chequers. The local hunt and the neighbours, already inconvenienced by the police cars, were not amused.

One evening in late summer of 1973, Elaine had a party of children to swim and have supper. Dusk was falling when I saw a Volkswagen car with foreign number plates come down the lane. It stopped outside the gate. Two men, bearded and unkempt, got out and came through the yard to the house. Two others stayed in the car. The police in plain clothes strolled casually out of the barn which they used as their guardroom and where they had their radio and telephone links and their weapons. I could see them talking. The men from the Volkswagen were clearly demanding something. The police, I could see, shook their heads and pointed back at the car. The two men gesticulated, obviously angry. Eventually they turned and went back to the car. I called out to the police and asked what the men had wanted. I was told that they had wanted to camp in the field by the house. By now it was growing quite dark and all the lights in the house had been switched on. The children's party was in full swing. I saw the Volkswagen reverse in front of the house and turn very slowly. The group in the car seemed reluctant to go. Then the car roared up the lane and the light from its headlights disappeared round the bend. I went back to my work. The children's party was still going strong. Suddenly all the lights went out – in the house and in the police guardroom. Pandemonium broke loose.

Some of the police rushed into the house with their rifles and stumbled to the upstairs windows. They believed that the cables had been cut at the end of the lane where the foreign Volkswagen and its bearded crew had disappeared. Elaine brought candles. I saw the frightened faces of the children. She led them all to the back of the house and sat them at a table. I joined her and we tried to play games. Soon police cars, summoned on the radio, screamed up the lane. Road blocks were thrown up. More and more armed men surrounded the house. Others came inside. The police felt sure that an attack impended. Their air of urgency could not be concealed from the children.

After an hour or so the lights came on. It had been a power failure, not sabotage. The grumpy, bearded foreigners had not been terrorists after all. So the extra police drove away, leaving the regular garrison behind. The unfortunate mothers who had been stopped at the road blocks arrived ashen-faced. They collected their children rapidly and drove off to the tranquillity of their own peaceful homes. The Rawlinsons at Douglaslake were not popular party-givers, save with some of the older boys who swanked that they had not been at all frightened and it was all a bit of a lark. But I remembered their faces. Elaine and the mothers did not think that it had been a lark at all.

Despite its beauty and that of its setting, we did not find it a happy house. Even after I had left government and most of the police had gone, we never found it a good house in which to live. A part of it, the oldest, twelfth-century part, had a dankness which no modern central heating relieved. We had it blessed, but we were not sad to leave it and to return to London in 1976. But perhaps it was the strain of our life at that time which turned us against Douglaslake. We had not given it much of a chance during those days when assassination threats and police protection were not so common as they are today.

During the week, however, my daily journey to work was a short, though escorted, walk. For there were also police at our flat in the Temple.

After I had arrived in the Law Courts the Legal Secretary, Tony Hetherington, would come to my room to hold the first conference of the day. After business with him, it was perhaps into the car and down the Embankment to the Lord Chancellor's office in the House of Lords for a conference with Quintin (usually fun); then to the Cabinet offices for a Cabinet committee (usually dull); then back at speed along the embankment to sandwiches over my table with Norman Skelhorn, the then Director of Public Prosecutions (usually disturbing). After the sandwiches, I might have to go in the car again to Westminster to answer parliamentary questions in the House; back to the Department for a meeting with Treasury counsel and then, very often, to Downing Street. Dinner would be eaten in the Commons dining-room from a menu known by heart. When the House rose, it would be back to our flat in the Temple with the red boxes which had to be cleared before bed. The person of whom I saw most, my constant companion, was my driver Albert Morley.

This programme, of course, varied considerably and it intensified immensely when there was superimposed the preparation for, and then appearances in, court. In the forty-five months of office, there were over thirty different cases in which I appeared as counsel, varying from those in which my part lasted only day-long or a few days, such as the V&G tribunal of enquiry or the Trident air-crash enquiry; to weeks at Winchester prosecuting in the IRA bombing case or arguing in the House of Lords in the *Sunday Times* thalidomide appeal. There were four separate sessions of appearances at Strasbourg, and two at The Hague. There were esoteric attendances in the room of the President of the Family Division on the sealing of the Royal Wills of the Dukes of Gloucester and of Windsor. There were the trips to Paris to attend the annual ceremony of the Paris Bar. And there was the regular weekly visit to Belfast.

In February of 1971 the board of Rolls-Royce announced that the losses of resources already committed to their RB–211 project of a new engine destined for service in Lockheed aircraft, combined with losses which would arise if the contract were terminated, were on such a scale that they were likely to exceed the net tangible assets of the company. The directors were in jeopardy of carrying on a business in breach of the Companies Act. The Rolls-Royce crisis had begun.

The government intervened. It was decided that it could not allow Rolls-Royce with its prestigious name and its involvement in defence to disappear. A new company was to be established, and the RB–211 contract was to be renegotiated. Complex legal problems arose, primarily over the fear that the trustee in bankruptcy of the old Rolls-Royce company in the US might seize the Rolls-Royce patents, of which there were over one thousand.

Jean-Pierre Warner, later first British Advocate General at the Court of Justice of the European Community and now a judge of the High Court, was then the junior Counsel to the Treasury in Chancery matters. He was the most distinguished lawyer then practising at the Chancery Bar. I sent him to New York and instructed leading US firms in patent and bankruptcy law. HMG was advised to acquire the Rolls-Royce US patents and license them. Henry Benson of the chartered accountants Coopers and Lybrand was brought in. Dan Haughton, the aggrieved President of Lockheed, came to No. 10. He had reasons to feel resentment. The Prime Minister then put Peter Carrington in charge of the intricate and anxious operation to save and revive the business and name of Rolls-Royce and its engine project.

On 24 March there was an all-night sitting in the House of Commons. I slipped home in the early hours for a bath and to change and then I returned to the House. With the House still in session, I was called at ten o'clock that morning to a meeting of ministers in the room of the Prime Minister about the Rolls-Royce crisis. Peter Carrington was flying that afternoon to Washington to meet on the following day with US Secretary of the Treasury Connally. A note was suddenly flipped to me across the table from Burke Trend. An hour later I was back at home. I collected a bag and was driven to Brize Norton to join Peter on board his VC-10 for his trip to the States. We worked away during the flight. When we landed at Andrews Field, Rowley Cromer, the Ambassador, was there to greet us. So was Mat Dick, my stepbrother-in-law.

How Mat got there and why he was there I have no idea. But there he was, standing at the bottom of the gangway among the official 'greeters'. They, of course, had no idea who he was. He had arrived, shaken them warmly by the hand, and joined the line. During this time whenever I went to Washington he always turned up. Admittedly he lived in George-town, but how he always worked his way into every official function that I ever attended I never knew. The following year on another visit I was scheduled to meet several Supreme Court and other senior judges for luncheon. Mat somehow got himself invited. He arrived at the luncheon before me. The judges mistook him for their official guest. He did not disabuse them. When I arrived I was nearly refused admittance. The hosts were clearly disappointed. The original Attorney General was far more colourful.

From Andrews Field Peter and I were taken off to the Embassy where we went straight into conference to prepare for the next day. Mat, I was relieved to note, had by now disengaged. We got to bed at 4 a.m. London time. I had been up all the previous night in the Commons and after the flights could sleep only fitfully. Next day we conferred with the unfortunate Dan Haughton and Lockheed, and then went to the US Treasury Department to meet Secretary Connally. By 6 p.m. that evening we were back at Andrews Field and flew off to London.

By then Peter was in his most xenophobic mood. For a man who professes to have little sympathy with foreigners he has had to pass a great deal of his life among them. He cheered when we took off. But probably it is all an elaborate Whig act. He had the remarkable facility of making everything, even this exhausting expedition, seem entertaining. The Thatcher Cabinet suffered immensely when he resigned over the Falklands invasion. He must have had a salutary effect on the Prime Minister, especially in her relations with and manner towards people; for he had an irreverence towards government. He had been a senior minister when she was little known and his lack of deference when she became Prime Minister must have been good for her soul. He also represented a tradition in the Conservative Party which is now wholly excluded from influence.

We landed at 7.30 a.m. London time. An hour later we were breakfasting with Ted in the flat at Downing Street. Then we went on to a ministerial meeting. I got home at two-thirty in the afternoon, and I felt that I had been struck on the head by a croquet mallet. Those were two rather special days out of the life of an Attorney General and the routine work of the office still remained to be done after we had got home.

The Rolls-Royce affair rumbled on for nearly a year. *The Times* said that the government had received the wrong advice. Henry Benson and I, with Jean-Pierre Warner and the Treasury Solicitor, and our (very expensive) New York lawyers, remained firm allies. We thought that together we might know better than the newspaper. Like all such crises the Rolls-Royce affair eventually subsided, only to be succeeded by some other.

That was the life, and always is the life. The pressures never cease. In my time if it was not Rolls-Royce, it was the IRA; or the V&G collapse or the Poulson affair. This last saw the departure of Reggie Maudling. Of the four leading young contenders for Harold Macmillan's Conservative crown a decade earlier – Heath, Powell, Macleod and Maudling – now only Heath survived. Quintin, his wig usually aslant, was frolicking in the Lords, being loved and loving it. All Ted's political heavyweight colleagues had gone. He was then on his own. He began to show his isolation. His temper shortened, and his touch with the parliamentary Party, so sure when he was Chief Whip, began to desert him.

I had my rows. On 14 December 1972 I had to advise the government on a matter of law. As was customary I had been briefed thoroughly by my own department lawyers, by those in the ministry concerned and by Treasury counsel. It is the Attorney General who is the constitutional legal adviser. Other ministers might be lawyers, but neither they nor the Lord Chancellor bear this responsibility. Their personal reflections upon technical matters of law and their legal opinions, expressed from the tops of their heads or their memory, are usually neither sound nor sensible. But they serve to cast doubt over the official advice which the Attorney General has to give. At the time I was sitting next to Margaret Thatcher. I remember that she made sympathetic, rather clucking, asides when all this broke out. The ministers in the end accepted my advice, but I left the meeting fuming. Back in chambers I made sure that Burke Trend knew that I was angry and that I would be very happy to hand in my cards. I told him that I could at once earn five times my present salary at the Bar and that my wife and family would be delighted.

I then flew off to Belfast on a routine trip, still growling and still shaking with fury. On my return I wrote formally to the Prime Minister. I said that Law Officers are professional advisers and not ministers to be instructed to carry out government policy; that their advice might be unpalatable and unwelcome and it is for ministers to accept or reject it; that their advice is not given without preparation or consultation with experts in the particular field of law; and that if he and ministers were inclined to listen to other advice on matters of law given casually without the discipline of research and responsibility and to criticize in discussion the advice of the Law Officers then the position of Law Officers becomes untenable.

I received a friendly and soothing message, and in the future I found that my legal row was much easier to hoe. The truth is that the strength of the position of an Attorney General depends upon how ready he is to leave. To do the job he had often to frustrate or thwart the plans, and thus the ambitions, of colleagues. He ought, in many ways, to be apart and separate from them. If his eye is set on another place in the administration, he will not provide that restraint for which, as in every walk in life, it is the duty of a legal adviser to call. But unless he is a toady, it is not a role which inspires love.

Chapter 23
In Fancy Dress

Each November the new Lord Mayor of London holds his annual banquet at which the principal guests are Her Majesty's ministers. It is a ceremonious affair, and the City fathers love it. It is the major civic event in the City calendar.

The line of the march, along which the guests are marshalled within the Guildhall to bring them to their host and to their dinner, is lined by incredibly old Beefeaters in ruffs and flat hats. Their gnarled fists grip their pikes on which they lean precariously, their knobbly knees and stringy calves are encased in scarlet tights, their old faces flushed or pale according, presumably, to years of indulgence or abstinence.

As well as ministers, a gaggle of judges in ermine and full-bottomed wigs is included among the guests. When I first attended as Solicitor General in 1962 the judge's wives were not included. The wives of the ministers were, so Elaine, in full fig, accompanied me. I too was in fancy dress, full-bottomed wig, knee breeches and black silk robe. As we made our way towards the entrance to the great chamber in which the Lord Mayor received his guests, I was suddenly taken aside by an official and asked to fall in behind the judges and march with them in their procession. 'I', said the man sternly, 'I shall look after Lady Rawlinson.' I said goodbye to a startled Elaine, who disappeared with her minder around the corner. I waited moodily with the judges. In the distance and out of my sight, I heard a voice boom, 'Lady Rawlinson.' There seemed to be a pause, and then a cheer and wild clapping. A moment later I understood what must have happened.

When Elaine left me she was escorted round the corner, her name announced, and she was launched under television arc lamps to walk alone between banks of seated City dignitaries the length of the great room to make her bow to the Lord Mayor. When she had first appeared and was announced, quite alone and a vision in a long white dress and decked in borrowed diamonds, there was for a moment a stunned silence. She presented a distinct difference from what had gone before. Then, led by two friends Gilbert and Denise Kilmarnock, the cheering had broken out, and it accompanied her throughout her long and lonely march. The entry of the legal procession (average age seventy) which followd her was a marked anti-climax. As I wandered along at the rear of this ancient and meandering column, I could appreciate the ordeal which she had endured and the delight which she had inspired.

Towards the end of the banquet, there comes the time when the loving-cup is solemnly passed. The orchestra breaks into a traditional air and the guests rise in pairs, one of whom receives the cup (which contains a singularly unpleasant brew), bows to the other in the pair who removes the lid, sips (lightly, if he is sensible) and hands over the cup. The other then drinks in turn, bows, turns and repeats the ceremony with his other neighbour who has risen to join in the fun, while the first in the pair guards the back of the second. And so on down the table and round the whole Guildhall.

When this ceremony began, a pair opposite to Elaine and myself was formed by a singularly solemn judge renowned for not seeing the funny side in anything and an elderly Labour Member of Parliament who was present as the escort of his wife, the Chairman of the London County Council. The solemn judge duly sipped and handed the cup to the elderly Member of Parliament, who seized it enthusiastically and drank copiously. Then, instead of turning and repeating the ceremony with a new partner, the old gentleman jovially handed back the cup to the startled judge. Taken aback at this unexpected turn of events, the judge felt obliged to take the cup and have another sip. He then handed it back. The Member of Parliament drank again, heartily and noisily. To the horror of the judge and to the delight of the spectators who were by now wondering happily how this delightful impasse would ever end, the Member of Parliament a little unsteadily once again handed it back to the judge. By now the judge had broken out into a muck sweat from the heat of his heavy robes, the unexpected nightmare in which he seemed to have become inextricably involved and the disgusting brew which he had been obliged too often to drink. Sadly an attendant, attracted by the jam which had clearly arisen in the circulation of the cup, hurried up and officiously intervened, persuading the enthusiastic drinker to turn and let someone else have a go. The solemn judge sank exhausted into his chair and the cup began to sail decorously down the table. The elderly Labour Member of Parliament looked across the table at me – and winked.

This habit of jumping into fancy dress on official occasions was not confined to England. Each year the Paris Bar invites an English Law officer to attend the Rentrée, the Séance Solenelle, which marks the annual opening of the Paris Law Courts and the start of their legal year. Usually the Law Officer is quartered with the Embassy. But one year that was not possible and I was put into the Crillon Hotel on the Place de la Concorde.

To fortify me for the ordeal which lay ahead (the ceremony is certainly not short), I had an omelette and a pint of champagne in my room and then climbed into my black robes, knee breeches, buckle shoes, lace jabot and full-bottomed wig. Then I had to make my way from my room to the ground floor and into the Embassy car which was to take me to the Palais de Justice. I descended very slowly in the open-ribbed cage of the old-fashioned elevator. As the lift approached the ground floor, I could hear some American tourists who were waiting for the elevator and who were discussing their plans for a trip that afternoon to Versailles. Suddenly, before their startled eyes, the lift cage disgorged my bewigged and black-robed figure. The jaws of the tourists, literally, hung suspended. All that I could do was to make them a bow and scuttle through the foyer and into the car. They came through the hotel to watch as the apparition was speedily driven away.

The Paris ceremony includes the delivery of two very lengthy *discours* by the two prize-winning new *avocats*, one of which traditionally had to be devoted to the life and career of some renowned *maître* of the Paris Bar; and a second to some great historical *procès* such as the trial of Louis XVI or of Captain Dreyfus. One one occasion, I was seated next to the Gaullist Minister of Justice; on my other flank was the dark-skinned, violently anti-Gaullist President of the Senate. The first *discours* was given by a very attractive girl, so attention was rapt and approval unanimous. The second, however, described the trial *in absentia* in 1880 for treason of General Boulanger who had threatened the overthrow of the republican regime in France. The General had eventually committed suicide in Brussels on the grave of his mistress, the Vicomtesse de Bonnemain. This tale clearly gave great scope to the astute young orator, and he took full advantage of it.

As the story unfolded there were numerous pointed and mocking references to 'M. le Général'. After a time the Gaullist Minister of Justice on my left began to scowl, and then to growl. He began to include me in his hardly *sotto voce* comments on the impertinence of the young pup. I bowed and nodded deprecatingly, and with that side of my face registered comradely outrage. But on my other side, each piece of mockery and illusion was greeted by chuckles of delight, accompanied by appreciative digs in my ribs, from the President of the Senate. Between scowling to my left and beaming to my right, I and my ribs had a remarkably uncomfortable afternoon.

This part of the occasion was followed by an evening reception in white tie and tailcoat. Among the guests one year were the Canadian Attorney General and his wife. They were from the prairies and had never before seen Paris. They looked rather lost. After a time, stimulated I admit by champagne, I suggested and they readily agreed that we should slip away and seek less formal entertainment. I took them to the Crazy Horse Saloon.

As soon as we arrived I realized that I had made a mistake. I had overlooked how we were dressed. We were immediately led by a distinctly impressed 'Maître d'hotel' to a table in the very front row. Soon the girls came on to the stage, only a few feet from our heads, and began, cheerfully and with great artistry, to take off all their clothes. The Minister's wife soon grew restive. The Minister, I could see, had begun to muse about the view his Bible-belt constituents might take of his attendance at such an entertainment. A moment later we were making a less dignified exit than we had made entrance, sped on our way by a volley of ribald jokes from the stage. When we parted our adieux were cool, as the worthy Canadians bade goodnight to their decadent European colleague.

These annual occasions were far more enjoyable when Christopher and Mary Soames were at the Paris Embassy. Then Elaine accompanied me and we stayed with them. The great house of Pauline Borghese was at that time the cynosure of the Faubourg St Germain. There could always be found abundant and exquisite food, social as well as political talk. At the feet of the smart, sharp Parisian ladies and their ministerial lovers there would perhaps be lying before the fire, sighing hugely and interrupting the latest gossip from the Elysée or the Hôtel Matignon, a large and bandaged labrador recovering from a recent hysterectomy. The visitors found it all very chic.

The only time that I ever wore my full-bottomed wig in action was before the International Court at The Hague. It was in the Iceland fisheries case during the Cod War. Until fairly recently, full-bottomed wigs were worn by QCs when appearing before the House of Lords. Now that has been abandoned. The Law Lords themselves have always worn everyday clothes. But I thought that at The Hague on behalf of Her Majesty's government I ought to try and cut a dash. The International Court makes an impressive scene, with all the international judges in their black velvet suits and white cravats seated on a great semi-circular dais. The advocate addresses them from a podium in the centre. So I decided to wear my long wig.

In these international cases counsel is required by the international law experts of his client state to stick very strictly to a script which Foreign Ministry officials and academic international lawyers spend hours honing and tempering. For they insist that each word carries some delicate diplomatic nuance, so that any departure from the text might lead to an immediate outbreak of hostilities; or if not that, to some severe financial consequence, probably to the Foreign Office vote and their salaries.

However, I decided that we ought to cut the length of the address, and I wanted to make more the speech of an advocate than of an academic, at which incidentally the Germans were known as the masters, droning on interminably without emphasis and with their noses buried deep in an immense tome. So on the principle of the correspondent who apologized for writing such a long letter since he did not have time to write a short one, we spent nearly the whole of the preceding night working on the speech, re-honing and re-tempering and shortening.

When I came to deliver it, like any barrister addressing a court, I paid the judges what I thought was the compliment of looking up from the brief and at them as often as I could. The Foreign Office officials, I was told by my junior counsel Gordon Slynn, grew pale and nervous, biting their fingernails lest I strayed as much as a pause from the sacred text. In the event we had a triumph for we won, due, I have to admit, to the fact that on the other side, the Iceland government, refused even to turn up and their half of the court was conspicuously deserted. But the attempt to shorten the text and to enliven the presentation paid off, for the Soviet judge expressed his approval. He had, apparently, a particularly agreeable appointment and, to his pleasure, he was able to spend the longer in enjoying it.

When we had left the court and I had packed away the long wig (which must have startled some of my audience), I said that the whole team of lawyers and officials must all have luncheon together. So off we went to an excellent restaurant. At the end of this celebration, one of the Foreign Office officials approached me with the bill and enquired who would pay. 'Send it to the Embassy', I said airily. A look of concern fell like a shadow over his polished face, that shadow which shows on the diplomatic countenance only when someone is mundane enough to mention money. I then swept away in the Embassy car heading for the airport and home. But, when I saw that we had plenty of time, I asked to be driven to the

Mauritshuis so that I could look at the Rembrandts. This meant a diversion from our direct route of only a few hundred yards. For that, I literally paid.

Back in London, that restaurant bill fluttered between the Foreign Office and the Law Officers' Department for months. Both refused to pay. A substantial file built up. Despatch riders shuttled between Whitehall and the Law Courts. After several months I was told that the Foreign Office had surrendered. In the end, I said complacently to Tony Hetherington, the Legal Secretary, they had behaved like the gentlemen I knew that they were. A week later I received from the foreign Office a personal bill for the use of one of their motorcars for a private visit to an art gallery. It was expressed in pounds sterling per kilometre at the very highest rate. It came to a little over one pound.

I have long considered that there are only two really professional diplomatic services, whom it is very difficult to best. The Quai d'Orsay is certainly one. The other? That bill confirmed me in my firm impression of which was the other.

Chapter 24
In the Fleet Street Doghouse

In June 1972 I shot myself badly in both feet. I tangled with *The Times*. Worse still, I tangled with their prestigious columnist, Bernard Levin. Worst of all, I caught him out in an error and made the most of it. Thereafter I became a prime target.

This quarrel with Bernard Levin arose in the summer before I became involved with the *Sunday Times* in the Thalidomide litigation, which was to involve me as both party and advocate. Bernard Levin had become angered by the prosecution of the publishers of IT (*International Times*) for the offence of conspiracy to corrupt public morals by publishing in their magazine advertisements under the heading 'Males'. In these advertisements homosexuals sought out other homosexual partners, describing in the columns of the magazine their particular tastes and requirements and offering financial and other inducements. At the trial the publishers had been convicted, and their appeals were later dismissed.

Bernard Levin was incensed. He argued that when I was Solicitor General in 1964 I as a Law Officer had given an undertaking in the House of Commons setting strict limits over prosecutions for offences against public morals and he accused me now as Attorney General of having deliberately breached that undertaking by authorizing this prosecution of 'Males'. Accordingly, he went on, it was surely time that I was politely told that I had had 'a good run for our money not to mention our liberties' and should now return with as much grace as I could muster to the backbenches and the Bar.

But Homer had nodded. I had neither authorized nor launched the prosecution of IT for publishing these advertisements. The prosecution had been authorized and commenced by my Labour predecessor, Elwyn Jones, before I had come into office. As to any breach of the undertaking which I had given in 1964, Elwyn had formed the view before he had agreed to the prosecution that a charge of corrupting public morals in this particular case would not conflict in any way with my undertaking. The judges before whom the case came, both at the trial and on the appeal, expressly considered the 1964 undertaking and agreed with Elwyn. So Bernard Levin was not only wrong about the law; he was also wrong on the facts. This was the hour when hubris struck. If I was to react at all (which I shouldn't have), I should have at most shortly corrected the facts. But for some reason I decided that on this occasion the official worm should turn. That was a great mistake. I should have known my place.

Anyhow I issued a formal statement which pointed out that Bernard Levin was wrong in law about the effect and meaning of the undertaking. Further that he was wrong on his facts as he had gone for the wrong Attorney General which, my statement pompously added, 'any check on the facts and press reports of the case must have necessarily revealed to any responsible commentator'. So there! But now the fat, or rather my fat, was well and truly in the fire. It fried there merrily for a long time to come.

Bernard Levin replied. He apologized for chasing the wrong Attorney General, then he returned to the attack in lively, limpid prose. Again I do not know what came over me but I just could not leave well alone. I authorized another statement pointing out acidly that the judges had expressly considered the matter of the undertaking and had decided that it had not been breached. And so the debate went on until eventually Bernard Levin announced, 'My final words on the IT case and the Attorney General.'

But it was certainly not his final word on me. I was to be taught a lesson. So my name, sometimes distorted and Germanized, began to pop up regularly in his articles, whatever the context and irrespective of the context. For instance, some misguided few might not want to stand when drinking the Queen's health, understandably none would want to stand when drinking, say the health of Sir Peter Rawlinson. A mountain was to be climbed because it was there, but who would want to climb Sir Peter Rawlinson? When some correspondents kindly but unwisely wrote in my defence, he invented a Society for the Protection of Sir Peter Rawlinson. Apparently, it had offices situated in 'the Thieves' Kitchen, Balham' and its honorary secretary was, strangely enough, Rabbi Moishe Ben-Rawlinson.

The mockery went on, feline and often funny. It went on so long and so regularly that eventually a mutual friend, Jamie Hamilton, enquired of Bernard Levin why he so often picked on me. The answer reported to me was that he claimed that it was not the person but the Office that was his quarry. I wondered. I suspected that I was being punished. In any event I had made a rod for my own back and it was being laid on by a master. Bernard Levin and I met for the only time many years later at a dinner party. Neither of us could then remember what on earth our row had been about. He was very pleasant, although he looked at me warily as if I might be going to lift his wallet. Once an Attorney General?

But these exchanges earlier in 1972 served perhaps to increase the acerbity between *The Times* Group and myself, first when the thalidomide litigation with the *Sunday Times* began in the autumn; and second when *The Times* campaigned in the following year for a tribunal of enquiry into the Poulson affair and I had chosen to prosecute.

The thalidomide litigation which I had with Times Newspapers was halfway through its journey up the hierarchy of the courts when on 13 January 1973 Harold Evans, the editor of the *Sunday Times*, appeared as a guest on Michael Parkinson's popular television programme. At that time he was by many considered to be a journalist hero, for he had been championing in the *Sunday Times* the cause of the pathetically disabled children born of mothers who when pregnant had taken the drug thalidomide marketed by the Distillers Company. The disabilities of these unfortunate children were horrendous. Some had been born with no limbs, others with stumps. Sympathy at their unhappy plight was universal. Litigation on their behalf had then been commenced against Distillers, and by 1972 there had been instituted some 389 claims for damages on behalf of the children against the defendant company.

To succeed in law, however, the claimants had to establish that the company had been negligent. This the company vehemently denied, and proof of their negligence which was needed if the claims were to succeed was going to be hard to establish. Negotiation had been taking place to reach a settlement of the claims and to obtain for the children and their families adequate compensation. Because the plaintiffs were minors, any settlement between the children and the company would have to be approved by the Court.

On his television programme, Michael Parkinson asked Harold Evans to tell viewers about the case. Accordingly he described the background to the story and then turned to the litigation with the Attorney General in which he and the *Sunday Times* were currently engaged. This litigation concerned the question whether articles which the newspaper wished to publish in support of the children's claims and in criticism of the defendant company were a contempt of court.

He explained to viewers that the previous September he had despatched a copy of an article which he proposed shortly to publish in the *Sunday Times* to the Distillers Company. The Company, he said, had replied by thanking him for sending this article and advising him that action would be taken. He then told viewers, 'Well, action being taken meant that there was a knock on my door and it was a letter from the Attorney General threatening me with prison if I continued the way I was continuing.' In answer to a question from Michael Parkinson, he stoutly added that rather than be silenced he 'would be prepared to go to prison'.

In reality the editor's role had been rather less heroic and more circumspect than might have been suspected from the impression given on television. The course of events had actually been as follows.

On 26 September 1972, four months before Harold Evans had appeared on the Michael Parkinson show, John Wilmers QC, counsel for the defendant Distillers Company, who were defending the action for negligence brought against them on behalf of the children, had come to see the Solicitor General, Geoffrey Howe. I was away in Strasbourg.

John Wilmers complained in particular about an article which Harold Evans had sent to Distillers and which his newspaper proposed shortly to publish. Wilmers claimed that the article was a blatant attempt to arouse public sympathy for one side in a pending suit and was an attack on the other party in an attempt to force or frighten the latter to abandon its legitimate defences in law. He said that to put pressure on a party in this way by using all the influence of a newspaper to mould public opinion against one side on behalf of the other was a contempt of court and an interference with the course of justice. Accordingly he requested the Attorney General, in the exercise of his role as the constitutional guardian of the public interest, to do his duty and to intervene.

The Attorney is certainly the guardian of the public interest, and the public interest certainly demands that none should seek to interfere with or influence the decision of a court which alone has the duty to decide issues in suits brought before the court. It was also in the public interest to prevent third parties from taking sides in a suit to the extent of frightening off either a defendant or a claimant. Further, it would be the Attorney's duty to intervene if it appeared that a contempt of court was about to be committed. The very fact that the editor had submitted the article to the defendants prior to publication seemed to indicate that the newspaper itself realized that it might give rise to just such an objection.

So the position was that on 26 September 1972, a party to a suit had lodged a formal complaint and had officially requested the Attorney General to perform his constitutional duty and consider whether the material submitted to him was, if it were to be published, a breach of the law.

In my absence overseas, Geoffrey Howe considered the article which John Wilmers had brought. A letter was then sent to the *Sunday Times* saying that the article had been complained about and that in Geoffrey's view the article could amount to a contempt; the letter concluded by inviting Harold Evans' comments. On the 28th Harold Evans politely replied, saying that he was very well aware of the limitations imposed by the law of contempt, that he contemplated that there would be further articles and that he would be grateful for any observations from the Law Officers' Department. He enclosed a short opinion from his own legal adviser who (confusingly) was called James Evans. Everything was thus very gentlemanly. No knocks on doors; no threats of prison.

On my return from Strasbourg I discussed the matter with Geoffrey, with Treasury counsel, with Tony Hetherington and with the other lawyers in the Department. I was extremely reluctant to get involved. If I did, obviously the reasons would either be misunderstood or they would be distorted, and I would end up (as of course I did) as the oppressor of the champion of the unfortunate disabled children. And with me, although it would have nothing to do with them, would be lumped the government.

However, there was my constitutional duty to perform and a formal complaint had been lodged. The principle concerning contempt of court seemed clear, namely that parties to a lawsuit and their advisers must be free to assess the evidence in the lawsuit and not be pressurized by public comment designed to whip up support for one side or the other. If the media were, in principle, allowed to take sides and lend their influence to one side or the other before a case came on for trial, parties might be deterred from defending or claiming. There then would have developed a very unhealthy and undesirable precedent for trial by media before impending trial by the Court.

While I was holding my conference, I was told that James Evans had come on the telephone and had said that the *Sunday Times* well understood the difficulties of the Attorney General and that the newspaper had no wish to embarrass him; and that if the Attorney's tentative view was that the article was a contempt, he would advise Harold Evans not to publish. He had then suggested that there should be mounted what he called 'a collusive action' to test the point of law.

On 5 October Harold Evans' lawyer wrote actually setting out the terms of the letter which he suggested should be sent to the *Sunday Times* on behalf of the Attorney and the terms in which the *Sunday Times* would thereupon reply. He concluded that this approach was the most constructive and sensible. This was indeed the 'very pineapple of politeness'. Still no knock on any door and still no threat of prison.

But I remained reluctant. I refused to take the matter to court unless the complainants, Distillers, failed to do so. They firmly declined and they again pointedly invited the Attorney to do his duty. I then suggested to the *Sunday Times* that they should go to the Court to seek a declaration that their proposed article was not a contempt of court and that I would then appear as *amicus curiae*, or friend of the Court, to assist the Court in its consideration of the law. The *Sunday Times*, however, excused themselves from taking this step because, they declared, the Court might not hear the matter for some time and they were anxious to get a decision and to publish as soon as possible. Whereas, they said courteously, if the Attorney would start the proceedings the matter would come before the Court far more speedily. This then was the 'mode' preferred and recommended by the *Sunday Times* for commencing what their own lawyer had suggested should be 'collusive action', in other words an agreed action to settle the matter of law over whether their article contravened the then law of contempt.

So it was eventually done, and so began the case of *Attorney General* v. *Times Newspapers Limited*. It had all been agreed between the Law Officers' Department and the newspaper but, as I had suspected from the very first, the Attorney General, and with him most unfairly the government, was soon cast as the villain, the scourge of a free press and a harsh, didactic official willing to see disabled children denied the help which they so sorely needed and which any man of compassion would have leaped to support. In the public image I made my position more personal by applying the principles which I followed in exercising the role of the Attorney as an officer of the Crown by appearing throughout all the hearings of the case in the English courts as the advocate. I was, accordingly, both party and counsel.

As a matter of law the English courts finally decided that the *Sunday Times* was wrong. In the first court, the divisional Court, it was held that the intended publication would be a contempt; the Court of Appeal allowed the appeal of the *Sunday Times* but the House of Lords (by five to none) restored the order of the divisional Court. Thus the view of Geoffrey Howe and myself that the proposed publication by the *Sunday Times* was, as a matter of law, an actual breach of the then English law of contempt was upheld by the highest English court. Subsequently Times Newspapers went to Strasbourg and succeeded there in convincing the Court of Human Rights by a narrow majority that the English law of contempt was a breach of Article 10(1) of the Human Rights Convention. But that had never been the issue in the litigation of the Attorney General with Harold Evans and the *Sunday Times*.

The English law was subsequently amended by the Contempt of Court Act 1981, which harmonized the law of England and Wales with the majority judgment at Strasbourg. But the 1981 Act still maintained the ultimate supremacy of the due administration of justice over the liberty to publish, although it shifted the balance a little in favour of the latter.

That then was the true story of how this litigation ever came about. As to 'a knock on my door and it was a letter from the Attorney General threatening me with prison ...' Well, well! But such is the stuff of which myths, and sometimes heroes, are made.

In between the autumn of 1972 and the spring of 1973, while the thalidomide litigation was proceeding through the courts, there came to a head ugly rumours about public corruption in the north-east. The architect John Poulson, with whom Reggie Maudling the Home Secretary had been associated in business during the years of opposition, was now facing public examination in bankruptcy.

I knew that a police investigation into the activities of Poulson was reaching its conclusion. But *The Times* was calling for a tribunal of enquiry. I was resisting these calls since I considered that the correct mode of proceeding was to implement the criminal law and, if there emerged sufficient evidence, to mount trials of John Poulson and a senior civil servant, William Pottinger. For if a tribunal of enquiry were to be set up, then Poulson and his associates would have to be granted immunity from prosecution and they would escape the punishment which I suspected that they richly deserved.

On 21 July 1973 the Director of Public Prosecutions came to see me. With him came the police. They handed to me their completed report. The Director recommended the immediate institution of criminal proceedings against Poulson and Pottinger. Accordingly I gave my consent and on the following day both men were arrested. The public hearings in the bankruptcy court had at once to be adjourned; press comment was stilled. This did not suit some of the newspapers, for they appeared to be rather more interested in running a sensational story than in seeing corrupt men brought to trial. But tried the two men were. Both were subsequently convicted and both imprisoned. In my view that was the best way of serving the public interest.

The Times was one newspaper which did not take kindly to the arrest of the two conspirators since this prevented the holding of a tribunal of enquiry into the whole matter, the course which they had been advocating. So they turned on the Attorney General, who also happened at the time to be litigating with their sister paper the *Sunday Times*. They published a weighty leader under the heading, 'Justice should never be secret.'

After the leader had declared that a trial of Poulson and Pottinger might not provide a sufficiently public explanation of the matter, the Thunderer thundered, 'a criminal trial may seem [to the Attorney General] a necessary price to pay for protecting the process of law. After all in the *Sunday Times* thalidomide case he has argued unsuccessfully in the Court of Appeal but for all one knows successfully in the House of Lords [this was prophetic; he had] that neither public interest, however great, nor the effluxion of time even if very long, should mitigate the rigour of the rules of contempt.' This was rather disingenuous shorthand for a necessarily complex argument over competing public interests.

The leader went on, 'In that case [the thalidomide case] more than four hundred children had been born mutilated; ten years later no adequate public inquiry into the circumstances had been held; yet the Attorney General was still prepared to argue that civil actions which could continue for another term of years, had to be protected against a newspaper article inquiring into the responsibility for the tragedy. A man who takes the view when four hundred children are involved after ten years in a civil case will certainly take it again when charges of public corruption are involved, after only a year of inquiries, in the more serious matter of a criminal case.' The leader concluded, 'Sir Peter Rawlinson in the thalidomide case ... and in this case had administered justice with the effect of limiting public knowledge.'

In the result, however, 'in the thalidomide case', the highest court in the United Kingdom was shortly to hold that what the *Sunday Times* proposed to publish was a contempt and in breach of the English law as it then was. In 'this case', the Poulson and Pottinger case, both men were convicted of serious crime and sent to prison and there was no limitation of public knowledge whatsoever. It had been demonstrated that the criminal law was adequate to expose wrongdoing and punish the malefactors.

The Poulson affair had already brought down one minister, the Home Secretary Reggie Maudling, whose incautious business connections with the architect during our years in opposition had left him open to attack. My experience during the troubled years 1962–4 made me very conscious of how gossip and rumour could unfairly destroy a public man, and so I received a nasty shock when on the day on which Poulson and Pottinger were to be arrested I learned that the name of another colleague, wholly innocent of any business connections with Poulson, was about to be publicly dragged into the murky story.

For on the day of the arrests of Poulson and Pottinger I had asked to come and see me Muir Hunter QC, who had been cross-examining the architect in his bankruptcy proceedings. Because the start of criminal proceedings would halt these hearings, I thought that it was only right to warn Muir Hunter of the arrests which were at that moment taking place.

He listened to what I told him, thanked me and said, 'Well, that has stopped the next stage of my cross-examination, which would have been interesting. I was just coming to a matter concerning the Chancellor of the Exchequer, Anthony Barber.' I froze. So my authorization the evening before of the arrests had effectively stopped the publicizing of the name of a second minister in the saga of the bankruptcy which the press was so avidly reporting! 'It was a quite innocent connection', went on Muir Hunter. 'Their children were friends and the Poulsons and the Barbers had shared between them the costs of a party which the children had held in Poulson's house. I was going to probe how Poulson's share of the costs were entered into his accounts.'

For a moment even the unfairness to Anthony Barber of dragging his name into the scandal because of a children's party escaped me. I could only think what use the press might make of this spectacular development. Obviously no one would believe that the Attorney General had not timed the arrests to stop the name of yet another colleague being brought into the Poulson affair. No wonder the Attorney General wanted to prosecute and not hold a public enquiry! I could already hear ringing in my ears the rumble of outraged editorial prose.

'Would you be prepared', I cravenly asked Muir Hunter, 'to let me have a letter saying that you told me about the Barber connection only after I had told you about the arrests and the adjournment of the bankruptcy hearing?' He would, and he did. I felt ashamed at even asking. For the letter was purely cover for my own back. And, even so, if the tale ever came to be told, it would probably not be believed.

All in all it had not been a triumphant period for personal public relations in the Law Officers' Department. Bernard Levin, thalidomide, a Poulson tribunal of enquiry. Before that the secret Dutschke hearings, which I describe in the next chapter. Some of the flak I had brought upon my own head. I was now clearly cast as a Law Officer who was determined to administer the law in secret.

It seemed a far cry from my days as the champion of the *Daily Express* in the D-Notice enquiry or my general retainer as leading counsel for the *Daily Mail*. I was now deeply esconced in the Fleet Street dog-house.

Chapter 25
Spies

I first learned about Anthony Blunt in April 1964 when I was still Solicitor General. John Hobson confided in me that Blunt was a traitor. Earlier in that year I had been sworn in as a member of the Privy Council, so I was bound by the Privy Council oath of secrecy.

By then I was anaesthetized against surprise. It had not been so very long since the exposure of Burgess and Maclean and Philby, and during the past eighteen months John and I had had Vassall and Ivanov in the Profumo affair. In the previous year I had unsuccessfully prosecuted Giuseppe Martelli, a nuclear research scientist, for an act preparatory to spying when there had been found in his possession one-time pads and shoes with hollowed-out heeled which swivelled and provided a secret cavity.

John, who was troubled, now told me that upon the request of the security services he had been persuaded to grant Blunt immunity from prosecution for his treachery. It had been represented to him that there existed no admissible evidence against Blunt, who steadfastly refused to make any admission. They were anxious to know how he, and who else, had been recruited, and what he had done when he was under Soviet control. It was represented that if Blunt were satisfied that his own skin was safe, he would reveal much of what the interrogators wanted to discover. One officer who was to do the interrogating of Blunt was to be Peter Wright.

John had no great confidence in the operation or the operators. He wanted to know first whether the information which the interrogators believed that they would obtain was worth more in the public interest than the prosecution and punishment of a traitor; and second, whether after they had obtained what they sought they would then at least expose the traitor. He had been assured that the information sought was of the greatest national importance, and that to expose Blunt after the interrogators had got what they wanted would only reveal to the Soviets that Blunt had at last been identified and would inhibit any further approaches which might in the future be required. Reluctantly John granted an immunity from prosecution for the acts of treachery limited, I understood at the time, to those committed prior to 1945 when Blunt had left the service. In fact, I believe that the actual inducement held out to Blunt which led to his confession in 1963 extended to total immunity for what he had done in the past.

Blunt was therefore interrogated again and among his interrogators was Peter Wright. Because of the inducement to confess and the immunity from prosecution Blunt could now be certain that his delicate frame would never languish, as it deserved, in jail. And so he talked. But those involved, among them Peter Wright, must either have not thought through what would eventually happen when, as was inevitable, Blunt's treachery was revealed by other sources; or they did not care. The price paid was certainly heavy. The masquerade of the great art historian, honoured by the Queen, was permitted to continue until the squalid story eventually was blown to the discomfiture of all. It must be hoped that the dividends obtained were worth it. In Moscow the friends who had fled and whose flight Blunt had facilitated must have smiled. For Blunt would only have told Peter Wright what the Soviets knew already, while their agents of those past years were fled or were by then of minimal importance or expendable. It was presumably an exercise in investigating penetration of the security services twenty years earlier and a search for any traitors still lurking undiscovered, perhaps by then in senior places in government service. Above all it was probably part of the hunt for the Arch Traitor in whose existence Peter Wright so fanatically believed. But Anthony Blunt was never likely to cheat on his real, true friends. Betrayal he had reserved for his country. All in all the Blunt exercise had not been a very successful operation.

Officially I was only informed about Blunt in 1972 when I was asked to advise whether the grant of immunity given by John in 1963 extended to any prosecution in the future. Studying what had been said to Blunt as an inducement to talk I had ruefully to advise that it did. Over the years when I heard of that figure sauntering between the Courtauld and the Athenaeum I thought how successful and clever Blunt had been. He had avoided exile; he had escaped prison. He had remained doing the work in which he delighted and in which he excelled. He could live where he chose, and after the change in the law he could live openly with whom he chose. Only at the very end was he exposed. I suspect that he was far too clever for Mr Wright.

I had been dissatisfied with the briefing which I had received in July 1963 when as Solicitor General I had unsuccessfully prosecuted the nuclear scientist Giuseppe Martelli for acts preparatory to spying. The prosecution had been founded upon a provision in the Act which made it a crime to prepare to commit espionage. No prosecution under this provision had previously been attempted. The Security Service chiefs, however, were anxious to proceed. I suppose that it was considered to be in the nature of an experiment. There was certainly no doubt that the man had in his possession the professional kit of the spy, but there was no evidence that he intended to communicate the secrets and he was acquitted. I felt at the time that I had not been fully informed by my 'clients' about the background and circumstances of this novel prosecution.

When I came back into office as Attorney General in 1970 I asked to see the legal adviser to the security services who was the officer who liaised between the Services, the Law Officers and the Director of Public Prosecutions. I made clear to him that I must be taken wholly into the confidence of the Service in all cases which were brought to me for the issue of my *fiat*, or I would refuse to give leave to prosecute. Without my leave no prosecution under the Official Secrets Act could be launched. From then on the legal adviser and I worked closely together over the next four years. Altogether he served his Service and the public interest with great distinction.

During these years there were five cases of offences against Section 1 of the Official Secrets Act in which I led as counsel for the Crown. All were concerned with spying for the Eastern bloc. In only one was there a plea of Not Guilty, that of Nicholas Prager. He was convicted by a jury and sentenced to twelve years' imprisonment. The incontrovertible facts in all these cases demonstrated not only the supply by the Russians or the Czechs of sophisticated and ingenious equipment to their agents in this country but also the extent of the intelligence effort made by the Eastern bloc to penetrate the defence and security interests of the United Kingdom.

But before I became involved in any of these major security cases, there arose another matter which brought in the Security Services and an appearance before a very unsatisfactory tribunal.

*

In 1968 Rudi Dutschke, a fiery revolutionary German student who openly advocated the use of force for political ends was shot in Berlin. That was the year when across the whole world student and protest violence was at its height. The wounded Dutschke was first taken to Italy, and in October 1968 an application was received at the Home Office on his behalf seeking permission for him to come to England to consult a specialist. He was already banned from entering France and Holland because of his revolutionary activities, and in the application it was volunteered that he undertook to refrain from political activity while he was in Britain. Jim Callaghan, the then Home Secretary, agreed that he could come for one month for medical consultation. In December he entered this country.

In January and again in July 1969 he was granted extensions of his permit for the purposes of convalescence. In January 1970 however he applied to stay to take a university course. Jim Callaghan granted him a further medical extension but informed him that if he wanted to stay to take a course of study he must make a fresh application because that would be an application based upon grounds different from the original grounds upon which he had been allowed to enter the United Kingdom.

In June 1970, on the change of government, Reggie Maudling succeeded Jim Callaghan as Home Secretary. Between January and June 1970 much information had poured into the Home Office concerning Dutschke's activities. When Dutschke duly applied to stay for a study course at a university, Reggie refused. Dutschke appealed against Reggie's decision.

Under an Act of the Wilson government in 1969 and the Aliens Order made under it, a special panel of the Immigration Appeals Tribunal had to be set up to hear any case where the decision to exclude an alien had been taken in the interests of national security or on grounds of a political nature. The principal ground of Dutschke's appeal was that he had kept his promise not to engage in political activities. Reggie knew better. So he referred the appeal to the special panel, to which evidence would be given about Dutschke's actual activities.

At the hearing of the appeal, the evidence of what Rudi Dutschke had in fact been up to would have to be given to the panel in secret session in order to protect the informants. There was, however, an unusual characteristic of the procedure provided for this tribunal. When secret evidence was being heard neither the appellant nor his counsel was allowed to be present. This awkward procedure had been conceived by our Labour predecessors, who had, incidentally, also appointed four out of the five members of the panel.

Since the appeal was in effect a challenge to the exercise of the discretion of the Home Secretary, it was thought appropriate that the Attorney should appear to represent him. Usually I enjoyed appearing as counsel but I did not relish this task.

Under the procedure of the Tribunal, I could be present when the secret evidence was given; Dutschke and his counsel, Basil Wigoder QC, could not. I was aware that evidence to be given in secret would tell of various places where Dutschke had visited, of what happened when he paid those visits, and whom he saw. This evidence would be given in the context of his personal undertaking not to engage in political activities. If accepted by the Tribunal it would be decisive. But Dutschke would be unable directly to challenge it. So I decided that it would be right at least to put to him in the public hearings the names of the places which those giving evidence in the closed session were going to say that he had visited during his 'convalescence'. At least he could then agree or deny that he had ever visited particular places and, if he chose, explain why he went there. The Tribunal would then be able to compare his account with that which they would later hear from witnesses in closed session. But such cross-examination in public session would have little meaning to those who would not hear the evidence in secret.

Dutschke duly gave evidence in open session. He vigorously denied that he had at any time broken his undertaking to refrain from political activities. In cross-examination I asked him whether he had ever paid any visits to various places, including Swansea and Port Talbot. Dutschke brushed this aside. He was dismissive of these foolish questions. I was obliged to leave the matter there. The commentators present at this part of the public hearing smiled condescendingly. Jim Callaghan, who sat in on the public hearings, later told the House of Commons that I was 'floundering'. It must have appeared so, because having put to Dutschke the names of various places, I was unable in public to suggest the true reason why Dutchke had chosen to visit them and what he had been up to while he was there. That would all be revealed later, but only to the Tribunal in secret session. The person who certainly did understand why those questions were asked was Rudi Dutschke himself. He knew only too well. For he knew whom he had met.

After hearing both public and secret evidence the Tribunal upheld the exercise of his discretion by Reggie Maudling, and Rudi Dutschke left these shores. Thereafter little was ever heard of him. But it had been an awkward and unsatisfactory process which Jim Callaghan and the Labour government had bequeathed. Soon the procedure on appeals against deportation orders was amended. But the appeal process in this kind of case has to remain a mixture between a judicial process and a review of an executive order.

In January 1971 there was a debate about the Dutschke case in the House of Commons. During the debate Michael Foot declared that if the freedom as defined by Reggie Maudling had been applied to Karl Marx, Mazzini, Garibaldi or Alexander Herzen, they would all have been excluded from our hospitable shores. The orator concluded, 'It is my belief that thanks to the folly and worse with which the Right Honourable Gentleman [Reggie] has dealt with this case, the name of Rudi Dutschke will be added to those famous names.'

Karl Marx, Garibaldi – and Rudi Dutschke! For the honour of the House, I am glad to report that Hansard faithfully records that when Michael Foot uttered those memorable words, Honourable Members cried, 'Rubbish!'

The criminal prosecutions in the 1970s in which I appeared for the Crown when I was Attorney General came after the Dutschke Tribunal. They were all relatively straightforward. A decade later it became not so easy to mount criminal prosecutions against spies and traitors. To secure conviction by a jury, witnesses have to appear before them and often the essential evidence to prove the guilt of the accused will disclose the identity of people whose anonymity may be essential for the security of the state. Or the evidence may disclose methods of surveillance or other security practices which it is likewise essential to keep secret. In the past it has been possible for a court to receive such evidence in camera, in secret, with reasonable confidence that it will remain secret because it is heard only by the judge, the jury and the lawyers, all of whom could be trusted.

It is now feared that if in the future a court goes into camera in a case involving state security, political activists in the guise of so-called 'clerks' or so-called 'experts' might be introduced into the defence team by being listed among those essential to remain in Court during the secret sessions, thus enabling them to learn confidential practices and the identity of witnesses. This is a new and disturbing factor. Added to that is the intense competition between newspapers and broadcasters which inclines them to be ready to publish matters which a generation of earlier editors might have forgone. Nowadays it is presumed that secrecy is always sought only in the interests of the system or of officials and bureaucrats and never in the genuine interests of the state. Some modern publishers demand to be personally satisfied of the details of the harm which it is alleged that a particular publication might do. They will rarely now take representations on trust. That would be considered the deferential conduct of times thankfully past. Only if personally convinced in the exercise of their own judgement will they agree not to publish. But the mere identification of matter sought to be published as sensitive, let alone any identification of the possible consequence of disclosure, may not be able to be done without endangering a source or a system which must be kept confidential. So the official has to decline to engage in this exercise of satisfying the publisher who is thereupon confirmed in his scepticism, while the official, for his part, doubts the responsibility of the journalist.

But the modern trial risk is the most serious. Traitors cannot be punished as they deserve unless they are prosecuted. The risk of a leak arising out of a trial can now outweigh the good of bringing these criminals to justice. It is exceedingly unhealthy for society and an undeserved comfort to spies and traitors if they were to suspect that they would not be prosecuted because the legal procedure can no longer provide at trial for the effective protection of state secrets and the identity of witnesses.

But these traumas only developed after I had left office. In my time there was still sufficient mutual trust between the lawyers, the press and the security services. In no case did we ever hesitate to prosecute.

On 31 August 1971 Oleg Lyalin, a Soviet Trade official stationed in London, was arrested for driving his car under the influence of drink. He refused to take a breathalyser test and at Tottenham Court Road Police Station he refused to give a blood sample. The next morning, 1 September, at Marborough Street Magistrates' Court he was released from custody on bail of £50. His surety was a Soviet official from the Embassy. But Lyalin did not leave the court in the company of his surety. He left the court alone and he did not return to his office. He collected his secretary, who was his mistress, and disappeared into a safe house under the protection of the British security service. Lyalin was a KGB officer and he had defected.

The successes of the British Service are not often acknowledged. The traffic in defectors has not only been eastward, and this defection of Lyalin was a major coup.

Lyalin never answered to his bail at Marlborough Street. He never reappeared. I entered a *nolle prosequi*, which meant that the charge against him was effectively quashed. But his failure to respond to his bail was noted. So was my action. My old client, John Gordon, 'Man of the People' of the *Sunday Express*, was outraged. In his column he angrily demanded an explanation. No man, he thundered, not even a foreign trade official, was above the law. He called for an immediate public enquiry. I offered no explanation. No enquiry was established. For in the month of September Oleg Lyalin was busy; and as a result I was busy too.

On 9 September the police went to a house in Upper Tollington Park, Finsbury Park, with a search warrant. In the bedroom of the house they found a portable radio with headphones connected to a tape-recorder. On the table beside the recorder were several sheets of paper on which had been written groups of figures, obviously a code. On the papers were notes of transmission frequencies and call signs. When the tape on the recorder was played, there could be heard a call sign and a message in code. The identical call sign and message recorded on the tape-recorder had been monitored a few minutes earlier by a government radio operator. The transmission had come from Moscow.

The occupants of the house were two Greek Cypriot tailors, Kyriacos Costi and Constantinos Martianou. They were both arrested. They had been caught red-handed. During the search of the premises by the police, Costi showed them some innocent-looking torch batteries whose tops unscrewed to reveal cavities in which were papers bearing numbers, and a small plastic pen in which was a rolled up film of a signal plan. From the bedroom Costi produced an ordinary dark green Venus pencil. When the top of the pencil was unscrewed, the body of the pencil was hollow, providing a hiding place for micro film and messages. Such was some of the equipment with which these modest spies had been provided.

Costi had originally been a member of the Young Communist League in London but after he had been recruited by a Soviet Intelligence officer he had been advised discreetly to resign. He had then received training in the receipt and despatch of secret signals both in London and in Moscow. In London some of his training was from a Soviet agent masquerading, as so many did, as a trade official and some from Oleg Lyalin himself. Constantinos Martianou had been recruited after he had paid a visit to the Russian Exhibition at Earls Court. He had also been in contact with Lyalin.

For any proposed legislation to replace the present Official Secrets Act, it should be noted that neither of these men had access to secret or official information. What they were equipped and trained to do was when required to pass on information received by them.

I prosecuted both at the Old Bailey. I had the tape with the Moscow call number and coded message played in court. Both men pleaded guilty and were sentenced to four and six years imprisonment respectively. They were small fish in the world of espionage.

One week after the police went to Upper Tollington Park, Srijiol Husein Abdulcalden was arrested. He was a student of Lincoln's Inn who had failed his Bar exams. He had been recruited by the KGB who directed him to seek employment with the GLC motor licensing department. This job had been specially selected for him by the KGB because they were anxious to know the index numbers of the cars of the Special Branch and the Security Service whose difficult task was to keep under surveillance the large number of so-called trade and other Soviet officials who were in fact Intelligence officers working in London. If the Soviet officials were able to identify the official cars, it would be easier for them to avoid observation. The large numbers of Soviet and other Intelligence officers operating in the city already made the task of the watchers extremely difficult.

The index numbers of these official cars were kept in a special file at the GLC and Abdulcalden was given the task by his masters to extract them and give them to his Soviet control. This Abdulcalden proceeded to do, but fortunately he was lazy and sometimes more inventive than industrious: he would then give to his paymasters imaginary numbers and this led to an agreeable amount of confusion and mystification for the Soviet agents. But the service which he genuinely provided enabled the agents often to evade the surveillance of the highly overstretched observers.

In February 1972 he was sent to prison for three years. Again for the reform of the Official Secrets Act it should be noted that the information which in this case was passed to the Soviet officials was not even classified information. It was just the index numbers of certain cars. But the information which was passed thwarted a task of national importance, the surveillance of spies.

In that busy month of September 1971, which began with the defection and debriefing of Oleg Lyalin, the government courageously tackled the mischief of the swollen numbers of Soviet officials, most of whom were known to be officers of the KGB. Ninety were expelled; fifteen who were absent from the country were refused permission to return. The strained resources of the watchers were much relieved. This effective expulsion of many KGB officers operating in Britain also brought further dividends beyond that of a welcome relief to the watchers. For the announcement of the expelled officials led to the emergence of two further traitors, one a civil servant employed at the British Embassy in Khartoum; the other a naval officer. In both these cases I again led for the prosecution.

Leonard Hinchcliffe was an administrative officer in the diplomatic service and in a position of considerable trust. A married man, he succumbed, he said, to blackmail by the Soviets concerning his relationship with a married woman when he was stationed in the Sudan in 1970 and 1971. He passed to his Soviet control, André, secret documents and for his services he later said that he had been paid about two or three thousand pounds. At an early meeting, André tore a page from his pocket-book and wrote, 'Received the sum of £1000'. On this slip of paper André demanded and got Hinchcliffe's signature. Thus in accordance with their standard practice the Soviet control had now in his possession proof of their relationship, and for Hinchcliffe there could henceforward be no escape.

Also in accordance with their customary practice, André established a system of recognitions for meetings. In London Hinchcliffe was to carry under his arm a copy of *Punch*. (Today, I suppose, that might very well make a person extremely conspicuous, but not then!) The control would approach and say, 'Could you show me the way to Alexandra Place?' Hinchcliffe had to reply 'I don't know. I have just come from the Sudan.' In Algiers, the greeting was, 'Didn't I see you before in Naples?' The reply was, 'It's possible. I was there in January.' Novelettish as all this sounded, this was in real life the actual code established by professionals to facilitate the passing of real and substantial secret information. I prosecuted him in April 1972 and he was sentenced to ten years imprisonment.

A month earlier I had been in Winchester at the trial of Sub-Lieutenant Bingham, a Royal Navy officer who had for two years been supplying the Soviet Naval Attaché, Lori Kuzmin, with naval secrets. These secrets included film and documents concerning Royal Naval equipment and devices, such as nuclear depth charges. Kuzmin set up with Bingham a complex system to pass to him the secrets which Bingham sold. It involved the use of hollowed-out artificial stones capable of holding documents and film which Kuzmin supplied. The 'stones' were made of putty, scorched on the outside and about the size of a cricket ball.

The arrangement was for Bingham to make a 'drop', that is to say to use the 'stones' as receptacles for the documents he was passing, and leave them among roadside piles of real stones at seven selected sites in the Guildford area from which Kuzmin would collect them. After Bingham had made a 'drop' he would leave an empty Player's No. 1 cigarette packet in a public telephone kiosk at Shalford. If Bingham ever needed to contact Kuzmin urgently at their prearranged place of rendezvous, he had to send to him a particular printed church notice. If Kuzmin was unable to come, he in turn sent Bingham a picture postcard of Big Ben. The secrets which this naval officer had passed were important and relevant to the defence against the ever-growing Soviet submarine fleet. Bingham's motive for treachery was money. He was sentenced to twenty-one years' imprisonment.

But before all these cases, I had gone north to Leeds to prosecute Nicholas Prager before John Widgery, the recently appointed Lord Chief Justice. I had settled that the trial should be held in Leeds partly because the Yorkshire police under Chief Superintendent Donald Craig had conducted a markedly efficient investigation and there seemed no call to hand this over to the Met. There was also another and graver reason to hold this trial outside London. Because of the identity of one of the witnesses whom I intended to call, it would be safer to try the case away from London, where the witness, who was 'on loan' from an ally overseas, could be more safely protected. Further, the court in Leeds had a facility which in this case was also important. From the steps which led up to the dock in the centre of the Leeds court ran an underground passage to the neighbouring prison. Thus a witness could be brought into the court shielded from the prying eyes of observers, and I knew that the witness who was to be called in the case against Nicholas Prager would be of very special interest not only to the press but also to others.

In Parliament, in response to questions why Oleg Lyalin had not answered to his bail and stood his trial on a drunk-driving case, I had revealed that he was a KGB officer who before his defection had been serving in that department in the KGB which was responsble for the organization of sabotage in the United Kingdom. The duties of that particular department, I told the Commons, included the elimination of individuals judged to be enemies of the USSR. I had no intention of allowing Lyalin to surface at Marlborough Street where he would be observed by his former colleagues, to whom he would now most certainly rank as an enemy of the USSR. For the same reasons I needed to keep away from the eyes of that menacing KGB department, and from the eyes of the world press, the witness whom I proposed to call in the trial at Leeds. Like Lyalin he was an Intelligence officer who had defected; like Lyalin, although a Czech, he would now rank as an enemy of the USSR. His name was Major Frantisek August.

Frantisek August had been an Intelligence officer serving with Josef Frolik, a one-time 'Labour attaché' at the Czech Embassy in London. They both had unrivalled knowledge of the Eastern-bloc spy operations which were so active in Great Britain. While serving in London they had concentrated on trying to penetrate the Labour Party. After the defection of both of these Czech intelligence officers, they gave to the Security Service the name of the Labour MP, Will Owen.

Owen had been prosecuted at the Old Bailey in the spring of 1970, just before we came into office. To his manifest surprise, he was acquitted. Later, safe from further prosecution, Owen spoke freely to the Security Service about his dealings with Czech Intelligence, which was, as it remains, a service of particular dedication and energy, directing much attention to the penetration of British society. I was determined that at the trial of Nicholas Prager in Leeds the jury would hear and see the defector Frantisek August in the flesh.

The counsel who had successfully defended Will Owen was James Comyn QC. I learned with relief that he had been retained for the defence of Prager. My delight arose not out of any disregard for James' talents as a jury advocate, but solely because it meant that in a case in which so much secret matter would be disclosed I knew that we had a counsel for the defence who could be wholly trusted. He was a redoubtable performer in court, deferring to no one, a robust and very effective advocate. For all his skill and expertise and his not infrequent success as counsel for the defence, his appearance on behalf of an accused in a spy case was always welcomed by the Security Service, who also knew that what was said when the Court went into secret session would never be betrayed by him. He would never allow any false 'expert' to be slipped into his defence team.

So in the Prager case all that we had to worry about, and that was quite enough, was whether James' very effective Irish blarney and charm would seduce the jury into error. Fortunately in the case of Nicholas Prager it did not.

Prager was the son of a Czech-born, British-naturalized father, and he himself had been born and raised in Czechoslovakia. As an adult he had come to England with his Czech wife and had joined the RAF. When he joined, he falsely declared that he was British by birth and that he had always lived in England. He became a radar operator at HQ Fighter Command. In 1956 he underwent positive vetting which wholly failed to show up the lies which he had told in his application to join the RAF. After the vetting he secured clearance for top-secret defence information. He was now in a position to obtain for the Russians, through the Czechs, the information which they so badly wanted and for which Prager had been targeted. The long years of preparation and waiting were at an end.

Among the devices to which Prager obtained access were Blue Diver and Red Steer, the radar jamming devices fitted to the RAF V-bomber force which enabled the aircraft to break through the Soviet radar defence screen and deliver nuclear bombs on to Soviet targets. The V-bomber force was at that time a major element in NATO strategy. The capability to penetrate the Soviet Union Air defence was an important factor in and justification for the British independent nuclear deterrent.

In fact, due to the treachery of Nicholas Prager, the Soviets knew every detail of the RAF anti-radar devices. The V-bomber force would not have been able to penetrate the Soviet defence screen. So the British deterrent, upon which much of NATO policy had been based during the 1960s, did not exist. The Soviets knew it and were able to frame their policy and strategy accordingly.

In 1961 Prager had left the RAF, his espionage mission accomplished. Thereafter he worked for English Electric. During the next ten years he spent much time in Prague. Eventually his activities during his service in the RAF were revealed to the Security Service by Frantisek August.

At the end of January 1971 his Yorkshire home was searched. It had been ten years since he had carried out his remarkable espionage coup, but nevertheless one-time pads (the message equipment of the professional spy) and other such kit were discovered in the house as if after an interval of ten years he was about to be reactivated from a decade as a 'sleeper'.

The trial began on 14 June 1971. Prager had confessed his treachery to the police. His bank accounts showed the receipt of sums of money while he was in the RAF which he would not at first explain. Then he admitted to the police that he had received the money from Czech Intelligence. His passport showed that he had been in Prague when he had pretended to be on leave in Hawaii. A sketch map for a meeting in Paris was found; it was of the kind supplied to their agents by Czech Intelligence. Prager had purchased a polaroid camera, at the time a relatively new device on the market. He admitted that he had used it to photograph the manual of the anti-radar jamming apparatus, Blue Diver.

At his trial he withdrew his confession, which he claimed was false and stated that he had made it only to protect his wife, who was the real spy. She, at the time of the trial, was of course conveniently safe in Czechoslovakia. The Court went into secret session on several occasions. The underground passage was used.

After a trial lasting eight days, Prager was convicted. The Lord Chief Justice sentenced him to twelve years in prison. In comparison to the other sentences imposed in cases of serious treachery, such as Blake's forty-two years, the Krogers' twenty, Vassall's eighteen, and in the following March Bingham's twenty-one, it was not a heavy sentence. On sentencing Prager, the Lord Chief Justice said that his offence was mitigated by the fact that ten years had passed since the treachery had been committed, during which no disaster had befallen this country as a consequence.

I found that last comment puzzling. What Prager had done had been to train himself for many months, if not years, in order to secure a position which would empower him to lay his hands on information which the Soviets badly wanted and which, when Prager had obtained it for them, had enabled the Soviets to neutralize the principal weapon of deterrence in NATO's armoury. As a result, the Soviets during the past decade had been able to balance their global policies with no fear of any threat from a substantial part of the military power of the West. Their diplomacy and military policy had been orientated in disregard of an important element in the fragile balance of power. The consequences of Prager's crime had been immense.

But sentences in spying cases are only meaningful in that they demonstrate the state's revulsion of treachery and deter to some extent the traitor at heart and to a greater extent the traitor for money. This last kind of traitor, the mercenary traitor, rarely manages to squeeze much out of his paymaster; for the traitor is inevitably trapped by the very fact of his first approach. He is compromised from the start. His visit or his meeting will have been recorded by those whom he has approached. The spymaster is in control from the outset and rarely has to be generous with his payments. So he pays parsimoniously, little by little , disparaging what he has been brought and ever demanding more and better.

One rule in the unequal relationship betwen the agent and his control is sacrosant. It does not matter whether the agent has been brought into the game through the 'honey-trap', the blackmail arising out of a sentimental or sexual attachment which has often been deliberately engineered; or whether he is an ideologue who seeks only to serve a cause. Whatever the circumstances, the spymaster will usually insist upon paying money and will ensure that there is evidence of the receipt. In this way, should the idealist weaken in faith or the blackmailed recover some resolve, there always exists the evidence of the sordid exchange of money. It is only the professional – who will have been trained and instructed to 'sleep' until got into place with access to the information which his controllers have targeted – who does not need to be compromised by the traditional pieces of silver. For every category of spy, however, gold in their business is rarely on offer.

The professional, Nicholas Prager, was the first of the spies whom I prosecuted between 1970 to 1972. Leonard Hinchcliffe was the last. Thereafter the criminal trials in which I appeared were those arising from the terrorist attacks by the IRA, namely the retaliatory raid after Black Sunday on the officers' mess of the Parachute Brigade at Aldershot and the bomb attacks on the Old Bailey and the War Office in London. After I had left office I prosecuted several more terrorist cases when I was leader of the Western Circuit.

From time to time there surfaced, out of the murk of the Irish scene, the Littlejohn brothers. Convicted in the Irish Republic of robbing banks to obtain funds for the IRA, they claimed to have infiltrated the organization on behalf of the British Secret Service and to have met a British junior minister. They asserted that they had been promised immunity from prosecution. They certainly had not by me.

It was then, as it is now, a commonplace in certain circles that the British system and British officials grotesquely exaggerate the security interest of the United Kingdom. Also it was then, as now, fashionable to scoff that the United Kingdom is today so unimportant that it has no secrets worth the stealing and that the last thing that the Soviets and the Eastern bloc would trouble themselves over were the puny defence interests of Great Britain. It is, such people claim, all a fantasy created out of the pathological bureaucratic obsession of Whitehall in wanting to keep everything secret.

But those who preached and still preach this doctrine cannot have troubled to study the evidence given in open court in the trials of the spies over the last twenty years. For, if the scoffers are right, what reason could there be for the constant operation in England of agents masquerading as 'trade officials' who are in reality trained Intelligence officers? Why was there mounted an operation to infiltrate the Labour Party at a time when Harold Wilson had labelled it 'the natural party of government'? These expensively trained Intelligence officers were not despatched to London to serve no purpose. The effort and expense would not have been expended by such professional and highly skilled Intelligence services if nothing worthwhile was to be gained for them from their highly organized operations in Great Britain. They would have been wasting their time.

But the scoffers were not correct, as the elaborate espionage operations which were continually being mounted by the Eastern bloc powers clearly demonstrate. The incontrovertible evidence given in open court in those five spy cases in which I appeared within the space of only two years spelt out some of the techniques of these operations. What were the publicized dividends which were won for the East? They were not trivial. They included the ability in the 1960s to neutralize NATO's V-bomber force; and in the 1970s securing details of Royal Naval nuclear depth-charges for defence against the Soviet submarine fleet. Out of this little batch of convicted spies, the haul included an officer in the Royal Navy, a former technician in the RAF, and an administrative officer in the Diplomatic Corps.

Recently there have been fewer criminal prosecutions for espionage. That may be due to the difficulty nowadays, to which I have referred, in maintaining confidentiality over the evidence when the court goes into secret session with the risk of identities and practices being revealed and the increased eagerness in modern times to publish, even at the risk of damaging national interests. The infrequency of criminal prosecutions is more likely to be due to such considerations than to any sudden downturn in the espionage activities of the Intelligence services of the Soviets and their vassals. If this is the reason, then it is a serious development. It is an additional reason for the urgent necessity for a more rational Official Secrets Act – which the media understandably demand – but also for an Act so framed that it will get the media off the back of the Security Service.

Fifteen years ago, Ewen Montagu QC, then Judge Advocate of the Fleet and a wartime officer in naval Intelligence (and the author of an earlier book, *The Man Who Never Was*), had written and was planning shortly to publish a book about certain wartime Intelligence operations. What Ewen had described in his book had all taken place a quarter of a century earlier. To some it would seem absurd to restrict any publication in the 1970s of what had happened in wartime twenty-five years earlier. To some, the official reservations would have seemed yet another example of the obsessive preoccupation of British officialdom with secrecy and of official restriction upon the freedom of publication. But certain systems and practices in use in the Second World War, though modified and modernized, were still proving useful. That these might be described by an author writing with the authority of Ewen's personal Intelligence experience and published at a particular time aroused concern. Burke Trend was then the Cabinet Secretary. He knew about the book and he asked me to talk with Ewen. This I did, and Ewen cut certain passages and publication was postponed. (The elderly J. C. Masterman was more obdurate and less amenable. He also had written of wartime activities but he was anxious to obtain the credit and for the world to know what he had done. So he published. The Crown rightly secured a substantial proportion of the author's royalties.)

It was possible to do this with Ewen because he accepted the burden of trust which he had assumed when he became engaged in naval Intelligence, and that the trust could last a lifetime. To him with his service experience, explanation could be given why publication was contrary to the national interest. The problem arises when an official request has to be made to someone without such experience and is met by the demand for identification of those particular subjects which on their face seem harmless and which it was said would harm the national interest. But official identification of areas of sensitivity can itself create the mischief it was hoped to avoid. So on occasion the only alternative may be to seek to ban the whole. That in turn is met by outcry about censorship, and officialdom is thrown back upon some general principle which appears to the media to go far too wide – such as the claim that there should be a lifelong bond of silence upon former officers of the Security Service.

To many, however, it seems obvious that where a person such as Peter Wright has voluntarily engaged himself to make his life's work in state security and national secrets, he should not be allowed in retirement to reveal them. For such an obligation is absolute. No resentment that a personal assurance about a pension has been dishonoured can excuse a breach of that bond. No more can the rejection of a theory that a former superior was a traitor, especially when that accusation had undergone internal and external investigation. In the 1970s and the aftermath of Watergate, the CIA was effectively destabilized and its effectiveness seriously weakened. The West suffered. A similar operation had been conducted earlier against the British Security Services, obviously facilitated by the exposure of the traitors within the service. The protracted search for other traitors, perhaps even more highly placed, for too long preoccupied the service, distracting operations and damaging morale. To some the Director General himself, Sir Roger Hollis, was a traitor. For others even greater game than Hollis was stalked. The mysterious virus which had killed Hugh Gaitskell and which led to his succession was the obsession of some; Peter Wright's was over the guilt of Hollis. When the accusation was rejected, but because some still remained dissatisfied, Burke Trend, the former Cabinet Secretary, passed a year in a personal investigation ultimately leaving the ghost of Roger Hollis uneasily at rest.

What then could be the purpose of a former officer in publishing a book? To show that he was always right and the others always wrong? To expose whom, and to expose what?

Under the present system the rules for former ministers and officials wanting to publish, provide that the author must submit his manuscript to the Cabinet Secretary. To a former official who wants to expose the misdeeds of his former official colleagues, that might not, I suppose, commend itself. But if the objective is genuine public exposure, the trouble of writing a book is hardly necessary. The evidence can be brought to the Director of Public Prosecutions who is independent of government. If, however, suspicion of all officialdom extends to distrust even of the Director and the purpose really is solely exposure, then there is the Opposition in Parliament, who are not usually diffident about making a public fuss if the fuss were to embarrass the Government of the day and the officials in its service. But if the paranoia goes so far that even the Opposition is not trusted because it is suspected that the exposure might embarrass even them, then there are powerful newspapers who are always rightly eager to mount an investigation into an official scandal and who much prefer themselves to investigate and expose public scandal than merely to publish the memoirs of an embittered public servant.

So if there is a genuine belief that wrongdoing in high circles has been perpetrated and must be exposed, there exist perfectly effective means for public revelation of official scandal, always assuming that there is something to be revealed. It is hardly necessary to hug the 'secrets' and write a book. If of course the object is less altruistic, then publishing a book without having it vetted is simply an exercise in making money out of the revelation of the confidences of public service. Where that public service is the Secret Service then it must be in the public interest to make every effort to stop the betrayal, or at least attempt to deny the betrayer the rewards of his betrayal. Accordingly, at whatever the cost and whether eventually successful wholly or in part, officialdom has no choice but to pursue a traitor to that service, if necessary to the ends of the earth. For the eyes of others who might be tempted are upon them and gentlemen with fat wallets and ready chequebooks are nowadays always waiting on the corner.

By doing it his way Peter Wright became one of the enemies of his service whom it was once his duty to catch.

Chapter 26
English Attorney General in Northern Ireland

'Dear Cur,' the letter began, 'I would like you to know I consider you are one of the worst of the scum boys. You are the lowest form of animal life i.e. a Catholic Tory M.P.. I hope you are proud of your fellow henchmen in Northern Ireland. Yours with the greatest of Disdain.' The letter was signed and came from Lancashire.

That, I felt, was a bit rough about my 'henchmen'. In fact I figured on their death list. By the date of the letter I was one of their prime targets, for I was responsible for their prosecution and the effort to ensure their conviction and imprisonment not only throughout the whole of England and Wales, but also, since Easter of 1972, throughout the province of Northern Ireland. But I was 'a Catholic Tory M.P.', and that I suppose was enough.

I had personal connections with Ireland, tenuous connections by blood, closer by association. The blood came through a Harrington grandmother whose family claimed kinship with the family of Edmund Burke and an illegitimate son of that old Duke of York who marched his troops up and down the hill and whose mistress made a good business out of the sale of army commissions. Two of my uncles had served with the Irish Guards in the First World War, and I and another in the second. I was very proud to have commanded Irish troops in war. The regiment had many officers, English as well as Irish, who were Roman Catholics. The chaplains to the battalions were always Catholic priests, usually Benedictine monks of Downside. The pipes and drums attended the Catholic church parade. In a regiment which recruited from both north and south of the border, there was no sectarian friction.

I had two married daughters, Mikaela and Haidee, both then living in Ireland, one in Kildare in the Republic, one in County Down in the North.

Neither of their then husbands was Catholic; both were, suitably for Irishmen, engaged in the business of horses. North of the border I had friends and sons of friends. One of these was Marcus McCausland, son of very old friends. Later, when he rashly but courageously sought secret meetings in a genuine search for reconciliation or at least understanding, he was callously murdered by the IRA. As a member of the British government I was from time to time the recipient of information about opinion in North and South. I was also the only senior Minister who was a Catholic. I knew little of Northern Ireland, while it had been almost a quarter of a century since my visits to Dublin on leave during the war. Nevertheless, I tried to convey to the government some of the atmosphere and mood of the Province and the Republic of which relations and friends wrote and spoke.

At this time Reggie Maudling, the Home Secretary, was the Minister indirectly responsible for Northern Ireland affairs. The Stormont government still bore the direct responsibility. The Troubles in Ulster had flared violently in 1969, when Jim Callaghan was Home Secretary. Throughout 1970 and 1971 the situation grew steadily worse. The bombing campaign began; assassinations became common; the army was constantly having to be reinforced. In August the governments of the United Kingdom and Northern Ireland introduced internment, detention without trial, in the face of the death and destruction which the IRA, now split between its Official and Provisional wings, was spreading throughout the Province. But Stormont had done this clumsily. Some citizens had been seized illegally; some, it was rumoured, seized out of spite. Later reports came of irregular methods of interrogation of people in custody. Charge and counter-charge were levelled by each community against the other. The killings mounted.

Until 1972 when I became Attorney General for Northern Ireland, I had had no direct experience of the Province. I had heard from certain friends, loyal to the Union, of discrimination against Catholics in jobs and appointments. I had heard of the prevalence of intense sectarian prejudice. Once I was talking with a man at a reception in Belfast. I spoke of a friend, Ambrose McGonigle, then a Lord Justice of Appeal, who in the war had won a Military Cross and bar. Did he know him, I enquired? The man said, slightingly, that he would not because Ambrose was a Catholic. I asked the man what service he had done in the war. He said that he had been in business.

After I had seen more of the Province and particularly more of its clerics of all denominations I began to understand that, just as many Anglicans could not identify with the bigoted Protestantism which they encountered in Northern Ireland, I, as an English Roman Catholic, could not identify with many of the Northern Ireland Catholics and their clergy. But I also met there some of the finest Christian individuals from both communities whom I have ever encountered.

On 30 January 1972, thirteen people were shot by the army in Londonderry. The Nationalists christened it 'Bloody Sunday'. The Irish Ambassador to London was withdrawn.

In February I had urgently to introduce into the House an Emergency Bill to restore to the army the lawful right to order the dispersal of crowds which had been successfully challenged in the Northern Ireland High Court. Only Bernadette Devlin, the fiery young member for Mid Ulster, seriously opposed the measure. But others took the opportunity to question whether the time had not come to look again at the question of a political initiative in Northern Ireland. The British Parliament had responsibility for the troops in Ireland, and internationally Britain was held accountable for all that was happening.

In the same month a 200-pound car bomb blasted the officers' mess of the Parachute Brigade at Aldershot, apparently in revenge for 'Bloody Sunday'. Seven died. In October of that year I led for the prosecution in the trial of three men accused of being responsible.

A whole Sunday in February was spent in conference at Chequers. Throughout March I attended frequent Cabinets and meetings at No. 10. Legislation was prepared for the United Kingdom to assume full power and to take direct responsibility. Few wanted this. It was a last resort. But the security situation was reaching a crisis.

Finally on 24 March the Prime Minister announced in Parliament that for a year Ulster was to be ruled direct from Westminster. The Northern Ireland Parliament was to be prorogued indefinitely and all its powers were to be transferred to the government in London. A new Secretary of State was to take over the executive powers. He was to be the genial Willie Whitelaw. As Attorney General of England and Wales, I was to become Attorney General of Northern Ireland. The announcement, at eleven o'clock on Friday 24 March, was greeted by a crowded House in silence. The gravity and the danger of the situation seemed to have imposed restraint. But in Belfast the shipyard workers stopped work and started to march. The 14,500 British troops stood to.

At two o'clock that afternoon I went to see Cardinal Heenan, Archbishop of Westminster. I told him that I had been invited by the Prime Minister to explain to him what the government intended to do and why. Later in the afternoon I was back at No. 10; then to the Law Courts to supervise the drafting of the legislation. As so often happens at times of crisis and maximum involvement, I had to go that evening to make a duty speech. It was to the Shipbrokers' Association at the Connaught Rooms.

It is occasions such as these, however friendly and understanding the hosts, which impose the worst burdens in public life. Seldom ever does anyone get these speeches right. Either you work like the devil to produce an amusing after-dinner speech (and nothing takes more preparation that that), and then you are criticized by some for being frivolous and for having insulted the occasion by saying nothing serious; or you deliver a heavy and prepared speech and are criticized by others for not making an after-dinner speech and surely the speech delivered need not have been so inordinately dull! Anyhow, I have a photograph of that particular occasion. Some are laughing; some look sour. What I am certain of is that on that evening I told no anecdotes about the Scotsman, the Englishman and the Irishman.

The following weekend and early week were spent in pressing on with the preparation of the Northern Ireland Bill which finally reached is Third Reading after an all-night sitting at 11.20 on Maundy Thursday morning. I made the winding-up speech, as I had on its Second Reading thirty-six hours earlier. Thirteen Ulster Unionists voted against the Bill. So did Enoch Powell.

That same afternoon I had to attend a Privy Council at Windsor, where the Queen had gone to spend Easter. Albert, my driver, and I encountered very heavy holiday traffic on the motorway, and we were caught in a mammoth traffic jam. It is a cardinal sin to be late for a Council and to keep the Sovereign waiting. That afternoon I committed it. This, I thought, as I sat in the car, was just what I needed after the previous frenetic days and nights. Eventually we swept into the Castle. I sprinted noisily up the long passages to the shock of the courtiers, and breathlessly expressed apologies to Godfrey Agnew, the Clerk, for conveyance to Her Majesty. I waited to be removed to the Tower. But I was excused. Back in London I went to bed and woke at lunchtime on Good Friday.

The week before I had seen Barry Shaw, a silk at the Northern Irish Bar who had been already provisionally selected by my predecessor in Ulster for the new post of Director of Public Prosecutions, Northern Ireland. The Province had not previously had a Director, and prosecutions had been left solely to the Attorney General. A permanent, independent officer was now to be appointed. Barry Shaw was a fine man, but as an Ulsterman he was understandably distressed by the sudden abolition of the Stormont government and Parliament. I had to persuade him to take on the new office under the new Westminster regime. It was good for Northern Ireland that he agreed. Thereafter he and I worked together in establishing a new Prosecuting Service independent of government and uninfluenced by the pressures which in that society were continually applied from both communities. It was due to the rock-like integrity and impartiality of Barry Shaw that the service gained the confidence and acceptance of both Unionist and Republican alike. He was ably assisted by the deputy whom he recommended, Barney McClusky, a Belfast solicitor.

After he had consented we held a small press conference in my room in the Law Courts in London to announce his appointment and that of his deputy. Barry Shaw was asked, 'What is your religion?' He answered, 'Presbyterian'. Then was asked, 'What is Barney McClusky's religion?' 'Roman Catholic', he replied. There were no further questions. The press conference was over.

I should have learned better from this, but at the time I did not fully appreciate its real significance. For to staff the new Prosecuting Service, I recommended to Barry that he should recruit lawyers with a previous record of experience of service for, and proven loyalty to, the Crown. He agreed and returned to Belfast to do this. Soon we had gathered together an experienced team, some of whom had served overseas in the Colonial Service as colonial Law Officers or Crown counsel. But what I had omitted to arrange was to ensure that to each the question was posed which had been asked at the press conference: 'What is your religion?' That was a question which up to then I would never have dreamed should be asked.

But it was reported back to me that it was being said, in rolling tones of Ulster thunder with long vowels and much thumping of lecterns, that the new English Attorney General himself was a Roman Catholic, and for this new service he had gathered together around him nothing but 'a nest of Roman Catholics'. It appeared that many of those who had been recruited on the basis of their proven past loyalty to the Crown in peace and in war were indeed Roman Catholics. Hastily I told Barry to try to balance the books. In this way was I introduced to a factor in public life which came wholly new to the English faces which were now to be seen in Belfast.

After appearing for the Crown at the Old Bailey in the trial of the spy Hinchcliffe in the morning of 17 April, I flew to Aldergrove, the Belfast airport. It was the first of the regular weekly visits which I was to make over the next two years. On this first occasion I stayed at Government House with Lord Grey of Naunton, the incumbent but soon to be dis-possessed Governor and a sometime barrister of New Zealand. During his distinguished career, crisis and trouble had pursued him wherever he served, from British Guiana and the emergence there of Forbes Burnham and his revolutionary government, to the Bahamas and the end of white minority rule and the ejection of the Bay Street Boys. Now he was encountering crisis in Northern Ireland.

His son was a member of my chambers and some years earlier I had been his guest for luncheon at Government House in Nassau. I had sat next to the black soul singer, Amalia Jackson. After a time she turned to me and asked dreamily how my meetings were going. I was a little taken aback, and then rather flattered. In my constituency, Epsom, the meetings were, I suppose, reasonable enough for modern times, but I was surprised that they should be of interest halfway across the world. I explained that they varied depending upon the occasion. She nodded, still dreamily, and asked how often I used the Albert Hall. I had the feeling that I was beginning to get out of my depth. Fortunately the Governor, on her other side, distracted her. I learned later that she had mistaken me for Billy Graham.

The day after my arrival on 17 April at Hillsborough, I enjoyed sensationally speedy legal promotion. I was called as a junior to the Northern Irish Bar, and seconds later promoted to the front row and granted silk by Robbie Lowry, the Chief Justice. The new Attorney General had been legitimized.

Over the next twenty-four hours, I met with the Army Commander, with the Chief Constable for the RUC and with the judges whose record of courage, integrity and dedication to the law and to the principles of justice shines through all the murky gloom of recent Ulster history. Many of them, including the then Chief Justice, have been personally attacked; some of them murdered; all abused and threatened. But they have remained true to their judicial oath. The Province and the tradition of the rule of law owe them a great debt.

But among the Bar there was some evidence of strain. Some of the Nationalist barristers, out of protest, were declining to prosecute. Relations between Unionist and Nationalist colleagues, who all shared a common library as in the Scottish system, were stretched to breaking point. Internment and the manner in which it had been operated and accounts of irregular and illegal interrogation were the principal causes. Barry and I addressed them. I promised, and Barry Shaw by his immediate example demonstrated, that prosecution would be impartial; the legality of any detention could be challenged in the courts.

The Bar used to hold extremely convivial dinners. It was the tradition at these dinners for the Nationalists to sing Orange songs, and the Unionists

Nationalist songs like 'The Wearing of the Green'. I revived the dinners; the singing began again. On these occasions I made a virtue out of necessity and, as a temporary Cockney, contributed 'Knocked 'Em in the Old Kent Road'. The Nationalists returned to prosecute.

With the army I had to emphasize that, however difficult it made their task, they had to operate under the rule of law. So if a soldier wantonly exceeded the appropriate level of force, he would be in jeopardy of prosecution. But I assured them that the Prosecution Service would not demand of them standards unreasonable when they were daily facing physical danger from sniper or bomber. The taking of the law cold-bloodedly into their own hands, however, could not be condoned. Further, we made clear that any one perpetrating or permitting brutality on those in custody would be prosecuted. Unlawful interrogation must cease.

From the so-called Nationalists came accusations that the new Prosecuting Service was just a tool of the Security Service and would do only what the English Secretary of State and the English Attorney General and the English Commander-in-Chief demanded. It would be used, they claimed, only against them. Priests as well as laymen peddled these wares and because of my religion I became a prime target. To them I gave the same answer I had given to Ian Paisley when he came into the Director's office: Barry would apply the law without fear or favour. And he did.

Yet over all these grave matters hung the unique Irish dimension. Robbie Lowry, the Chief Justice, regularly went south to judge at hunter trials or eventing; and a senior civil servant excused himself in the middle of a security conference with Willie over a serious crisis concerning the border with the Republic by announcing that he had to leave since he was due in Dublin to attend a meeting of the Irish rugby selectors. Willie threw up his hands in bewilderment. His Scots as opposed to my Irish Guards experience had not prepared him for this. But he went about his task, affable, avuncular, often engagingly incoherent and understandably bewildered as he wove his way through the intricacies and complexities of the novel Irish political scene.

Chapter 27
At Strasbourg – The IRA Bombers – Sunningdale

In December 1971, the government of the Irish Republic brought the United Kingdom government before the European Commission of Human Rights over the alleged mistreatment of political detainees. It claimed under articles of the European Human Rights Convention, in particular under Article 3, which related to the methods of interrogation of those in custody, Article 5 (imprisonment without trial), Article 14 (discrimination in the exercise of internment powers), and Article 2 (the taking of life).

Preliminary hearings were fixed to decide whether or not the complaints should be admitted for a full hearing. This came before the Commission in Strasbourg in September 1972. A year earlier I had appeared before this Commission on behalf of HMG in respect of complaints made by East African Asian United Kingdom passport-holders. I was the first British Law Officer to appear before it. Only recently had HMG by treaty agreed to the determination by the Commission of applications by individuals.

Unlike the International Court at The Hague or the EEC court at Luxembourg, I did not find the European Commission of Human Rights and the Court, which both sit at Strasbourg, impressive bodies. They had an inflexible and, I thought, an ill-ordered procedure; moreover they were generally manned at that time by judicial officers who had been selected by each individual state, none of which had chosen senior national judges. Some of the commissioners appeared at that time to have a poor command of English and yet they did not seem to feel obliged to avail themselves of the facility of the simultaneous translation. Some read during the oral submissions. Some, by their questioning of the advocates, or by their attitude and conversations during the lengthy breaks in the hearings for coffee which the commissioners and counsel all took together, displayed attitudes which seemed inapt for their judicial role. The proceedings were meant to be confidential but leaks to the press about the cases and their probable result were endemic. On occasions it was only vehement protests by the lawyers which kept to 'photo sessions' the press and television cameras, which nevertheless hovered round the Palais de Droits. The confidentiality rule which had been laid down by the Commission itself was regularly breached. Press conferences at the doors of the court, on the stairs leading to the court and in the foyer of the Palais were commonplace features of every hearing of every claim, and since the character of most of the claims had usually a strong political flavour, the opportunity was presented and readily taken for effective public representations of a complainant's case.

As is not unusual when any international body is charged with exercising what is technically a judicial function, namely the interpretation of a treaty, there was always a political flavour about the proceedings at Strasbourg. Further, a 'human rights' industry had grown up, encouraged by the elasticity of the interpretation of the treaty and the inevitable compromises often inherent in a process in which an international group of judicial officers each appointed by a separate state and all usually academics or former members of national Foreign Services are given the task of adjudicating upon the alleged transgressions of a member state.

But, to my mind, the real failing in both Commission and Court was in the calibre of the commissioners and even the judges to whom lay appeal from the Commission. If the present system of exercising this jurisprudence is to continue, then each state must ensure that there are appointed national judges of stature and quality who should be drawn from the highest ranks of the national judiciary of each member state. The judges who are then appointed should each serve for a term and then be replaced by others from their national Bench. In this way the national Bench of judges in each state would acquire experience in the jurisprudence of Strasbourg. The presence of judges selected from the ranks of judges of the superior courts, who would be jurists of international repute and who could be relied upon to exercise their task with strictly judicial rigour, would go far to remove the whiff of political prejudice and expediency which pervades much of the proceedings at Strasbourg.

Alternatively, each state could incorporate into the corpus of its own national law the provisions in respect of human rights, and make appeal on these issues lie from the national courts to the European Court at Luxembourg. This would eliminate the judicial apparatus in Strasbourg and the participation in European judicial affairs of representatives from states, such as Sweden and Switzerland and Malta, who are not members of the Community.

In September 1972 I looked forward to the preliminary hearings by the Commission at Strasbourg of the complaint by the government of the Republic of Ireland (the state case) with neither confidence nor professional pleasure. I had collected, however, a formidable legal team to assist me in representing HMG, for I had insisted to the Foreign Office and to the Treasury upon briefing the then Treasury 'devil', Gordon Slynn. Whenever I had to appear in any case at home or overseas, I always insisted that Gordon should also be briefed, for I always felt more comfortable with him beside me. He was very able. I also had Godfray Le Quesne QC instructed so that, if the matter went further and into lengthy proceedings which I could not attend, Godfray could lead for HMG. I reckoned that he was the most able lawyer among all the first rank of silks then practising. Later, for the witness hearings I brought in the criminal silk, John Hazan. Their companionship would be comforting during the handling of this disagreeable and difficult task.

Godfray was a particularly old friend. Also he lent an air of grave respectability to our team which I felt that the Foreign Office would appreciate; for he looked like an archdeacon. Even off-duty he was always garbed in clerical black, and he invariably wore, above his gold-rimmed glasses, a black Homburg hat. He was a teetotaller, but we always charged him an equal share of the bill for our luncheons and dinners for he ate enormously. He was an excellent companion to have on an assignment which was not going to be easy.

On the day before the hearing began in October 1972, and sometimes during the excessively lengthy luncheon adjournments which the commissioners liked to take, we drove up into the forest and walked around the Lodge built like a fortress by the Hohenzollerns after the seizure of Alsace in the war of 1870. But mostly we had little time for anything other than the preparation of our submission or reply. My principal concern over the hearings was in relation to certain methods of interrogation which had been used in about a dozen cases by the security forces in Northern Ireland before Westminster took over, such as hooding, the use of continuous high-pitched sound and making prisoners lean in a certain stance against a wall. I considered their use wrong, and that no amount of expediency, not even helping to counter the murderous campaign being waged against the population by the terrorists, justified such methods of trying to obtain information from those in custody. The government had set up two committees of enquiry to look into allegations that had been made about these methods, and in March 1972 the Prime Minister gave an assurance that they would never be used in future as an aid to interrogation.

Further there had been undoubted irregularities in the application by the authorities of the powers to detain without trial. But, following the assumption of direct rule by Westminster, many of those wrongfully or illegally detained, or who had been violently and systematically ill-treated while in arrest, were bringing civil actions for damages against the state without restriction by the authorities. Inevitably some unworthy claimants were among those who had brought these claims, but some claims were genuine and they were not defended by the Crown.

The hearing of the Republic's state case in Strasbourg began that October in 1972 and concluded at the end of several days of submissions on behalf of both governments. After some months of deliberation, the Commission dismissed the accusation by the Republic under Article 2 of the Convention as inadmissible. This was a welcome success since this had impugned the security operations in the field by the Army. The claims under other articles were remitted for a full hearing, which was eventually fixed for the first days of October in 1973.

That year had been a better year for those anxious to improve relations between the governments and peoples of the United Kingdom and Ireland, although there seem always to exist surprisingly many on both sides of the border and the Irish Sea to whom that is something which they never wish to encourage. But to most the meeting of the Prime Minister of the United Kingdom and the Prime Minister of the Republic at Baldonnel airfield near Dublin on 17 September 1973 was a significant move in the attempt to improve the relationship and to seek settlement of the age-old political differences. This meeting was primarily concerned to confirm the agreement to hold in England later in the year a Tripartite Conference, to which the principal political parties in Northern Ireland would be invited.

But it had also been agreed, or so I understood, that it was desirable to avoid taking the Republic's state case against the United Kingdom before the Commission at Strasbourg to the stage of hearing evidence of witnesses, and that the Strasbourg procedure of the promotion of a 'friendly settlement' by the Commission should be promoted by both governments. This decision was heralded as an important augury for the success of the proposed Tripartite Conference and it appeared to demonstrate the desire of the two heads of government to avoid all the bitterness of public litigation in an international forum.

Or so it was believed by HMG. On 20 September an approach was accordingly made on behalf of HMG to the Acting President of the Commisson to set in hand the promotion of the procedures for a friendly settlement of the proceedings at Strasbourg between the two states, leaving aggrieved individuals wholly free to prosecute their individual claims against HMG. However, shortly after the Baldonnel meeting some disturbing signals began to come from Dublin, and profound disquiet arose over the attitude of the Republic's lawyers.

On 1 October I arrived in Strasbourg with my legal team. I had temporarily left the lengthy trial at Winchester where I was leading the prosecution of the IRA active service unit commanded by the Price sisters, which earlier in the year had bombed the Old Bailey and an army office in Whitehall; I was to return to the trial when I had finished at Strasbourg.

On arrival I was concerned to hear that all the complaints against the British government before the Commission might still be continued by the Republic. It seemed essential to make plain to the Irish that our approach to the Acting President of the Commission had been made in good faith following the prime ministerial meeting on 17 September, and that it had been made in the expectation that the Republic would react positively.

I was also personally disturbed because one claim by the government of the Republic was that the use of the objectionable methods of interrogation amounted to the use of torture as an 'administrative practice'. This, if persisted in, amounted in the jurisprudence of Strasbourg to an accusation that British ministers had been responsible for and had knowledge of a practice of which we had been wholly ignorant and which, when we learned of it, we had banned. The ministers against whom this accusation had to be directed were the Prime Minister, the Secretary of State Willie Whitelaw and myself as Attorney General. The sustaining of this accusation before the Commission was resented, and I hoped that in the new mood of reconciliation after Baldonnel it would be abandoned.

Because of the disquieting news from Dublin which had followed the welcome agreement between the two Prime Ministers, I sought out a meeting with my opposite number, Declan Costello, the Irish Attorney General, who was in Strasbourg to present the case for the Republic. In the language of international communiqués, the exchanges between Mr Costello and myself when we met were certainly 'full and frank'. When we parted I realized that there seemed to be little likelihood of any positive reaction by the Republic to the approach by the Commission to promote a 'friendly settlement' of the state case, despite the apparent agreement at Baldonnel. I thought, however, that the personal position of British ministers would be made clear and that the accusations concerning an 'administrative practice' would not be pursued. But after our meeting I could not entirely fathom whether I had been in discussion with the lawyer or the client. I reported to No. 10 on the telephone.

The next day Mr Costello opened the case for the Republic. Nothing had been abandoned. That evening I spoke again with the Prime Minister in London. Then I settled down with our team to pass many hours of the night changing the submissions which after the 'bonhomie' of Baldonnel we had prepared. Next morning, still resentful, I delivered our amended submissions in rebuttal of the litany delivered the day before.

The argument before the Commission lasted all week. At its conclusion an enquiry by the Commission concerning the promotion of a 'friendly settlement' was welcomed by me. But it takes two to dance, or at least it used to, and in Strasbourg I definitely had no partner.

Two days later I was back in Winchester at the trial of the IRA terrorists. At least with them I knew where they stood.

I next met the Republic's Attorney General in December at the Tri-partite Conference at Sunningdale. We were not very friendly. I feared the use to which the enemies of Anglo-Irish friendship might put the persistence of the Republic in pressing the Irish state case at Strasbourg. Next year, when all had collapsed, I had no doubt that those responsible for the decision to persist in that case had contributed to the ruin.

Back from Strasbourg, I began on 29 October 1973 my final speech to the jury in the trial at Winchester of the IRA bombers of London. In summarizing the case for the prosecution against each of the accused in turn, I had to speak all that day, all the next and for half of the third – a total of over twelve hours. In November the jury returned their verdicts – guilty, on all save one. The one acquitted was a young girl. After arrest she had given the police a statement explaining her role in the operation. After the verdict she was saluted by the others who had been convicted. They held in their hands silver coins which they clinked together. One coin was flung at her. It was the symbolic gesture of the price of betrayal – pieces of silver.

When commentators review the conviction of IRA terrorists by English courts, they often fail to comprehend the technique of this fanatic organization which lays claim to the life-long loyalty of its members. These armchair critics make much of confessions to the police given in private which at the public trial are withdrawn. The commentators often use this to reflect upon the conduct of the interrogators. But they overlook the grip which this organization tries to retain on the people it has recruited. For it preaches that its arm extends beyond the courts and the prisons, and that its vengeance stretches beyond the sentences which have to be served and beyond the protection of any government. In fact it does not, but the discipline of terror is formidable. The oath to the organization is for life. They seek to portray that, like the Mafia, the tentacles of their IRA terror reach beyond any haven.

When the Winchester trial was over, I was driven back to my house in Sussex. The armed police in the barn at my gate checked me in. The Special Branch Officer sat in my hall. As darkness fell, the guards patrolled, and stared at the woods through their infra-red viewfinders. Next morning Albert Morley drove me to London, travelling – as he was permitted to do for security reasons, and much to his enjoyment – well over the legal speed limit.

As we passed through a village I happened to look up from my seat in the back of the car, where I was working on the papers from my red box which were spread out beside me. I noticed that a car was parked facing us on our right in the oncoming lane of traffic. Suddenly another car pulled out from behind it. Our path was effectively blocked and we had to come to an abrupt halt. I saw the Special Branch officer sitting in the front beside Albert take out his pistol, slip the safety catch and place it on his lap.

This, I had to remind myself, was the English countryside in 1973. Then the other car pulled aside and we went through. I went back to my papers.

On Wednesday 5 December 1973 I attended a briefing at No. 10 for the forthcoming Tripartite Conference which was to open at the Civil Service College at Sunningdale the next day. Attending the Conference were to be Prime Minister Cosgrave of the Irish Republic and his ministers; the Ulster Unionists with former Northern Irish Prime Minister Brian Faulkner at their head, the Social Democratic and Labour Party and the Alliance Party from the Province; and the Prime Minister of the United Kingdom with the new Secretary of State, Francis Pym, appointed only a few days earlier, and myself.

The Conference sat throughout the Thursday, and then on that night the participants were driven back to London to dine at No. 10 as the guests of Ted Heath. As was the custom which he had established, Ted Heath had glee singers to sing grace at dinner. This on another occasion had proved a notable strain upon the straightfacedness of a certain Permanent Under-Secretary when a guest at No. 10, and who was unprepared for song before he settled down to his dinner. He was not alone in having difficulty in controlling himself. I have seen shoulders, not those of the then Prime Minister, heave and shake as the singers got into their second verse; for some found it excruciatingly comic. Those of us who regularly attended such dinners were prepared, and the Irish guests had been warned. So they too were ready.

As ever Ted made one of his felicitous speeches at this Irish dinner. On the occasion of another which he had earlier given for all the heads of the civil service departments and to which he had asked certain ministers, he invited us to join with him in the toast by the ephemeral to the permanent. At this Irish gathering he was equally gracious and graceful, so unlike his performance in the formal set-pieces which he delivered in Parliament or on the platform. The Irish, who had not before encountered this facet of a remarkable man, were pleased. The choir sang Irish airs. Everyone and everything, including the English eyes, were smiling. If only, I thought, we could be left unpressurized, we here on this evening could surely settle our differences. Despite the past we were all heirs to a similar tradition and culture. We had far more in common than we had in conflict. We even rather liked each other.

But that, I suppose, was the wine talking. Next day we were all back wrangling at Sunningdale. All that day until one in the morning, all the next day and all the next night. I then drove home to Sussex and slept for two hours until noon. By two in the afternoon we were back at the Conference until nine o'clock that night. Finally, all was agreed and a communiqué signed. Even a photograph was taken, although not a group photograph, for the great are seldom great at sharing out credit.

The communiqué issued after the Sunningdale Conference set forth that the Irish government had accepted and solemnly declared that there would be no change in the status of Northern Ireland until a majority of people in the Province desired a change in that status. The British government solemnly declared that if in the future the people of Northern Ireland should indicate a wish to become part of a united Ireland, the British government would support that wish. That, ordinary people might be forgiven for thinking, ought to satisfy ordinary people in Northern Ireland.

The communiqué went on to announce that the two governments had agreed to establish a representative Council of Ireland (a concept at least sixty years old) with a council of ministers, a consultative assembly, a secretary general, a secretariat and a headquarters. Studies were to be put in hand to promote the economic health of the whole island, including tourism and sport; a joint commission was to be set up to consider the complex legal problems affecting both nations, including extradition and the establishment of a common law enforcement area in which an all-Ireland court might have jurisdiction. It was agreed that a formal conference would be held in the New Year 1974 to consider the reports of these studies.

We drove away from Sunningdale rather happy. We parted as friends. On 10 December, Ted Heath made a statement in the House of Commons. Many dared to hope, English and Irish, Catholic and Protestant. So did my family in the north and in the south of Ireland.

Forty-eight hours later I was back in Strasbourg. There it was confirmed that the Irish government was going to pursue its state case before the European Commission. The British government was still going to face the much resented Irish allegation that the British security forces had subjected detainees to inhuman treatment in accordance with an institutionalized practice, an 'administrative practice'. The jolly hosts at the recent feast were still to be in the dock, personally accused by their recently so jolly guests. The blarney of Sunningdale, those 'smiling eyes', the glee singers and the wine at Downing Street, all that seemed very far away as I sat in the Palais de Droits listening to the Irish lawyers.

The claim was pursued, despite the fact that HMG had already demonstrated to the Commission that if any person had been subjected to illegal interrogation when in custody, he or she could freely bring claims for damages against the Crown, and already some claimants had been awarded substantial pecuniary awards in the Northern Ireland courts. Moreover, apart from the Irish government state case, individuals were bringing their own cases before the Commission at Strasbourg. By December 1973 seven had been admitted as appropriate for hearing by the Commission and were due to be heard. It might have required some political courage for the Irish government to abandon the state case, but it could have been done. The individuals who claimed to have been injured had their personal remedy. Nothing could be gained from one government fighting the other.

In the light of the Sunningdale communiqué and the mutual determination to move into a new phase of Anglo-Irish co-operation and friendship, the persistence of the Irish government forty-eight hours later with the claim that the inhuman treatment of prisoners had been institutionalized by the British government inevitably blasted many of the sentiments which had flowered at the Conference and did much to destroy the hopes which had been raised so shortly before. Whoever advised the Irish government to proceed at Strasbourg bears some responsibility for destroying the chance of opening a new chapter in Anglo-Irish relations.

A decade of more death and destruction was to pass before another attempt could be made to revive the concepts of Sunningdale. By then, in

1983, the bloom had gone. The moment had been lost. Doubt of good faith and suspicion of blarney, those spectres at so many Anglo-Irish feasts, had returned within a few hours of the earlier parting as friends. Strasbourg reopened wounds and left scars.

It was the Belfast UCW strikers in May 1974 who principally brought down the agreement forged at Sunningdale. But the hawks in the Irish government had played into their hands. Whoever it was who made the decision to proceed with the Irish state case at Strasbourg in December 1973 also contributed to the ruination of an honest attempt to build a better bridge between neighbours.

After my experience in Northern Ireland I find it difficult to believe that the Irish situation is capable of resolution during the lifetime of the present generation. No one who knows anything about it believes that it is. The visiting politicians from overseas, anxious to win support at home, are reported asking why the soldiers do not go home. But where is 'home'? And what would a Dublin government do if the Province were left to the heavily armed gunmen? Were the Republic to become outward masters of the whole island, they would encounter apart from the IRA a hard core of dedicated and energetic people who would resist with great unity and stern purpose. Bar an unthinkable deportation executed with all the ruthlessness which the Marxists employed upon Russian and Chinese peasants, the island and the world must go on living with a land mass of which one smaller part is determined to be excluded from the larger. On other land masses in others parts of the world, when people of different and alien culture inhabit contiguous lands, geographically artificial frontiers exist and are respected. Like it or not, it seems that will have to happen in the island of Ireland for many years to come.

On 28 March 1972 Willie Whitelaw, the first Secretary of State for Northern Ireland, had expressed in Parliament the hope that the Bill which gave to the British Parliament full power over Northern Ireland could provide a fresh start which must be used 'to promote feelings of tolerance, understanding, fairness, and impartiality'. The minority, he declared, must be won away from the gunmen. Greater fairness, and impartiality in social and employment fields have been instituted, but the gunmen, still sustained by some ignorant Irish-Americans and supplied with weaponry by America's enemy Libya, have not yet been defeated. On my first morning visit to the Law Courts in Belfast, in April 1972, the sounds of several explosions shook the building. The bombings are now fewer in number, but often more severe in extent. The dead of Enniskillen lying among the artificial poppies by the memorial to The Fallen, demonstrated in 1987 the implacable will of the perpetrators.

The struggles in Ireland have coincided also with a time when the authority of the Churches has declined. In the United States, foolish sentimentalists of Irish descent, ignorant of Ireland, pour out dollars while what a sixteenth-century Pope, Julius II, called the *gioco del mondo*, the game of the world, continues to be played out to the benefit of the suppliers of arms whose sole interest is in perpetuating strife. The battle will surely go on, for Ireland has its own place in world strategy, lying across the western supply flank of NATO. It will inevitably remain divided, either as now causing men and material and money to be diverted to contain the threat of Sinn Fein; or, in an Ireland from which the British troops have been withdrawn, leaving in place an alienated minority and an army and an economy wholly incapable of dealing with the IRA, who are as much the enemies of the Republic as they are of the United Kingdom. It would then become a cockpit for ever-increasing violence.

Times of hope come and go, but no more than in the Middle East does there exist a ready solution to this intractable tribal and religious conflict. Only patience and time might bring relief. Seven English Secretaries of State and four Attorneys General have sat in Hillsborough and the Royal Courts of Justice, Belfast, since in 1972 Willie Whitelaw in the House of Commons expressed the hope that the initiative of direct rule might win the minority from the gunmen, offer a better chance of dealing with violence, and lead to a settlement of a centuries-old problem. Sixteen years have passed and few of those hopes have been fulfilled. The more blatant discrimination may have been reduced if not eliminated; genuine grievances which existed may have been excised. That the war still goes on demonstrates that it is not social inequality or discrimination that it feeds upon: it feeds upon naked, atavistic, tribal hatreds. Neither modern politician nor soldier, but only cardinals and bishops and priests and reverends and preachers and elders can reach into such bitter hearts. The men of God bear much of the responsibility for the ills and unhappiness of that island. Like the politicians they have been found wanting.

For myself I was very sad at the swift evaporation of the spirit which, for a short time, had sprung from the efforts, principally of Ted Heath, at Sunningdale. I should like to have been a part of a success over Ireland far more than, say, Rhodesia. But, in the end, both ended in failure. Nineteen-seventy-three was expiring with a bitter flavour. I would not be returning to Strasbourg. Within those twelve months I had prosecuted to conviction the IRA bombers; I had defended the British government and colleagues from accusations of connivance at institutionalized torture; I had negotiated and argued at Sunningdale; I had been weekly in and out of Belfast trying with Barry Shaw to ensure the impartial administration of the prosecution of offenders; on New Year's Eve itself I had been at the Cabinet Offices and No. 10 on the business of Ireland. Like so many who have gone before, I was getting weary of it.

So it was good to go later that evening of New Year's Eve to a party given by Elizabeth and Rex Harrison. Elizabeth was the second Welsh Mrs Harrison, yet for some idiosyncratic reason was a fierce partisan of Richard Crookback and a passionate enemy of the Welsh Tudors. So the evening might well be weirdly Celtic. It would not, however, be Irish. After the past year, I was glad of that.

Chapter 28
The Decline of the Law Officers

A year earlier, in the autumn of 1972, I had 'lost' Geoffrey Howe as Solicitor General. In a way he had never wholly been with me, because from the very start he had been assigned to special duties, although when he was free he gave trenchant help to the Department. But I was aware that his heart lay more with politics than the law, and in the government re-shuffle that autumn he had joined the Cabinet. I knew that I would miss his companionship but I was glad for him. I watched with pleasure as he began his journey along the road which was to take him to the Treasury and to the Foreign Office, in the first of which he laid the foundations for the subsequent economic revival for which others obtained the credit; and in the second he provided the Western Alliance with that ballast of intellect, character and good humour which was so greatly needed, first in the awkward time of the 'Iron Lady' and later in the heady days of *glasnost*.

Ted then asked me whom I recommended he should appoint to succeed Geoffrey. The field was narrow. Of the silks then in the House, Michael Havers had probably the most practice, but it was in the criminal courts only. He had little experience of substantial civil work and this would inevitably make the burden for him heavy, as indeed it did then and later. However, I had appeared in many criminal prosecutions for the Crown over the past years and I reckoned that I would be able to divert some of this work to a Solicitor General with experience in the criminal courts. Above all I certainly needed full-time help, since Northern Ireland had been added to my patch earlier in the year. So I eventually recommended Michael Havers to Ted and he was appointed.

The days rushed past, with an endless stream of Cabinets and Cabinet committees, consultations to hold, documents to study, written advices to give and courts to attend. The pace was, as it always is for the Law Officer, relentless.

In government the pressure of events is always so great that there is never time to stand aside and reflect. It is only when 'recollected in tranquillity' that it is possible to assess what actually happened or, more important, what ought to have happened. Only much later, looking back after nearly twenty years, can I now see that the historical and traditional concept of the Law Officers' role on which Harold Macmillan had lectured me in 1962 was, even in my time, coming to the end of its long and honourable life. Recent developments have confirmed that the ancient conception of the office no longer accords with the style and the demands of modern government.

The traditional role of the Attorney General was that of Counsel to the government. In the nineteenth century he still came from his chambers in the Temple to the Cabinet and gave his advice. He would then withdraw and return to his private law practice. He and not the Lord Chancellor was, as he still remains, the constitutional adviser on law to the Cabinet. He held only a retainer from the Crown and he still engaged in private practice. That custom ended earlier this century, but it was only after the Second World War in Hartley Shawcross's time that the Attorney began to be paid a full ministerial salary in lieu of the retainer and brief fees which he had hitherto received for appearing for the Crown in court and for the legal Opinions which he gave to ministers.

For the Law Officer faithfully to execute his responsibilities to the Crown, as opposed to those required of him by the administration of which he is a member, he must be regularly in court. But when he is in court he is not immediately available for consultation by ministers, and they find that inconvenient. Even in the early 1970s it was beginning to be put about that the Attorney, like all ministers, should put the convenience and the interests of the administration before that of any other. Even in those years irritation if not exasperation used to be delicately conveyed down the wire from Whitehall to my chambers in the Law Courts whenever I as Attorney was in court and not at immediate beck and call. Over the past decade and a half that attitude within government has grown, with more and more talk about the need to shift the priorities in the Attorney's duties from their Crown to their ministerial character. To mark this change it was suggested that the Law Officers' Department should leave its present quarters in the Royal Courts of Justice in the Strand and be brought to an office in Whitehall, a move which would not only be administratively convenient but would also significantly mark the definitive change in the character of the office.

The Westland incident in 1985 (when a legal opinion from the Solicitor General contained in a letter was deliberately leaked by government and the Secretaries for Defence and for Industry both resigned) was a murky story involving, it was said, No. 10. Whoever did authorize the leak, it was a manoeuvre in the political game and a flagrant breach of the strictly enforced rule over the confidentiality of Law Officers' opinions. It showed that, at heart, what the modern administration really wanted was tame 'in-house' legal advisers, creatures of the government more in the style of the retained family or company solicitor than of independent officers of the Crown.

The less and less frequent appearances of the Law Officers in the courts over the past fifteen years confirms the change in the service which they are now required to provide. This withdrawal from regular appearance in the courts signifies the end to the old tradition. In these circumstances, the Attorney ought, in this new situation, to retire from his position as titular Head of the Bar and if he has become merely a ministerial legal adviser who no longer appears in court, he has no intrinsic need even to hold the rank of Queen's Counsel. He would then necessarily have to give up his quasi-judicial responsibility for criminal prosecutions and his task as the guardian of the public interest. In effect the old office will have been abolished.

But it was not only the role of the Law Officers in the House of Commons which has recently met with change. For in 1987 there was an alteration in the qualifications hitherto regarded as essential for the holder of the office of Lord Chancellor, who is the minister charged with the administration of the English civil law, the management of the English courts and the selection of the English judiciary. In the past he has been required to possess the qualification of having been trained in the English law, called to the Bar of England and Wales, and to have practised in the English courts. This was believed to afford to the judiciary, which a Lord Chancellor heads, some assurance of independence. North of the border in Scotland many of the equivalent functions (although not the headship of the judiciary) are exercised, in effect, by a Scottish lawyer, the Lord Advocate, trained and experienced in the different and distinct Scottish legal system.

But in 1987, with the appointment of Lord Mackay of Clashfern, a former Lord Advocate and a Scottish jurist of distinction, that tradition was abandoned. The selection of Lord Mackay as Lord Chancellor was, in fact, widely welcomed, for it was felt by many that after the long reign of Lord Hailsham this Scotsman would bring a breath of fresh air to the office. That he was personally well fitted for the post, none had any doubt.

These personal qualities, however, should not disguise the significance of the fact that for the first time there sat upon the Woolsack, charged with the responsibility of administering the English (not the Scottish) law and of selecting the English (not the Scottish) judiciary, a man who had never been trained in the English law and who had never practised in the Law Courts in the Strand or in the Old Bailey or in the Crown Courts throughout England and Wales.

The Lord Chancellor has, moreover, the duty personally to select from those who have hitherto been fellow practitioners those suitable for appointment to the English Bench. For the Scottish Bench, selection is made by the Scottish Lord Advocate. Admittedly in England Lord Hailsham's long tenure of office contribued to a decline in personal selection, for by the end of his reign it had been seventeen years since he had himself been in practice in the English courts. Of his immediate predecessors, Elwyn Jones had been only six years from practice; Gerald Gardiner six; and Reggie Dilhorne two. But with the appointment of Lord Mackay it became quite obvious that the new Lord Chancellor could not possibly have personal knowledge of English practitioners. Necessarily, therefore, the selection for legal appointments in England has come to be done by officials, by anonymous civil servants and judges recommending new judges. This cannot be constitutionally desirable. In these new circumstances the selection of the judges should be placed upon a more formal basis by the creation of a statutory Judicial Appointments Commission, with publicly appointed commissioners, a system some have long advocated.

There are other consequences. Logically, if a Scottish lawyer is qualified to administer the English law and make the appointment to the English courts of English lawyers, then in the United Kingdom an English lawyer must be equally qualified to fill the post of Scottish Lord Advocate. It is fanciful to believe, however, that an English minister as Lord Advocate would ever be acceptable to Scotland. Be that as it may, the position in England now is clear. The old tradition of actual practice in the English courts as a necessary qualification has been abandoned and in consequence there is now no reason why the post of Lord Chancellor should not in future be filled by an academic lawyer, by a solicitor unversed in litigation, or even by some legally qualified Cabinet member who had never practised in the courts. Thus from now on, the office must be open to any who have some legal qualification of whatever discipline or experience. The political opportunity for Prime Ministerial selection has been greatly extended, and the judges themselves should now be starting to feel uneasy.

There remains the ultimate consequence. The Lord Chancellor is both a judge and a leading member of the Cabinet of whichever political party is in power. The Attorney General is constitutionally responsible for all criminal prosecutions but is also elected to the House of Commons under a party label, as is the Solicitor General. There have long been those who consider it objectionable in modern times to retain the historic anomalies which give to the three political Law Officers judicial and quasi-judicial powers. The critics have demanded that these offices ought to be swept away and replaced by a system which wholly separates the political from the judicial function. In their criticism of the present system they also point to the illogical division in ministerial responsibility for the law, where at present civil law rests with the Lord Chancellor and criminal law with the Home Secretary who is a senior political Minister, responsible for the police and the prisons and for whom, as the reformers point out, no legal qualification has ever been required. For the Home Secretary is not a Law Officer at all. Thus under our present quirky system, responsibility for administering the civil law and prosecuting offenders is allotted to the Lord Chancellor and the Attorney General respectively, but it is the Home Secretary who is responsible for the efficacy of the criminal law and for order on our streets. Logically this makes little sense.

The case for reform of the whole system has been further strengthened by the fact that with the development of legal aid the Lord Chancellor's Department has become in recent years a significant spending department, with an annual vote of five hundred million pounds. Yet it remains the only department with no minister answerable for expenditure sitting in the House of Commons, the House responsible for supply. This may not long remain acceptable to Parliament, and if it were to demand that there should be a minister answerable to the Commons this would bolster the call for review of the whole constitutional position of the Law ministers. From this there could emerge that for which the reformers have long sought; namely a unified Ministry of Justice, with a political minister in the Commons responsible for the supervision of all municipal law, both criminal and civil; for the administration of the courts; for the prosecution of offenders; for the police; and for the management of prisons.

It is no wonder, therefore, that in 1988 for the first time in history the judges felt impelled to appoint from among their number a Council of Judges, a council which is presumably intended to be the representative body designed to look after the interests of the English judges who in former times were content to leave the protection of their constitutional independence in the hands of a Lord Chancellor.

Despite these major consequences, the recent changes occasioned no challenge from the English legal profession. Indeed the appointment of the Scottish jurist to head the English judiciary was greeted with pleasure. That was a striking tribute to James Mackay, the Lord Chancellor who broke the mould. But the absence of question has clearly demonstrated that what the profession requires today above all is ministerial efficiency over the supervision of the law and in the administration of the courts. It is a tacit acknowledgment that the office of Lord Chancellor in its old form is of little actual importance, save as the ceremonial representative of an ancient but now irrelevant tradition.

That all this has gone unchallenged must have been greeted with immense satisfaction in Whitehall. Quietly and without fanfare, there has been brought about not so much reform as revolution in the role of the traditional Law Officers of the Crown. For Whitehall has at last succeeded in clearing the way to transform them into ministerial legal servants, government legal eunuchs. The post of Lord Chancellor has become that of just another political bureaucrat in the Cabinet which is open in the future to any minister with some knowledge of law, while those of the Attorney and Solicitor Generals have been transformed into that of tame legal consultants to their master or mistress, the Prime Minister. It has been neatly accomplished, and without any debate either in Parliament or the profession over whether the eunuchs will give a better service to the administration of the law. But sooner or later this part of the Thatcher revolution in government will require to be legitimized. Over the political horizon, for better or for worse, there must now loom the spectre of a unified Ministry of Justice, with its ministerial head just another post for political careerists.

The Great Seal and the wigs can be locked away into the museum. The ghosts of the great Crown Law Officers of the past must be stirring uneasily in their graves.

Chapter 29
Ted Heath and Margaret Thatcher

Although I did not know it, in that summer of 1973 my time in office was drawing to a close. We went to stay for a week with our friends Rex and Elizabeth Harrison in Rex's house high up on the hill above the harbour of Portofino. It was necessary to take a jeep up the first part of the steep hill and then clamber up the remainder on foot. From the house there was a panoramic view over pinewoods down to the sea. One evening we stood on the balcony looking down on a fierce fire which had broken out in the woods below. No fire appliance could ever have reached us if the fire had spread up the hill. After a time the flames died away, leaving great blackened scars on the hillside.

In the morning we bounced across the bay in the speedboat and lunched on the other coast. In the evening Elizabeth laid the dining-room table with five extra places. For whom? we asked. 'For Rex's former wives', she said. 'They haunt this place.'

One night we stayed up late playing Rex's old songs on tape. He could remember few of the words. Elaine and Elizabeth talked through the night, casually waking me in the early morning to pull a recalcitrant cork in the final bottle of champage. The only policeman in evidence was one carabiniere who struggled up the hill resentfully and soon went thankfully down. It would take, he said, a parachute commando to storm Rex's eyrie. So we were left peacefully alone.

That year, 1973, after the IRA trial at Winchester, the police presence at home and around the family greatly increased. At the time I figured on the IRA death list. The family scene was growing understandably tense. The strain of the constant police guard was telling, especially upon Elaine and our young daughter Angela. Save for the week at Portofino, Elaine and I had not been away together and I had been on almost constant duty from early morning until late at night for nearly four years. I saw nothing of our friends, only lawyers and politicians. Most of all, I saw my driver, Albert Morley. Elaine had never enjoyed any of the pomp of officialdom and government. She had been left to make a life of her own.

The end of the old year and the start of 1974 had brought with it the three-day week followed by the miners' strike. These domestic troubles had followed the outbreak of war in the Middle East the previous autumn and the phenomenal hike in oil prices. Later came the secondary banking crisis.

On 7 February I attended a Privy Council at Clarence House. The Queen was overseas. So the Queen Mother and Princess Margaret, as Councillors of State, presided. No new Councillor was to be sworn in, and unlike my début with Lord Merthyr ten years earlier the ceremony went impeccably. It was the last Council I ever attended. At Clarence House Jim Prior confirmed that there was to be an election. I knew that Peter Carrington, the chairman of the Party, had been recommending it for some weeks.

I began my campaign in my Epsom constituency on my own, for Elaine was on her annual visit to her widowed mother in Newport, Rhode Island. Twice during the campaign I had to break it off and fly to Belfast. On the second occasion I had to stay there for several days with the comparatively new Irish Secretary, Francis Pym, dealing with a threatened police strike. Resentment at the Republic's persistence in their claim at Strasbourg even after the Sunningdale agreement, and apprehensions over the proposal for a Council for Ireland, were rumbling menacingly throughout the Province.

At Epsom the public election meetings were well attended; at my last over five hundred came. But during the local canvass our team were struck by the negative reaction which we were encountering from the expensive houses and the well-to-do in the grander villas. In the modest houses, support was solid. 'Who runs the country?' ran the slogan, 'the government or the unions?' The people in the smaller, poorer houses understood very well. In the richer, support faded as the campaign progressed. It seemed certain that there would be a heavy Liberal vote. This we knew could put in Labour, the last thing which the foolish rich desired. My election agent thought up a dreadful personal slogan which he made our people stick along the rear windows of their cars. 'I'm a Sir Peter Supporter'. I sent it to my son Anthony at school, who thought it great.

Elaine could not get home until two days before polling day, and one Saturday during the campaign I collected Angela from the convent for her weekend away from school. Then I was suddenly summoned to No. 10.

So Angela had to sit outside in Downing Street in my car, a pale little figure still worried about assassins. Inside, while I waited, I gossiped with Robert Armstrong. Peter Carrington came in from Smith Square, the Party headquarters. 'Bad luck,' he said to Robert. 'It looks as if you lot have got us for another four years.' Ten days later we were out – for five years. That was the last time I set foot in No. 10.

Downing Street and Chequers had been much improved as houses by Ted, especially Chequers. He had introduced his personal taste and flair and Chequers was far more attractive than it had been when Harold Macmillan was the occupant. But Macmillan had Birch Grove, so he was not greatly interested. Ted obviously enjoyed the house and, like any house which is loved, it responded. The same was true of the staff. There was a story that Harold Wilson got on excellently with his colleagues and poorly with the servants; and that Ted got on vilely with his colleagues and famously with the servants. Certainly the servants at his official houses were greatly attached to him.

He was not easy. He had built for himself that outer carapace inside which lived the very private and sensitive person who was ever struggling to get out. He found the small change of social life truly difficult. He could not flirt with women or tease men. So he brushed all that aside as being unimportant and trivial and a waste of precious time. But in reality a part of him was longing to carry off all those things which a man of the world finds so easy. It would have helped him very much if he could have acquired that comfortable facility. Not that he was ever a bad host. His houses were graceful; the flowers abundant; the food and drink excellent. But an easier air could have helped his commerce with his colleagues, none of whom at the end of his time in the leadership ever approached his political stature, equalled his native intelligence or rivalled those tastes of the cultivated man which he so conspicuously demonstrated.

There was just one occasion which stays in my memory and which illustrates how the use of just a few clumsy words could create a wrong impression and arouse an unnecessary reaction which did not facilitate the business that he had in hand. In itself it was unimportant. No one suffered. It was all forgotten very soon. It was, to witness, rather funny.

It arose out of a security flap. Several of us, including certain grand officials who had responsibility in the security field, were suddenly summoned to Chequers. It was the middle of the holiday season, and we all scrambled and bustled from our homes to meet the call. The day was very hot, but we thought it right to wrap ties around our necks and clamber into jackets. I had been lucky for a helicopter had brought me from Sussex. When we were assembled we stood in a formal little group in the Great Hall, waiting for our host, the Prime Minister. He strolled in from the garden, dressed comfortably and appropriately in a pair of linen trousers and an open shirt. It was a particularly fine summer afternoon. It was his house. For all that it mattered to us, he could have been dressed in bathing trunks.

'Good heavens!' he greeted us. 'How incredibly pompous you all look!' I could see official faces redden and necks swell over the recently buttoned-up collars. The remark was, of course, intended as a pleasantry. But the words used were just the wrong words with which to address his visitors, sweating slightly on that hot afternoon from the effort to meet the summons to confer with their Prime Minister. They were simply ill-chosen words for that particular moment, whereas I had so often heard from him words perfectly chosen and perfectly timed, whether the occasion was a dinner at No. 10 or a welcome delightfully addressed to a Commonwealth Prime Minister. But those were official occasions and this was informal, almost social, and the words, meant jocularly and designed to put us at our ease, were awkward and wrong. As a result it was not a wholly sympathetic group which was then led into the small white drawing-room to begin the conference.

It was said that Ted used to be urged to take aside at each ten o'clock division in the House of Commons a backbencher who had earlier spoken in the debate and tell the fellow what a good speech the Whips said that the man had made. By doing this each parliamentary evening he would have made disciples for life, and over the years there would have been many. But, so the story goes, he demurred. He had not heard the speech himself; he could not readily accept the judgment of others; and he was too honest to pretend. The story was probably apocryphal. What is true is that if Ted could have acquired a more cosy, comfortable style, he would not have lost the leadership of the Party.

I found him always impressive and I liked him personally. His loneliness, somehow epitomized by the solitary hours which he spent at his piano, and that hidden but nevertheless real longing to be accepted as one of 'the Club', aroused affection in those who had the lesser, easier talents but who lacked the greater which he so obviously possessed. I certainly had my differences with him in government, but it was easier for me than for some to be independent. I was in a sense a technocrat. And I would quite gladly go: I had no desperate desire to remain in government.

But with many colleagues Ted was brusque and all too blunt. When

Margaret Thatcher was a member first of his Shadow and then of his real Cabinet, he did not treat her well. Or, more exactly, he did not treat her right. After the putsch, when a well-organized lobby led by those two improbable conspirators Airey Neave and Keith Joseph, overthrew him and crowned Margaret, his resentment may have been fuelled by a subconscious sense of disquiet; for he had not handled her well. For him she was neither sensitive nor clever enough. But then she was, probably, always quite impossible to handle.

I first saw her in 1959 when the then Attorney General, Reggie Manningham-Buller, had called a meeting of all Conservative MPs who were barristers, irrespective of whether they were practising or not. Soon after the meeting had begun, I noticed in the committee room a pretty girl. She had a creamy pink and white complexion, and beautifully, too beautifully, coiffed fair hair, not a single strand out of place. But there was a rather prim pursing about the lips. To look at, she was certainly far better than any other girl I had ever seen in the House. Raymond Asquith once described Diana Manners at Aston Tyrell as 'a black tulip in a garden of cucumbers'. This girl in the committee room was not exactly a Diana Manners nor even a yellow tulip, for there was something altogether a little too severe about her.

At first she sat silent, not demure since she sat very straight and she turned her head from side to side quizzing everyone else in the room. She was observing the 'cucumbers', her male colleagues, around her. I thought that she examined particularly balefully the stout and stalwart figure of the Attorney General, Reggie Buller. By now the usual bores in their black jackets and striped pants had begun to 'contribute', as they liked to call it, to the discussion. I watched the girl with the bright hair and I could see that she was winding herself up ready to join in. When eventually she did, it was certainly not with the diffidence of a briefless barrister which she was, nor with the hesitancy of a very newly elected raw MP, which she also was. She spoke even then (it was some prosaic legal topic which we were discussing) with a vehemence rather too exaggerated for the subject and, I noticed, with an irritating emphasis on the wrong word, a habit she has never wholly lost. It was obvious that her 'contribution' had been designed merely to attract attention. She had of course attracted notice from every man in the room before she had ever opened her mouth. But that was not the kind of notice which she sought.

I do not suppose that was the first time that Margaret Thatcher ever spoke in the Palace of Westminster, but it was the first time that I had ever heard her.

The matter in her speech was not important and at the end of the meeting she was cheerfully swatted down by Reggie as impartially and as robustly as he always swatted everybody. But she had achieved her purpose, which was to serve notice that here was, if not a brain – the proof of that would come later – then certainly a personality to be taken into the reckoning. So we all smiled benignly as we looked into those blue eyes and at the tilt of the golden head. We, and all the world, had no idea what we were in for.

Later, on the circuit of Conservative circles, we encountered her and her husband. Denis was even then the same brisk, bluff company director who from those very early days acted out the part of consort with good humour although with a shade more condescension than he came to do a decade and a half later. The couple appeared as odd and rather quaint recruits to our backbench Tory world, the girl earning male admiration which she seemed to enjoy while at the same time making efforts to show that such tribute by itself was not enough. On these Party occasions she appeared rather over-bright and shiny and, with the women, wary. In the House and in the Party committees she soon won a reputation for making remorseless 'contributions' as relentlessly as any of the striped-pants-and-black-jacket-brigade, although what she said was usually sensible, the matter better than the manner. She rarely smiled and never laughed.

Half a dozen years later after I had been Solicitor General and was a Privy Councillor, and she had been a junior Parliamentary Secretary in the same administrations, we used to sit next to each other amiably enough at the meetings of the Shadow Cabinet. I thought at that time that she was rather agreeable and in those days unspoilt, even if demonstrably ambitious and strangely insensitive. She certainly talked. How she talked! And she certainly irked the Leader. Instinctively he seemed to bridle at her over-emphasis. I was rather on her side because I believe that she honestly did not realize how irritating she was.

But after another half a dozen years when she became a minister, all that changed. Then she only said what was needed. By then she had won her spurs and when they were on her boots for all to see there was not the same tiresome need to draw attention to herself. For by then she was a minister and a good minister too. It was only when the boots got very big that some of the unnecessary nonsense returned and the lack of generosity so sadly noticeable.

When I was Attorney I found her supportive rather than otherwise in any differences I had with the Prime Minister. But that, I suppose, only arose out of opposition to the person with whom I was then temporarily in dispute. There was such obvious antagonism between Ted and Margaret that anyone could have foretold that if ever opportunity presented itself, the political dagger would be cheerfully slipped out of the stocking-top and into the substantial frame of her Leader. They were enemies, naked and unashamed, and they had been from the start.

She and I were never close, and for her politics were intensely personal. I did not support her challenge to Ted in 1975, but by then I had left the front bench and I was Chairman of the Bar. Three years later, reluctantly and on the insistence of others, she put my name forward to Prime Minister Jim Callaghan for a peerage. After she had become Prime Minister I was not included when she entertained at No. 10 the Society of Conservative Lawyers. When I finally retired from the Bar in 1985 I spoke with Robert Armstrong, then Secretary of the Cabinet, offering in my retirement to do some voluntary public work where my experience might prove useful. There was reported back to me the magisterial response. 'He can expect no preferment from me!' 'Preferment' was not what I had been talking about, but I suppose that by then, for her, preferment was what life had all become.

Margaret Thatcher has found a role which she has played with deter-mination and courage. But Edward Heath, as he sits slumped in his seat below the gangway in the House of Commons, must surely feel that much of her achievement has been due to his pioneering efforts during the early days of his premiership when he set out to break the mould in which British politics had been fixed for twenty-five years. Then he lost his major lieutenants, the dash for growth was hobbled by the failure to corral the unions, and the war in the Levant finally blew him away.

There was a significant occasion right at the start of his days in power which illustrates what he had to face. Soon after he had become Prime Minister and after he had announced his initiative to curb for the first time the power of the unions, which no postwar government had dared to attempt, he gave a dinner party at Chequers for Harold Macmillan, to which he invited those of us in his present government who had also served in senior positions under Harold. We were not many.

At the end of dinner, the moment appeared to have arrived for a speech from our former Prime Minister, and we were all poised to receive it. At this date, the great Stockton-Macmillan speech had not yet been conceived. That came a decade later, when it became known and loved as the Great Speech. Those who heard it never tired of its repetition, for it was a work of art. It began in stately manner with the funeral procession of Queen Victoria led by Captain Ames, the tallest man in the British Army. This solemn introduction was followed by a somewhat quizzical reverie upon the number of domestic servants then in service in Edwardian English homes. That done, the orator – apparently emotionally overcome during the next passage but happily only temporarily – led his audience through the mud of Flanders in one war and the sands of the Western Desert in another. Rallying after these plaintive memories of 'old, unhappy, far-off things and battles long ago', the tone sharpened and the speech trotted along, gathering pace as it reflected on the role of the British as Greeks and the Americans as Romans and concluding in fine scorn over the sale of the family silver.

But after that dinner at Chequers in 1970, it did not seem as if there was to be any speech at all, for our new Prime Minister abruptly scraped back his chair and led us all from the dining-room into the Long Gallery. There Harold was seated down in front of the fire. I was on a window-seat talking with Peter Carrington. Suddenly Ted announced, 'Harold would like to make a speech'. And Harold, a silver-topped ebony cane between his pale, delicate hands, did.

The speech which he then made was, in part, the prototype of the Great Speech of later years. However, this speech began not with the funeral of Queen Victoria but with an affectionate reference to our splendid young leader. I knew then that we were in for trouble. And we were. The words of the speech flickered like the lights from the flames of the fire around our splendid young leader's prematurely silvered head as, after this acknowledgement to our host, the elder statesman then turned to urge restraint. We must remember, said the sage, that the men from Stockton and the Yorkshire coalfields had fought and died with him at Ypres and Passchendaele and he had seen their sons march past their Sovereign in triumph in the great parade after the victory in North Africa. Here the orator flicked away what appeared by the gesture to be the ghost of an inconvenient tear. Happily only temporarily overcome, he went on gravely to reflect that we had at last become as a nation truly one people. No one and indeed no organization of our people must be crushed. Caution, he counselled, staring into the fire, caution and, above all, restraint.

On this grave and ominous note of warning, the oration rolled to its sonorous end. Our 'splendid young leader' thanked Harold without noticeable warmth, save to offer him and us a glass of whisky.

The significance of that speech given in the firelight on that evening in Chequers was that it spelt out the anxiety and alarm felt by the great exemplar who had presided for so many years over the previous Conservative government. It was delivered in the vintage tones of the politics of the 1950s and 1960s and spoken in the accent of all those who had moulded postwar political history. It revealed that the Old Guard reckoned that Ted, by giving notice that he intended to challenge the trade-union barons, was launching an abrasive initiative which threatened to blast the spirit of consensus under which the country had been governed since the end of the world war. It was a stern, paternal warning against dividing the One Nation which the past quarter-century had at last created, and it demonstrated how in 1970 the mould of the 'Butskellite' era was far tougher and harder to crack than it would be a decade later after the defeat of Ted and the second, raffish reign of Harold Wilson, when the unscrupulous exploitation of power by the trade-union bosses had finally brought the nation to the end of its toleration of their holding the nation to ransom.

Margaret Thatcher deserves, and characteristically takes, the credit for what she has achieved in reviving the fortunes and spirit of the nation. She has certainly won for herself the right to an eventual statue in Parliament Square. But when in years to come her shade mounts her plinth to take her heroine's place among the English heroes, her shade, in justice, ought to make at least a bow to her Conservative predecessor. He himself may never be rewarded with such a monument but in far more difficult circumstances he started the process which she was given the chance to complete. He had, after all, made easier her path.

In life politicians are not renowned for giving credit if that might somehow detract from their own, so Margaret Thatcher's shade will of course do no such thing. The spirits of those two enemies, even with all passion spent, could never bring themselves to make to each other even so much as the sign of ghostly obeisance.

As the February election of 1974 drew to its close, and despite the earlier optimism of Peter Carrington, it became clear to those of us canvassing in the suburbs around London that all was not going well. The substantial haemorrhage of support from the Conservatives to Jeremy Thorpe's Liberals pointed inevitably to the return of Harold Wilson. As we knocked on the expensive doors of the larger houses, we realized that it would be the voters in those houses who would make this happen.

On polling day, after the tour of the polling booths in my constituency, Elaine and I set off to drive home from Epsom to our house in Sussex to spend the night watching the results on television. As usual, the Epsom count would be held on the following morning. We had both cars with us, so we drove home separately. The police car followed me. On the drive back I pondered the future. I thought that the Conservative government might have just lost or just won the election. Whichever way it went, it was probable that the result would be close.

As I approached the end of my journey, I pulled up the car in the woods above our house, which lay below me with the armed platoon in the barn. I wanted to think for a while. The police car stopped behind me. One of the police walked up to where I was sitting in the darkness in my car. I said that I wanted to stay there for a little while. He walked back to the police car. I could hear them radioing down to the house below.

Sitting there in the dark, released from all the exhaustion and pre-occupation of electioneering, I began to think about our family and what lay ahead. I thought principally of Elaine and myself. She had given to me the whole of her adult life. How had I repaid her gift? What had I given to her. Not a great deal, while latterly I had imposed upon her and our children a life of perpetual tension with constant separation and almost total lack of companionship. All this by my choice. Should any woman, I wondered, be asked to tolerate for long such a life?

In any event, did I myself hanker so greatly for the life which I had been leading? I had no consuming political ambition. I had served three prime ministers and I had held both Law Officerships in the Commons. As for the Lord Chancellorship, I would have liked that, but at the time when I was sitting there in my car and deciding my future I was barred as a Catholic from holding that office. The Bar, by contrast, had always been my first and truest love. The excitement of a trial, the infinite variety of problems and personalities which the barrister encounters, that was what I really enjoyed. So what was it all about? For what was I forcing my family to live this unnatural life in the fortress farmhouse which lay below me down the road which led through the dark woods?

During the past months I had become increasingly conscious of how the total immersion in politics which service in a government demands begins to affect everyone involved. It had begun to dawn on me that in government we all became such immense bores!

When I was a minister I honestly could not fathom why anyone with whom I talked was not deeply interested in and concerned with the politics of the day. I was genuinely surprised when I discovered that there actually existed intelligent people who were not! It was only later when I was right out of it all that I realized that most sensible people find that the arts, or the countryside, or food or stamp-collecting, or making music, money or love, indeed almost anything, was more worthwhile than politics. And I also began to realize that politicians never actually talk to anyone. They either lecture or they canvass. Suddenly it appeared to me to be all very tedious, and rather comical. And then there was the dark side, that false friendship of rivals, of competing colleagues, all with their hidden daggers. I had witnessed some of that from the sidelines and the spectacle had never been pretty.

So as I sat there in the dark I balanced up what I might be in danger of losing against what I still had and what I might not always have if the election was won. To my shame, I began for the first time seriously to think about Elaine, the person whom I had married and taken from her homeland as a girl nearly twenty years before, and about the actual life which I had given her.

For myself, I was now halfway through my fifties. I had no original ideas to contribute to political thought. I had no group or cabal to which I was in principle allied. I had been only a journeyman politician with some early idealism for service and some useful qualifications, when what I really in my heart would have liked to have been was an artist-advocate! That had been a youthful dream, but at least I still had time to live the life of a real barrister.

All our little family group had been in some way bruised by the life which I, the husband and father, had imposed upon them. I realized now that the only practical political family must have the children grown and long since gone. There had been some among us like that, and they were those who flourished in the unreality of public life. They were the ones who bloomed in the artificial sunlight of official engagements. They were the teams of husband and wife who thrived on being a part, and an important part, of an official function and who beamed with genuine satsifaction at the greeting of rhythmic clapping to which they made their entrance into the dinner of mass-produced food, with the plummy toast-master and the speeches, good, indifferent, mostly bad, and the whole rigmarole of official pleasure.

Those who genuinely enjoyed the official round were naturally those who were most caught up in the manic obsession with the world of public affairs and politics which to some greater or lesser degree infected us all. The full extent of how infectious it was and how it drove out awareness of so much else, I only fully comprehended when the field had been fled and the keep abandoned. Only then, in remembrance of times past, did I recognize it as a form of madness.

So I made up my mind there and then in that darkened car, which in the February night was rapidly growing intensely cold, that I was not prepared to risk the loss of that which I loved most. I started the engine and drove down through the woods to our home.

Epilogue
Return to First Loves

Elaine and I sat before the fire, watching the election results coming through. The anticipated swing from Tory to Liberal made Labour the largest single party. Early next morning No. 10 telephoned to discuss the constitutional position. The advice was not difficult to give. Over the weekend Jeremy Thorpe came and went from Downing Street. On Monday 4 March the government resigned, and I cleared my desk in the Attorney General's Chambers. On the Wednesday I attended my second reception-for-departing-ministers at Buckingham Palace, and I moved back for the second time into my old chambers in King's Bench Walk. This time it was for keeps.

That same day I was instructed to advise the ruler of a Gulf state and I earned in a few hours half a Law Officer's annual salary. In the Inner Temple I was approached to stand for election as vice-chairman of the Bar, which meant that, if elected, I would be Chairman in the following year. I spoke with Pat Neill, the sitting Chairman of the Bar, and I agreed to stand and was elected. The Bar was about to enter a new organization, the Senate of the Inns of Court and the Bar, which had just been established. Ironically, ten years later I chaired a committee which abolished it, and I served as its last President.

During that first week after the general election defeat I wrote to Ted. It was twelve years since I had first joined the front bench. I had done quite a stint as its legal adviser. Now I resigned and retired to the backbenches. He replied, in very generous terms. When I saw him a few days later I asked him how he was. 'Shell-shocked', he replied.

I fought my last parliamentary election a few months later in the autumn of 1974. I then told the constituency chairman that I would not fight another. To part after twenty-three years from those who had been so kind to me was indeed a wrench; but it was the only sadness which I felt. I knew that Christopher Soames was anxious to return to the House of Commons and after talking with him I suggested his name to the chairman of the Epsom Conservative Association. But later, at a critical moment for the constituency, he became very ill. The Epsom Association were determined not to delay in finding a successor candidate because the Labour government was a minority government dependent for its survival on Liberal support and no one could be certain when an election might come. The Association chose Archie Hamilton.

From the date of my decision in the dark, cold car on the last day of February in 1974 until I retired from practice in 1985, I had eleven years of intensely enjoyable activity at the Bar. On my retirement the computer print-out recorded in the official Law Reports over ninety entries of reported cases in which I had appeared as counsel.

During those last years of practice I happily trailed my wig or my briefcase from the Law Courts in London or the Western Circuit which I led for seven years, to Hong Kong, to Singapore, to South America, to Texas, to Strasbourg. I battled for sugar owners against President Forbes Burnham of Guyana, who for some reason gave me a stuffed crocodile and thereafter used to send me boxes of Havana cigars given to him by his friend Fidel Castro. One box was even delivered to me – at what I felt was the rather irreverent request of President Burnham – by hand of the Archbishop of Canterbury. I advised another President, that of Nigeria; I appeared for Jimmy Goldsmith against *Private Eye* and *Der Spiegel*; for Mel Tormé, who came to my chambers with his American lawyer Marve Mitchelson who then abruptly told his client to shut up; for Keith Richards and Mrs Ronnie Wood of the Rolling Stones; for Indira Gandhi, Arnold Goodman personally, 'Union Jack Hayward', Hong Kong property developers, Malaysian tycoons and, of course, for the *Daily Mail* against the Moonies.

There was an odd postscript which came after I had retired. I appeared as the 'Challenging Counsel' in a television enquiry into allegations of war crimes said to have been committed during service in the German army by the President of Austria, Dr Kurt Waldheim. We had to study almost ten thousand pages of documents and the statements of almost four score 'witnesses'. My task was to probe and challenge the accusations. We spent ten days recording the hearings, which were edited down to five hours for television transmission and sent out all over the world. An international panel of five leading judges dismissed the allegations. Before the hearing some complained about the propriety of the process. After it was over Dr Waldheim certainly did not, and it served to put on record and identify the facts and to dispel rumour.

As I listened to the judges' verdict I knew that this really was the end of my life as an advocate. I bundled up the papers and was driven home. I felt like the proverbial war-horse finally put out to pasture

Elaine became a most successful interior designer. I painted many more bad pictures. We had holidays together in Newport, Rhode Island; in Bangkok, in Honolulu and the island of Maui; in Tuscany, in Crete and mostly in beloved Provence.

We were very happy.

Index